A Book of Men
VISIONS OF THE
MALE EXPERIENCE

A BOOK
OF MEN

VISIONS OF THE
MALE EXPERIENCE

Edited by

Ross Firestone

STONEHILL PUBLISHING COMPANY, NEW YORK

ISBN: 0-88373-040
Library of Congress Catalog Card Number: 75-40595
Book Design by Jon Goodchild.
Original collage engravings by Jim Herder.
Cover Design by Rubin Pfeffer.

First Printing.
Printed in the USA.

ACKNOWLEDGMENTS

My gratitude to those who have
helped make this book possible:
the many publishers who have
allowed me to include material they control,
Carmen Barone, Susan Bergholz, Jonathan Cott,
Alan Douglas, Gail Firestone, Jon Goodchild,
Jim Herder, Beverly Kowalsky, Rosanne Leacy,
Esther Mitgang, Rubin Pfeffer, Ken Schaffer,
Nat Sobel, Jeffrey Steinberg, Thorn Welden,
Heather White, and Basil Winston.

Contents

3. *Husbands* 169

Franz Kafka/ Cyril Connolly/ A. S. Neill/ Huey P. Newton/ Floyd Dell/ Vincent Van Gogh/ Stephen Spender/ Sherwood Anderson/ James Agee/ Eugène Ionesco/ Piri Thomas/ Malcolm Muggeridge/ Groucho Marx/ Max Frisch/ John Wain/ William Carlos Williams/ August Strindberg/ Bertrand Russell/ Alan Watts/ D. H. Lawrence/ John Fowles/ Havelock Ellis/ Henry Miller/ Dalton Trumbo/ John B. Koffend/ Lenny Bruce/ Paul Goodman/ Ernest Jones/ Aldous Huxley/ Raymond Chandler/ Thomas Bell/ Theodore Roethke

4. *Fathers* 253

Eugène Ionesco/ Cesare Pavese/ Malcolm Muggeridge/ Jakov Lind/ Edward Hoagland/ Charles Bukowski/ Bertrand Russell/ William Gibson/ Vladimir Nabokov/ Henry Miller/ William Saroyan/ August Strindberg/ W. C. Fields/ Henry de Montherlant/ Edward Weston/ Georges Simenon/ F. Scott Fitzgerald/ William Carlos Williams/ Dalton Trumbo/ Robert Graves

To
RAY AND LOU
AND
GAIL
AND
SIMON

Foreword

My purpose in this book is to express the varieties of male experience, the diverse ways we come to terms with our maleness as we move through our years as sons and lovers, husbands and fathers.

To get as close as possible to the tangible realities of men's lives, I have largely limited my selection to personal writings—autobiographies, journals, letters, diaries and the like. More theoretical pieces have been included only when their abstraction is infused with the urgency of self-revelation.

The men brought together in this collection span the twentieth century and exemplify the range of possibilities most familiar to our time. The few I have chosen from the nineteenth century seem no less modern to me in their preoccupations and perceptions.

I have looked for writings that pinpoint the essence of a recognizable situation or attitude. Each selection resonates for me with some sort of truth about what it means to be male. There is no single, all-containing truth, of course. Life is much too slippery for that. So the insights expressed in one piece may be followed by different, even opposing insights in the next.

For all that, there is, I think, a single common voice running throughout this book from beginning to end. It hints to me of the common, unifying core of human maleness so often obscured by all the different forms our lives take and all the different ways we respond to them.

1. Sons

C. G. Jung

Yet another image: I am restive, feverish, unable to sleep. My father carries me in his arms, paces up and down, singing his old student songs. I particularly remember one I was especially fond of and which always used to soothe me, *"Alles schweige, jeder neige...."* The beginning went something like that. To this day I can remember my father's voice, singing over me in the stillness of the night.

I was suffering, so my mother told me afterward, from general eczema. Dim intimations of trouble in my parents' marriage hovered around me. My illness, in 1878, must have been connected with a temporary separation of my parents. My mother spent several months in a hospital in Basel, and presumably her illness had something to do with the difficulty in the marriage. An aunt of mine, who was a spinster and some twenty years older than my mother, took care of me. I was deeply troubled by my mother's being away. From then on, I always felt mistrustful when the word *love* was spoken. The feeling I associated with *woman* was for a long time that of innate unreliability. *Father*, on the other hand, meant reliability and—powerlessness. That is the handicap I started off with. Later, these early impressions were revised: I have trusted men friends and been disappointed by them, and I have mistrusted women and was not disappointed.

Memories, Dreams, Reflections

Kenneth Patchen

CAREER FOR A CHILD OF FIVE

At night, when I can't sleep,
When the faces won't back,
When horror touches my chest
And I start up screaming . . .

It was long ago in a strange land,
Child, that I shall kill you

My mother got the palms from the hands
Of the priest himself; and being doubly blessed
As they were, she would put them on the bureau
Near candles, where their shadows reeled
A devil's walk through my childhood.
But I never cried, being too near terror.

You may repeat your nice prayers,
Child, that I shall kill you

Then one night, after hours of torment,
I started to say all the foul words
That boys had taught me; beginning
Softly . . . then louder, louder,
Until mother came and put soap
In my mouth to rub them away.

Was ever son so willed in love,
Child, that I shall kill you

And now, when I can't sleep,
When shadows bring the boy back,
It's always he who is able to cry;
The foul words remain to me.

Alan Watts

I am sure I was—at least until puberty—overly dependent
on my mother, though I cannot remember anything even
faintly resembling an Oedipus complex. On the contrary, I
was disappointed in the fact that she did not seem to me as
pretty as other women, and I couldn't abide the expression
she wore when she first woke up in the morning. But, at least
when I was little, she understood me, and always believed in
me—or perhaps in her idea of me, for when I was naughty she would say that it just wasn't like *me* to do such a
thing. She also gave me the impression that God had it in
mind for me to do a great work for the world, and it is probably just as well that I remember this subtle reinforcement of
my ego. It gave me comfort in the face of childhood sick-
nesses and dangers. Somehow it seemed that she disliked her
own body, perhaps because she had had so much sickness just
after marriage, and when she spoke of people being very *ill*
she would swallow the word as if it were a nasty lump of fat,
and take on a most serious frown. As I was an only child (she
had two miscarriages and a baby boy who lived only two
weeks) I think I picked up her anxiety for my survival and
became something of a physical coward.

But she made up in personality for what she lacked in
my conception of prettiness, and my father adored her, always. They would hold hands under the dining table at

meals, and he would hug her like a bear. Although she never sang and couldn't hold a tune, she had a musical and lilting speaking voice which held authority without forcing it. Having now become gently cynical about human nature I can say with some amazement that her eyes were as honest as her conscience, and that, though she may have been squeamish about things of the body, she was never at any time malicious, mean, greedy, conceited, or untruthful. I could never imagine what sins she was confessing in church when she joined in saying, "But thou, O Lord, have mercy upon us most miserable offenders." The "us" must have meant me. The only unpleasantness I ever found in her was her annoying habit (especially to an Englishman) of probing for your real emotions when you were trying to keep a stiff upper lip. When I once berated her for this, rather forcefully, she said, "I think I'll go and shed a tear."

Although my parents suffered through two horrendous wars and the Depression, which hit them hard, I cannot imagine being born to a more harmonious and unostentatiously virtuous couple. Yet I feel that I never quite gave them what they wanted. I don't know what that was, and perhaps they didn't either. But I was a weird child. I was a fantast who believed in fairies and magic when all the other children had given them up for twaddle. I preferred watching birds to playing cricket. I adopted a strange and un-English religion, and went off on my own to a far country. They said I had "imagination," which was good but dangerous, and the neighbors would speak of Mrs. Watts as "Alan Watt's mother." I told anyone who would listen endless tales of fantasy and of blood-and-thunder. I would conduct funeral ceremonies for dead birds and bats and rabbits instead of learning tennis. I read about ancient Egypt and Chinese tortures and Aladdin's lamp instead of "good books" by Scott, Thackeray, and Dickens. I have no idea how I came to be so weird, but never for a moment have I regretted that I forgetfully reincarnated myself as the child of Laurence Wilson Watts and Emily Mary Buchan, at Rowan Tree Cottage in Holbrook Lane, in the village of Chislehurst, Kent, England, almost due south of Greenwich, on the morning of January 6, 1915, at about twenty minutes after six, with the Sun in Capricorn, conjuncted with Mars and Mercury and in trine to a Moon in Virgo, with Sagittarius rising, and under bombardment in the midst of the first World War.

In My Own Way: An Autobiography

Bernard Shaw

Technically speaking I should say she was the worst mother conceivable, always, however, within the limits of the fact that she was incapable of unkindness to any child, animal, or flower, or indeed to any person or thing whatsoever. But if such a thing as a maternity welfare center had been established or even imagined in Ireland in her time, and she had been induced to visit it, every precept of it would have been laughably strange to her. Though she had been severely educated up to the highest standard for Irish "carriage ladies" of her time, she was much more like a Trobriand islander as described by Mr. Malinowski than like a modern Cambridge lady graduate in respect of accepting all the habits, good or bad, of the Irish society in which she was brought up as part of an uncontrollable order of nature. She went her own way with so complete a disregard and even unconsciousness of convention and scandal and prejudice that it was impossible to doubt her good faith and innocence; but it never occurred to her that other people, especially children, needed guidance or training, or that it mattered in the least what they ate and drank or what they did as long as they were not actively mischievous. She accepted me as a natural and customary phenomenon, and took it for granted that I should go on occurring in that way. In short, living to her was not an art: it was something that happened. But there were unkind parts of it that could be avoided; and among these were the constraints and tyrannies, the scoldings and browbeatings and punishments she had suffered in her childhood as the method of her education. In her righteous reaction against it she reached a negative attitude in which, having no substitute to propose, she carried domestic anarchy as far as in the nature of things it can be carried.

I myself was never on bad terms with my mother: we lived together until I was forty-two years old, absolutely without the smallest friction of any kind; yet when her death set me thinking curiously about our relations, I realized that I knew very little about her. Introduce me to a strange woman who was a child when I was a child, a girl when I was a boy, an adolescent when I was an adolescent; and if we take naturally to one another I will know more of her and she of me at the end of forty days (I had almost said of forty minutes) than I knew of my mother at the end of forty years. A contemporary stranger is a novelty and an enigma, also a possibility; but a mother is like a broomstick or like the sun in the heavens, it does not matter which as far as one's knowledge of her is concerned: the broomstick is there and the sun is there; and whether the child is beaten by it or warmed and enlightened by it, it accepts it as a fact in nature. . . .

Shaw: An Autobiography

Hermann Hesse

My father was different. He stood alone, belonging neither to the world of the idols and of my grandfather nor to the workaday world of the city. He stood to one side, lonely, a sufferer and a seeker, learned and kindly, without falseness and full of zeal in the service of truth, but far removed from that noble and tender but unmistakable smile—he had no trace of mystery. The kindliness never forsook him, nor his cleverness, but he never disappeared in the magic cloud that surrounded my grandfather, his face never dissolved in that childlikeness and godlikeness whose interplay at times looked like sadness, at times like delicate mockery, at times like the silent, inward-looking mask of God. My father did not talk to my mother in Hindu languages, but spoke English and a pure, clear, beautiful German faintly colored with a Baltic accent. It was this German he used to attract and win me and instruct me; at times I strove to emulate him, full of admiration and zeal, all too much zeal, although I knew that my roots reached deeper into my mother's soil, into the dark-eyed and mysterious. My mother was full of music, my father was not, he could not sing.

Childhood of the Magician

Henry Miller

Even the earliest memories of my mother are unhappy ones. I remember sitting by the stove in the kitchen on a very special kind of chair and talking to her. Mostly she was scolding me. I don't have pleasant memories of talks with her.

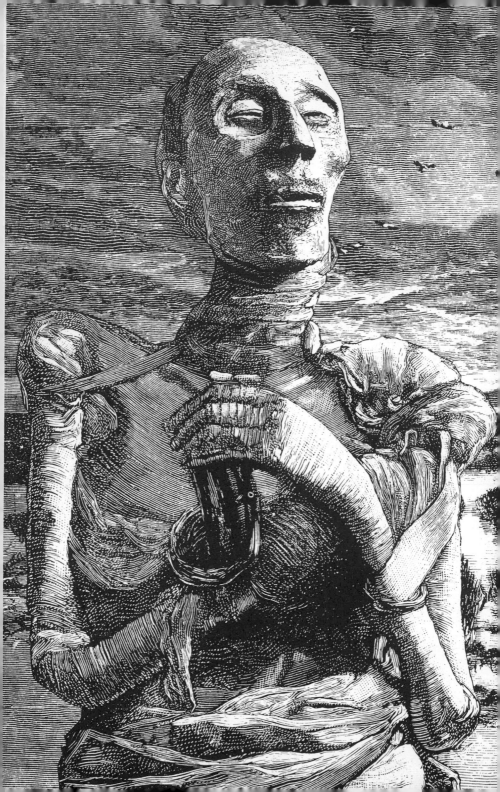

Once she grew a wart on her finger. She said to me, "Henry," (remember I'm only four years old) "what should I do?" I said, "Cut it off with the scissors." The wart! You don't cut off a wart! So she got blood poisoning. Two days later she came to me with her hand bandaged and she says, "And you told me to cut it off!" And BANG, BANG, she slaps me. Slaps me! For punishment. For telling her to do this! How do you like a mother who does that?

My sister was born mentally retarded; she had the intelligence of a child of about eight or ten. She was a great burden in my childhood because I had to defend her when the kids called, "Crazy Loretta, crazy Loretta!" They made fun of her, pulled her hair, called her names. It was terrible. I was always chasing these kids and fighting with them.

My mother treated her like a slave. I returned to Brooklyn for two or three months while my mother was dying. My sister was down to a skeleton. She was walking around with pails and brushes, mopping the floor, washing the walls, and so on. My mother seemed to think that this was good for her, that it gave her something to do, I suppose. To me it seemed cruel. However, my mother had put up with her all her life and there's no doubt but that it was a heavy cross to bear.

You see, my sister couldn't attend school because she was so backward. So my mother decided to teach her herself. My mother was never meant to be a teacher. She was terrible. She used to scold her, crack her, fly into a rage. She'd say, "How much is two times two?" and my sister, who hadn't the faintest idea of the answer, would say, "Five, no—seven, no—three." Just wild. BANG. Another slap or crack. Then my mother would turn to me and say, "Why do I have to bear this cross? What did I do to be punished so?" Asked *me*, a little boy. *"Why is God punishing me?"* You can see what kind of woman she was. Stupid? Worse than that.

The neighbors said she loved me. They said she was really very fond of me and all that. But I never felt any warmth from her. She never kissed me, never hugged me. I don't ever remember going to her and putting my arms around her. I didn't know mothers did that till one day I visited a friend at his home. We were twelve years old. I went home from school with him and I heard his mother's greeting. "Jackie, oh Jackie," she says. "Oh darling, how are you, how have you been?" She puts her arms around him and kisses him. I never heard that kind of language—even that tone of voice. It was new to me. Of course, in that stupid German neighborhood they were great disciplinarians, really brutal people. My boy friends, when I'd go home with them, would say, "Defend me. Help me. If my father starts to hit me, grab something and let's run."

I had no real contact with my mother when I was grown. I saw her briefly when I came back from Europe after being away ten years. But after that I had no contact with her until she became ill. Then I went to see her. Still the same problem—we had nothing in common. The horrible thing was that she was really dying this time. (You see, once before I had gone to see her when she was supposed to be dying.) She lasted three months before passing away. That was a terrible period for me. I went to see her every day. But even when dying she was that same determined tyrannical person dictating what I should do and refusing to do anything I asked her to do. I said to her, "Look, you're in bed. You can't get up." I didn't say, You're going to die, but I implied it. "For the first time in my life I'm going to tell you what to do. I'm giving the orders now." She rose up in bed, thrusting out her arm, shaking her finger at me. "You can't do that," she yells. There she was, on her deathbed, and I had to push her down with my hands around her throat. A moment later I was in the hall sobbing like a child.

Sometimes now in bed I say to myself, You have

reconciled yourself with the world. You don't have any enemies. There are no people you hate. How is it you can't
conjure up a better image of your mother? Suppose you die
tomorrow and there is a hereafter, and you encounter her.
What are you going to say when you face her? I can tell you
now she'll have the first and last word.

A weird thing happened when we were burying her. It
was a freezing cold day with the snow coming down thick.
They couldn't get the coffin angled right to lower it into the
grave. It was as if she was still resisting us. Even in the funeral parlor, before that, where she was on view for six days,
every time I bent over her one of her eyes would open and
stare at me.

My Life And Times

G. I. Gurdjieff

My father had a very simple, clear, and quite definite view on
the aim of human life. He told me many times in my youth
that the fundamental striving of every man should be to
create for himself an inner freedom toward life and to
prepare for himself a happy old age. He considered that the
indispensability and imperative necessity of this aim in life
was so obvious that it ought to be understandable to everyone without any wiseacring. But a man could attain this aim
only if, from childhood up to the age of eighteen, he had acquired data for the unwavering fulfillment of the following
four commandments:

First—   To love one's parents.
Second—To remain chaste.

Third— To be outwardly courteous to all without distinction, whether they be rich or poor, friends or enemies, power-possessors or slaves, and to whatever religion they may belong, but inwardly to remain free and never to put much trust in anyone or anything.

Fourth—To love work for work's sake and not for its gain.

My father, who loved me particularly as his first-born, had a great influence on me.

My personal relationship to him was not as toward a father, but as toward an elder brother; and he, by his constant conversations with me and his extraordinary stories, greatly assisted the arising in me of poetic images and high ideals.

Meetings With Remarkable Men

Jean-Paul Sartre

A father would have weighted me with a certain stable obstinacy. Making his moods my principles, his ignorance my knowledge, his disappointments my pride, his quirks my law, he would have inhabited me. That respectable tenant would have given me self-respect, and on that respect I would have based my right to live. My begetter would have determined my future. As a born graduate of the Ecole Polytechnique, I would have felt reassured forever. But if Jean-Baptiste Sartre had ever known my destination, he had taken the secret with him. My mother remembered only his saying, "My son won't go into the Navy." For want of more precise information, nobody, beginning with me, knew why the hell I had been born. Had he left me property, my childhood would have

been changed. I would not be writing, since I would be someone else. House and field reflect back to the young heir a stable image of himself. He touches himself on *his* gravel, on the diamond-shaped panes of *his* veranda, and makes of their inertia the deathless substance of his soul. A few days ago, in a restaurant, the owner's son, a little seven-year-old, cried out to the cashier, "When my father's not here, *I'm* the boss!" There's a man for you! At his age, I was nobody's master and nothing belonged to me. In my rare moments of lavishness, my mother would whisper to me, "Be careful! We're not in our own home!" We were never in our own home, neither on the Rue le Goff nor later, when my mother remarried. This caused me no suffering since everything was loaned to me, but I remained abstract. Worldly possessions reflect to their owner what he is; they taught me what I was not. *I was not* substantial or permanent, *I was not* the future continuer of my father's work, *I was not* necessary to the production of steel. In short, I had no soul.

The Words

James Baldwin

I was the only child in the house—or houses—for a while, a halcyon period which memory has quite repudiated; and if I remember myself as tugging at my mother's skirts and staring up into her face, it was because I was so terrified of the man we called my father; who did not arrive on *my* scene, really, until I was more than two years old. I have written both too much and too little about this man, whom I did not understand till he was past understanding. In my first memory of him, he is standing in the kitchen, drying the dishes. My mother had dressed me to go out, she is taking me someplace, and it must be winter, because I am wearing, in my memory, one of those cloth hats with a kind of visor, which button under the chin—a Lindbergh hat, I think. I am apparently in my mother's arms, for I am staring at my father over my mother's shoulder, we are near the door; and my father smiles. This may be a memory, I think it is, but it may be a fantasy. One of the very last times I saw my father on his feet, I was staring at him over my mother's shoulder—she had come rushing into the room to separate us—and my father was not smiling and neither was I.

His mother, Barbara, lived in our house, and she had been born in slavery. She was so old that she never moved from her bed. I remember her as pale and gaunt and she must have worn a kerchief because I don't remember her hair. I remember that she loved me; she used to scold her son about the way he treated me; and he was a little afraid of her. When she died, she called me into the room to give me a present—one of those old, round, metal boxes, usually with a floral design, used for candy. *She* thought it was full of candy and *I* thought it was full of candy, but it wasn't. After she died, I opened it and it was full of needles and thread.

This broke my heart, of course, but her going broke it more because I had loved her and depended on her. I knew—children *must* know—that she would always protect me with all her strength. So would my mother too, I knew that, but my mother's strength was only to be called on in a desperate emergency. It did not take me long, nor did the children, as they came tumbling into this world, take long to discover that our mother paid an immense price for standing between us and our father. He had ways of making her suffer quite beyond our ken, and so we soon learned to depend on each other and became a kind of wordless conspiracy to protect *her*. (We were all, absolutely and mercilessly, united against our father.) We soon realized, anyway, that she scarcely belonged to us: she was always in the hospital, having another baby. Between his merciless children, who were terrified of him, the pregnancies, the births, the rats, the murders on Lenox Avenue, the whores who lived downstairs, his job on Long Island—to which he went every morning, wearing a Derby or a Homburg, in a black suit, white shirt, dark tie, looking like the preacher he was, and with his black lunch-box in his hand—and his unreciprocated love for the Great God Almighty, it is no wonder our father went mad. We, on the other hand, luckily, on the whole, for our father, and luckily indeed for our mother, simply took over each new child and made it ours.

No Name In The Street

Soren Kierkegaard

Johannes Climacus
or
De omnibus dubitandum est
a story

His home did not offer many diversions, and as he almost never went out, he early grew accustomed to occupying himself with his own thoughts. His father was a very severe man, apparently dry and prosaic, but under his frieze coat he concealed a glowing imagination which even old age could not dim. When occasionally Johannes asked his permission to go out, he generally refused to give it, though once in a while he proposed instead that Johannes should take his hand and walk up and down the room. At first glance this would seem a poor substitute, and yet, as with the frieze coat, there was something totally different concealed beneath it. The offer was accepted, and it was left entirely to Johannes to determine where they should go. So they went out of doors to a nearby castle in Spain, or out to the seashore, or about the streets, wherever Johannes wished to go, for his father was equal to anything. While they went up and down the room his father described all that they saw; they greeted passers-by, carriages rattled past them and drowned his father's voice; the cake-woman's cakes were more enticing than ever. He described so accurately, so vividly, so explicitly even to the least details, everything that was known to Johannes and so fully and perspicuously what was unknown to him, that after half an hour of such a walk with his father he was as much overwhelmed and fatigued as if he had been a whole day out of doors. Johannes soon learned from his father how to exercise his magical power. What first had been an epic now became a drama; they talked while walking up and down. If they went along familiar ways, they watched one another sharply to make sure that nothing was overlooked; if the way was strange to Johannes, he invented something, whereas his father's almighty imagination was capable of shaping everything, of using every childish whim as an ingredient in the drama which was being enacted. To Johannes it seemed as if the world were coming into existence during the conversation, as if his father were our Lord and he were his favorite, who was allowed to interpose his foolish conceits as merrily as he would; for he was never repulsed, his father was never put out, he agreed to everything, and always to Johannes's satisfaction. . . .

While thus there was being developed in him an almost vegetative tendency to drowse in imagination, which was in part aesthetic, in part more intellectual, another side of his soul was being strongly shaped, namely, his sense for the sudden, the surprising. This was not accomplished by the magic means which commonly serves to rivet the attention of children, but by something far higher. His father combined an irresistible dialectic with an all-powerful imagination. When for any reason his father engaged in argument with anyone, Johannes was all ears, all the more so because every-

thing was conducted with an almost festive orderliness. His father always allowed his opponent to state his whole case, and then as a precaution asked him if he had nothing more to say before he began his reply. Johannes had followed the opponent's speech with strained attention, and in his way shared an interest in the outcome. A pause intervened. The father's rejoinder followed, and behold! in a trice the tables were turned. How that came about was a riddle to Johannes, but his soul delighted in the show. The opponent spoke again. Johannes could almost hear his heart beat, so impatiently did he await what was to happen—It happened; in the twinkling of an eye everything was inverted, the explicable became inexplicable, the certain doubtful, the contrary evident. When the shark wishes to seize its prey it has to turn over upon its back, for its mouth is on its underside; its back is dark, its belly is silver-white. It must be a magnificent sight to witness that alternation of color; it must sometimes glitter so brightly as to hurt the eyes, and yet it is a delight to look upon. Johannes witnessed a similar alternation when he heard his father engage in argument. He forgot again what was said, both what his father and what the opponent said, but that shudder of soul he did not forget.

. . . What other children get through the fascination of poetry and the surprises of fairy-tales, he got through the repose of intuition and the alternations of dialectic. This was the child's joy, it became the boy's game, it became the youth's delight. So his life had a rare continuity; it did not know the various transitions which commonly mark the different periods of growth. When Johannes grew older he had no toys to lay aside, for he had learned to play with that which was to be the serious business of his life, and yet it lost thereby nothing of its allurement.

. . . Wherever he surmised a labyrinth, there he must find a way. If once he began such an enterprise, nothing could make him leave off. If he found it difficult, if he grew tired before having finished, he used to adopt a very simple method. He shut himself up in his room, made everything as festive as possible and then said in a loud and clear voice, *I will it*. He had learned from his father that one can do what one wills; and his father's life had not discredited this theory. This experience had imparted to Johannes's soul an indescribable sort of pride. It was intolerable to him that there should be anything one could not do if only one willed it. But his pride was not at all indicative of a feeble will; for when he had said those energetic words he was ready for anything, he then had a still more lofty goal, namely, to penetrate by sheer will the jungle growth of difficulty. This was again an adventure which aroused his enthusiasm. So his life was at all times romantically adventurous, although for his adventure he did not need forests and distant travel, but only what he possessed—a little room with one window.

Although his soul was early attracted to the ideal, yet his trust and confidence in reality was in no wise weakened. The ideal which he was nourished upon lay so close to him, all came about so naturally, that this became his reality, and again in the reality around him he might expect to discover the ideal. His father's melancholy contributed to this. That his father was an extraordinary man was something Johannes got to know later. That he astonished him, as no other man did to the same degree, he knew; but he was acquainted with so few people that he possessed no scale with which to measure him. That his father, humanly speaking, was something out of the ordinary was the last thing he would learn in the paternal house. Once in a while, when an old friend visited the family and entered into a confidential conversation with his father, Johannes would hear him say, "I am good for nothing, cannot accomplish anything, my one wish is to find a place in a charitable institution." That was not a jest, there was no trace of irony in his father's words, on the contrary there was a gloomy seriousness in them which alarmed Johannes.

. . . Johannes, whose whole view of life was, so to say, hidden in his father, inasmuch as he himself saw only very little, found himself involved in a contradiction, which baffled him for a long time, the suspicion that his father contradicted himself, if not in other ways, at least by the virtuosity with which he could triumph over an opponent and put him to silence. So Johannes's confidence in reality was not weakened; he had not imbibed the ideal from writings which taught him that the glory they describe is, indeed, not to be found in the world; he was not formed by a man who knew how to make his knowledge precious, but rather to make it as unimportant and worthless as possible.

Journals

Theodore Roethke

MY PAPA'S WALTZ

The whiskey on your breath
Could make a small boy dizzy;
But I hung on like death:
Such waltzing was not easy.

We romped until the pans
Slid from the kitchen shelf;
My mother's countenance
Could not unfrown itself.

The hand that held my wrist
Was battered on one knuckle;
At every step you missed
My right ear scraped a buckle.

You beat time on my head
With a palm caked hard by dirt,
Then waltzed me off to bed
Still clinging to your shirt.

Neal Cassady

. . . The reading of *The Count {of Monte Cristo}* had been my
first mighty excursion into extended thought, and together
with the motion picture *The Invisible Man*, it had for a long
time given my imagination all it needed. Walking home
from school I often became momentarily lost, so absentmind-
ed was I while under the influence of a great daydream that
followed threads of plot to an end and then continued with
its own imagery until all thoughts were suffocated under
their very number.

There was no ebbing in the love of literature that had
sprung forth, and while henceforward I was to pursue its
gleanings in a satisfied solitude I still looked to Father for tu-
toring of my quizzical mind in the meaning of things the
movies portrayed. Yet, this was an indecisive teaching, for he
himself was seldom sure of anything. That is, if he did know
a particular answer but it could be one or two or more
things, he would evade positive pronouncement because the
habit of non-commital speech was too strong in him to allow
for any direct statement when there was a chance of error.

Since beginning to drink he had maintained the safety of unformed opinions in consequence of his need to agree with any idea expressed. This was especially apparent when he was soberly talking; indecisive to the core in the long repression of his timid ego, his numbed mind refused to crystallize anything and made adroit sidesteps of even the most trivial of beliefs that it might be called upon to take a stand. Such an instance of this retrogression, that clearly showed the decline his mental grovelling had caused to his potency of reflection, occurred when I asked him what the word *kill* meant in the movie title *Four Hours to Kill.* After an explanation that it meant to murder someone, there came to him the idea that it might mean to pass time. His mind, though quickly confused, must have known this to be right, yet perversely his nature felt obliged to filter through a haze of thoughts for a difficult third possibility which, although unfound in minutes of intense thinking, was believed better to be sought after than to risk a rash decision on one of the two more likely meanings of the word.

Coupled with The Drunkard's intellectual hesitance, and in more than ordinary measure, was its twin trait of meekness. In his weakness Father accepted complete subjugation to the power of his vice and, thus gripped by its onslaught, his unrebelling slavery to drink produced the sustaining force for a saintlike gentleness he always displayed when sober. Deeply penetrated by the destroying excess of an uncontrolled flaw, his soul assumed the guilt which made unquestionable the right of his suffering. Without evident bitterness, he would innocently accept the torment administered him as though unaware that he could protest. In him this Christian virtue of "turning the cheek" was no pretension, for the low esteem in which he held his drunkard's self made for a near-genuine humility over his Sin. Being feebly involved in his own fault, he could not be demanding, and so was blinded to the faults of others. The humble attitude created by his exaggerated self-debasement is shown in the fact that while my brothers, Jack in particular, beat and villified him for years with cruel and brutal arrogance, I never heard him speak in other than terms of highest praise for them. These abject stupidities were not the hypocritical utterances of fear; rather they were motivated by his honest feeling of their superiority and the inner acceptance that the base things they said of him were all quite true.

Of course, being such a doormat made almost everyone like Dad, and it was seldom that his servility went unnoticed by those who saw him regularly. Even among the non-violent personalities of the bleak bums with whom we associated there were comments like, "Neal wouldn't hurt a fly." and "Give the barber another drink, he's so damn timid he might forget to speak up." From Mother and the few other women he later knew came, "Neal's such a nice man, so loving and considerate if only he could stop drinking." And from my brothers: "Neal's okay when he's sober, but that's not often enough."

My concern in the matter was, at first, only expressed by an ever-increasing exasperation at the need to prod and pry at the edges of his intellect before he would say Yes or No about anything in question. It was not until later that I resented his being pushed around and then I became doubly put out with him, for he remained an inert mass while I, dumb with child ignorance of life, alternately goaded and pleaded to make him stop taking such abuse. But right now about the only thing that got me down was the absurd torpidity of his movements, especially when drunk. After our Saturday night on Curtis Street, which invariably ended with my punching him awake from an inebriated snooze, as in the harsh glare of the houselights curious people looked on with embarrassed stares while they filed out, I would stagger him home in anguished frustration that his slowmotioned gait was unnecessarily prolonging the mortifying trip.

He somewhat hindered my dashing about on our Sundays too, but not then needed to hold him upright, I directed his steps from afield instead of beneath his crushing weight and so his irritating slowness became more the normal adult lagging behind the scampering boy. Since I was in a fever of excitement it made little difference to my inattentive mind, attuned only to flushed joy of exploration, what might be the cause of Father's present languidity. I now appreciate that with an aching head or queasy stomach and enduring the severe nervousness of the "shakes," his weak smile frequently requesting rest can be seen as the sick grin of a man with a certain bravery. For I gave him no letup because Sunday was "my day," and I made him tramp from morn to night over the miles of countless wonders that I set out to find.

The First Third: A Partial Autobiography

William Golding

My father was a master at the local grammar school so that we were all the poorer for our respectability. In the dreadful English scheme of things at that time, a scheme which so accepted social snobbery as to elevate it to an instinct, we had our subtle place. Those unbelievable gradations ensured that though my parents could not afford to send my brother and me to a public school, we should nevertheless go to a grammar school. Moreover we must not go first to an elementary school but to a dame school where the children were nicer though the education was not so good. In fact, like everybody except the very high and the very low in those days, we walked a social tightrope, could not mix with the riotous children who made such a noise and played such wonderful games on the Green. I did not question these contradictions.

But at eight or nine the standard of education did not matter. My father could see to that. He was incarnate omniscience. I have never met anybody who could do so much, was interested in so much, and who knew so much. He could carve a mantelpiece or a jewel box, explain the calculus and the ablative absolute. He wrote a textbook of geography, of physics, of chemistry, of botany and zoology, devised a course in astro-navigation, played the violin, the cello, viola, piano,

flute. He painted expertly, knew so much about flowers he denied me the simple pleasure of looking anything up for myself. He produced a cosmology which I should dearly love to pass off as all my own work because he never told anyone but me about it. He fell hideously and passionately in love with wireless in the very earliest days and erected an aerial like the one on a battleship, and had some unused qualifications as an architect. He hated nothing in the whole world unless it were a Tory, and then only as a matter of principle and on academic lines. He stumped the country for the Labour party, telling the farm laborers that the Labour party did not want to exploit the workers the way the Tories did; it simply wanted to do away with them. He stood proudly and indignantly with my mother on the town hall steps under the suffragette banner, and welcomed the over-ripe tomatoes. He inhabited a world of sanity and logic and fascination. He found life so busy and interesting that he had no time for a career at all. But that was all right. His children would have the career in his place and restore the balance of nature. He and my mother brought us up with a serious care which he gave to nothing else but wireless and politics.

The Ladder And The Tree

Sherwood Anderson

A boy wants something very special from his father. You are always hearing it said that fathers want their sons to be what they feel they cannot themselves be but I tell you it also works the other way. I know that, as a small boy, I wanted my father to be a certain thing he was not, could not be. I wanted him to be a proud silent dignified one. When I was with other small boys and he passed along the street, I wanted to feel in my breast the glow of pride.

"There he is. That is my father."

But he wasn't such a one. He couldn't be. It seemed to me then that he was always showing off. Let's say someone in our town had got up a show. They were always doing it. At that time it would have been the G.A.R., the Grand Army of the Republic. They did it to raise some money to help pay the rent of their hall.

So they had a show, the druggist in it, the fellow who clerked in the shoe store. A certain horse doctor was always in such shows in our town and, to be sure, a lot of women and girls. They got as many in it as they could so that all of the relatives of the actors would come. It was to be, of course, a comedy.

And there was my father. He had managed to get the chief comedy part. It was, let's say, a Civil War play and he was a comic Irish soldier. He had to do the most absurd things. They thought he was funny, but I didn't think so.

I thought he was terrible. I didn't see how Mother could stand it. She even laughed with the others. It may be that I also would have laughed if it hadn't been my father.

Or there was a parade, say on the Fourth of July or on Decoration Day. He'd be in that too. He'd be right at the front of it. He had got himself appointed Grand Marshall or some such office, had got, to ride in the parade, a white horse hired from a livery stable.

He couldn't ride for shucks. He fell off the horse and everyone hooted with laughter but he did not care. He even seemed to like it. I remember one such occasion when he had done something ridiculous, and right out on the main street too, when I couldn't stand it. I was with some other boys and they were laughing and shouting at him and he was shouting back to them and having as good a time as they were. I ran away. There was an alleyway back of the stores on Main Street and I ran down that. There were some sheds, back of the Presbyterian church, where country people stabled horses during church on Sundays and I went in there. I had a good long cry.

Or I was in bed at night and Father had come home a little lit up and had brought some men with him. He was a man who was never alone. There were always men hanging around him. Before he went broke, running a harness shop, when he had the shop, there were always a lot of men loafing in there. He went broke of course because he gave too much credit. He couldn't refuse it and I thought he hadn't any sense. I thought he was a fool. I had got to hating him. I'd be upstairs in bed in the front room of the little house we lived in and he'd bring his crowd of men friends and sit with them on the front porch of our house.

There'd be men I didn't think would want to be fooling around with him but they did. There might even be the superintendent of our schools and a quiet man who ran a hardware store in our town. Once I remember there was a white-haired man who was cashier of the bank. It was a wonder to me they'd want to be seen with such a windbag. That's what I thought he was. I know now what it was that attracted them but I didn't know then. Now I think it was because life in our town, as in all small towns, was at times pretty dull and he livened it up. He made them laugh. He could tell stories. He'd even get them to singing. If they didn't come to our house he'd get such a crowd and they'd go off, say at night, to where there was a grassy place by a creek. They'd cook food there and they'd drink beer. They'd sit about listening to him while he told his stories. I knew that most of the stories he told were lies.

He was always telling stories about himself. He'd say this

or that wonderful thing had happened to him. It might be something that made him look like a fool. He didn't care. If it was a story, he'd tell it.

He was like this, let's say an Irishman came to our house. Right away Father would say he was Irish. He'd tell what county in Ireland he was born in. He'd tell things that happened to him in Ireland when he was a boy. He'd make it seem so real, telling little details of his life as a boy in Ireland, that, if I hadn't known where he was born, in a county down in southern Ohio, I'd have believed him myself.

If it was a Scotchman the same thing happened. He became a Scotchman. He'd get a burr into his speech. Or he was a German or a Swede. He'd be anything the other man was.

I think now they all knew he was lying but they seemed to like him just the same. As a boy that was what I couldn't understand.

And there was Mother. How could she stand it? I wanted to ask but never did. I was afraid. She was the kind you didn't ask such questions. . . .

We had gone broke, down and out, and do you think he ever brought anything home? Not he. If there wasn't anything to eat in the house, off visiting he'd go. He'd go visiting around at farm houses near our town. They all wanted him. Sometimes he'd stay away for weeks, Mother working to keep us fed, and then home he'd come bringing, let's say, a ham. He'd got it from some farmer friend. He'd slap it on the table in the kitchen. "You bet I'm going to see that my kids have something to eat," he'd say and Mother would just stand there looking at him and smiling at him. She'd never say a word about all the weeks and months he'd been away, not leaving us a cent for food. Once I heard her speaking to a woman in our street. It may be that woman had dared to sympathize with her. "Oh," she said, "it's all right. Don't you worry. He isn't ever dull like most of the men in this street. Life is never dull when my man is about."

I'd be up in my room and Father'd be down on the porch with some of his crowd. This would be on a summer night. He'd be spinning some of his tales. Then I didn't understand but now I know he never told any lies that hurt anyone. I know now that he just wanted to give people a show, make them laugh. He knew how bitter tasting life gets to almost everyone that lives. He had I think some notion of putting a kind of color on life, touching it here and there with a bit of color. I think he wanted to wash it over with color and I think Mother knew.

I was up there in my room and I was awake. I was filled often with bitterness, hearing my father go on and on with his tales, and often I wished he wasn't my father. I'd even invent another man as my father.

To be sure I wanted to protect my mother. I'd make up stories of a secret marriage, that for some strange reason never got known, as though some man, say the president of a railroad company or maybe a congressman, had got married to my mother, thinking his wife was dead and that then it turned out she wasn't.

So they had to hush it up but I got born just the same. I wasn't really the son of my father. There was a mysterious man somewhere in the world, a very dignified quite wonderful man who was really my father. You get the point. I even made myself half believe some of these fancies.

And then there came a certain night. Mother was away from home when Father came in and he was alone. He'd been off somewhere for two or three weeks. He found me alone in the house.

He came silently into the house and it was raining outside. It may be there was church that night and that Mother had gone. I was alone and was sitting in the kitchen. I had a book before me and was sitting and reading by the kitchen table.

So in came my father. He had been walking in the rain and was very wet. He sat and looked at me and I was startled for, on that night, there was on his face the saddest look I have ever seen on a human face. For a long time he sat looking at me, not saying a word.

And then something happened to me.

There are times when a boy is so sad, he doesn't quite know why, that he thinks he can hardly bear to go on living. He thinks he'd rather die. The sadness comes mostly when it has been raining or it comes in the fall when the leaves fall off the trees. It isn't anything special. It is just sadness.

So there was Father on the rainy summer night. He was sad and looking at him made me sad. He sat for a time, saying nothing, his clothes dripping. He must have been walking a long time in the rain. He got up out of his chair.

"You come on, you come with me," he said.

I got up and went with him out of the house. I was filled with wonder but, although he had suddenly become like a stranger to me, I wasn't afraid. We went along a street. At that time we lived in a little yellow frame house, quite far out at the edge of our town. It was a house we hadn't lived in very long. We had moved a lot. Once I heard my mother say to my father, "Well, I guess we'll have to be moving," she said. She said we were back three months on our rent and that there wasn't any money to pay it with. She didn't scold. She even laughed. She just took it as a fact that when the rent got far behind we had to move.

I was walking with my father and we went out of the town. We were on a dirt road. It was a road that led up a little hill, past fields and strips of woodland, and went on over the hill and down into a little valley, about a mile out of town, to where there was a pond. We walked in silence. The man who was always talking had stopped talking.

I didn't know what was up and had the queer feeling that I was with a stranger. I don't know now whether or not my father intended it so. I don't think he did.

The pond at the edge of the town was quite large. It was a place where a creek had been dammed and was owned by a man who sold ice in our town. We were there at the edge of the pond. We had come in silence. It was still raining hard and there were flashes of lightning followed by thunder. We were on a grassy bank at the pond's edge, when my father spoke, and in the darkness and rain his voice sounded strange. It was the only time during the evening that he did speak to me.

"Take off your clothes," he said and, still filled with wonder, I began to undress. There was a flash of lightning and I saw that he was already naked.

And so naked we went into the pond. He did not speak or explain. Taking my hand he led me down to the pond's edge and pulled me in. It may be that I was too frightened, too full of a feeling of strangeness to speak. Before that night my father had never seemed to pay any attention to me.

"And what is he up to now?" I kept asking myself that question. It was as though the man, my father I had not wanted as father, had got suddenly some kind of power over me.

I was afraid and then, right away, I wasn't afraid. We were in the pond in darkness. It was a large pond and I did not swim very well but he had put my hand on his shoulder. Still he did not speak but struck out at once into the darkness.

He was a man with very big shoulders and was a powerful swimmer. In the darkness I could feel the movement of his muscles. The rain poured down on us and the wind blew and there were the flashes of lightning followed by the peals of thunder.

And so we swam, I will never know for how long. It seemed hours to me. We swam thus in the darkness to the far edge of the pond and then back to where we had left our clothes. There was the rain on our faces. Sometimes my father turned and swam on his back and when he did he took my hand in his large powerful one and moved it over so that it rested always on his shoulder and sometimes as we swam thus I could look into his face. There would be a flash of lightning and I could see his face clearly.

It was as it was when he had come earlier into the kitchen where I sat reading the book. It was a face filled with sadness. There would be the momentary glimpse of his face and then again the darkness, the wind and the rain. In me there was a feeling I had never known before that night.

It was a feeling of closeness. It was something strange. It was as though there were only we two in the world. It was as though I had been jerked suddenly out of myself, out of a world of the school boy, out of a world in which I was ashamed of my father, out of a place where I had been judging my father.

He had become blood of my blood. I think I felt it. He the stronger swimmer and I the boy clinging to him in the darkness. We swam in silence and in silence we dressed, in our wet clothes, and went back along the road to the town and our house.

It had become a strange house to me. There was the little porch at the front where on so many nights my father had sat with the men. There was the tree by the spring and the shed at the back. There was a lamp lighted in the kitchen and when we came in, the water dripping from us, there was my mother. She was as she had always been. She smiled at us. I remember that she called us "boys." "What have you boys been up to?" she asked, but my father did not answer. As he had begun the evening's experience with me in silence so he ended it. He turned and looked at me and then he went, I thought with a new and strange dignity, out of the room.

He went to his room to get out of his wet clothes and I climbed the stairs to my own room. I undressed in darkness and got into bed. I was still in the grip of the feeling of strangeness that had taken possession of me in the darkness in the pond. I couldn't sleep and did not want to sleep. For the first time I had come to know that I was the son of my father. He was a storyteller as I was to be. It may be that on the night of my childhood I even laughed a little softly there in the darkness in my bed in the room. If I did, I laughed knowing that, no matter how much as a storyteller I might be using him, I would never again be wanting another father.

Memoirs

J. R. Ackerley

Child psychology is a tedious subject and if I advance one or two facts about my early childhood, I do so in no seriously scientific spirit or belief in their significance. I was a persistent bed-wetter. My Aunt Bunny told me that, like my brother, I was an accident and a "little unwanted" and that some attempt was made to prevent my arrival also. Possibly it was more perfunctory, possibly that instinct for self-preservation I have mentioned preserved me; at any rate I emerged a robust and healthy child, but became a persistent bed-wetter. Psychology, I believe, has abandoned a theory it once held that bed-wetting is a kind of unconscious revenge mechanism; I am sorry if that is so, for it seems to me an amusing notion that I might have been pissing upon a world that had not accorded me the wholehearted welcome my ego required. But whatever may be thought of that theory now, my parents could hardly have known of it then, for child psychology was not invented, nor would my father, I hope, have had the impudence to beat me for my behavior, which he eventually did. A good deal of patience, it is true, must have been expended upon me for years, and many a good mattress did I ruin until I slept permanently upon rubber sheets. Then came a time when the practice ceased, then it began again in my early teens. I myself, of course, knew nothing about it, only that at first it was pleasantly warm, then unpleasantly cold, and in the resumed cycle I used to dream, I recollect, that I was standing in a urinal—a devilish dream, for what more natural than to pee? At any rate, when I began once more to ruin the new and unprotected mattresses with which I had at last been entrusted, my father denounced it as "sheer laziness," to which, I fancy, he had long attributed it, and taking down my trousers in front of my protesting mother he beat me upon the bare bottom with his hand.

This is not recommended treatment, I believe, for my particular weakness, or strength, whichever it was, nor is it recommended for building up a relationship of love and confidence between father and son, and I still faintly remember the embarrassment and humiliation I felt when I pulled and buttoned up the trousers he had taken down before laying me across his knees—though, memory being what it is, I can't be sure that this was on that particular occasion, for he beat me for other things as well, though not often and not hard, and if these chastisements had upon our future relations any effect, I certainly never bore him any conscious grudge.

Another disadvantage to which he may be thought to have put himself in regard to us children was that throughout our formative years he was what may be called a "weekend" father, if as frequent as that. Having accidentally produced us all and concealed us, first in Herne Hill, where I was born, then in Herne Bay, where my sister was born two years later, he removed us again, at the turn of the century, to Bowdon in Cheshire, his own homeland, where we were accidentally discovered by his business friends. He himself was working in Covent Garden and had a flat in Marylebone where, according to Aunt Bunny, he led a gay free bachelor's life—"all the fun of the fair," as she put it—and to which my mother was never invited. We were therefore brought up and surrounded by women, my mother, aunt, grandmother, his sisters, old Sarah and various nurses, governesses, and maids, while he himself was an irregular weekend visitor: in 1900, for instance, eighteen months after my sister's birth, he departed with Stockley for Jamaica on a business trip. It was not until 1903, when he removed us again, this time to the first of the three houses we were to occupy in Richmond, Surrey, that he lived with us and we became a united family.

Such a father might well be an awe-inspiring figure to small children, and that was the aspect he sometimes assumed. For of course we were as naughty and disobedient as children are likely to be when reared almost entirely by sweet, kind, doting women in whom all sense of discipline is lacking. My poor, dear, scatter-brained mother to whom, in particular, we paid so little heed, would sometimes be driven by our unruliness, impertinence, or downright cruelty to say, "I shall have to tell your father when he comes," and occasionally, provoked beyond endurance, she did—and that was how I got my beatings. The dogs too. We always had household dogs, and my father was dispenser of justice to them also, for no one but he would "rub their noses in it" to house-train them, or take punitive action against them, the "good hiding," for other offenses. It is fair to say that he came to us generally in the guise of Father Christmas, loaded with presents; but if we or the dogs were in disgrace he came as a figure of retribution, and it may be that, for this reason, he did not perfectly earn his way into my childish heart. But I would not care to make too much of all this as affecting the confidential relationship he himself offered my brother and me some years later.

My Father And Myself

Floyd Dell

But ... how has it happened that a child stoic has turned into Little Lord Fauntleroy? A stoic is one who no longer expects anything good. But in whom has he placed his naive and boundless trust? In whom can a child place his trust, but in his all-powerful, heroic, wonderful, beneficent father? And when he finds that he is not a prince but a pauper, he is cruelly disillusioned in his father. He has, in fact, lost the godlike, all-powerful father of his childhood, as if by death; this jobless workingman who sits around the house trying to maintain authority over growing children who are supporting the family, is no such personage as the father that the boy lost one Christmas Eve. Who is he, and what the boy can do about him, remains to be seen. But evidently he can be, at present, no model, no hero, no masculine influence in his son's boyhood, no guide along the pathway of life, no evoker of ambition.

There remains the Mother. A little, bent, ailing, tireless

woman, she is yet, within her own realm, an all-powerful Goddess. And her own realm is not just the kitchen where she bends over the hot cook-stove, or the table, where she sits anxiously on the edge of her chair so as to be ready to jump up and serve her husband and children. Her realm, for her youngest son certainly, is the Ideal Universe. . . . Before I could see very much of the wide world myself, it was already there in my mind, a far-flung world taken on trust from her teaching lips, a world that extended in Time as well as in mere Space. It grew in my mind, that Ideal Universe, until it was infinitely vaster than the small world which my young body inhabited, the small world of which I could learn something for myself by my five senses. The Picture of the World in my mind stretched out farther than my swift little legs could ever run, on and on past the farthest hills that my young eyes could see—out, out beyond the familiar house and yard, the half-explored neighborhood, the partly-glimpsed small town, out past Pike County itself, into America, an America come to by my pioneer ancestors as a free country, a country to be proud of, with Washington and Lincoln to reverence, a flag to cherish as a soldier's son; out, out to a world beyond that, the older world from which Columbus came, with knights and heroes in it, Greece and Rome to remember, China and Africa to civilize and explore. This firm clear sketch that my mother drew for me, after being gradually disentangled from the other pretend-world of giants and fairies and dragons, was presently being filled in at school by women like my mother, beautiful and wise and good and firm and kind—at least, some of them were. And always, before I came to anything as I went further and further into the world, before I could hear it, see it, smell it, touch it, taste it, I had it already in my mind, in its place among other things, explained and understood in advance. Books were taking up the work; the Ideal Universe grew every day larger, brighter, more orderly, more understandable, more complete.

And all this Ideal Universe, her gift to me, was filled with a sense of *ought* and *must*—her laws, which I must obey. Whom should I trust, if not her? Whose opinion or taste or authority could I rank above hers? Not my father's, not my brothers' or sister's, not the neighbors'. If she wanted me to wear curls, that was surely little enough to do for her. There was no possibility of my being anything else but a "mamma's boy."

So that was how the fiercely cold child-stoic that crept into my mind upon Christmas Eve had turned me into Little Lord Fauntleroy. He had given me the strength never to want anything that a father could give; lest I be disappointed. But he had no power to shield me from the inexorable radiance of a mother's love.

Homecoming: An Autobiography

Andre Gide

It is Pascal, I believe, who says that we never love people for themselves, but only for their qualities. I think it might have been said of my mother that the qualities she loved were not those of the persons she tyrannized over, but those she wished them to acquire. At any rate, that is how I try to explain her unremitting efforts to work on other people, and me in particular; and I was so excessively irritated by this that I am not sure my exasperation had not ended by destroying all my love for her. She had a way of loving me that sometimes almost made me hate her and touched my nerves on the raw. You whom I shock, imagine, if you can, the effect of being constantly watched and spied upon, incessantly and harassingly advised as to your acts, your thoughts, your expenditure, as to what you ought to wear or what you ought to read, as to the title of a book. She disliked, for instance, that of *Les Nourritures Terrestres,* and as there was still time to change it, she never wearied of returning to the charge.

Wretched questions of money too had for the last few months brought an added cause of irritation into our relations: Mamma used to give me a monthly allowance, which she considered ought to be enough for me—three hundred francs, if I remember rightly—two thirds of which I used regularly to spend on books and music. She did not consider it prudent to put the money that came to me from my father—I had no idea what it amounted to—at my free disposal; and she took care not to let me know that at my majority I had a right to it. But it would be a mistake to think that any personal interest was at the bottom of this; she was solely actuated by a desire to protect me from myself, to keep me in leading strings, and, what exasperated me most of all, by a kind of feeling of what was proper and so to speak, *congruous* for me to have, and this she measured by her own estimation of my necessities. The accounts she showed me when I became aware of my rights, were, she tried to make out, all in my favor; people talk of the "eloquence of figures"; with Mamma every column was a speech for the defense; she wanted to prove that I should find no advantage in any other arrangement, that my monthly allowance was as much or more than my rightful income; and as my board and lodging were charged to me, it appeared to me that the best way of getting out of the difficulty was to propose, on the contrary, to pay *her* an allowance during any time I should spend with her. It was by this compromise that our differences were settled.

But, as I have said, this fortnight that we spent together after a long separation, was a cloudless one. I certainly brought a great deal of good will to it on my part, as if some presentiment had warned us both that these were the last days we should pass together; for Mamma, on her side, was more conciliatory than I have ever known her. The joy of finding me less deteriorated than she had imagined from my letters no doubt disarmed her; I felt in her nothing but a mother's love, and I was happy to be her son.

I now began to wish for the resumption of our life in common, which I had ceased to think possible, and planned to spend all the summer with her at La Roque. It was settled she was to go there first to open the house and it was possible that Emmanuèle might come and join us. For, as if to seal our more perfect understanding, Mamma had at last confessed to me that she wished for nothing so much as to see me marry my cousin, whom she had long looked upon as her daughter-in-law. Perhaps too she felt her strength failing and was afraid of leaving me alone.

I was at Saint-Nom-la-Bretèche, staying with my friend E. R. until it should be time for me to join her, when a telegram from our old Marie suddenly summoned me. My mother had had a stroke. I hurried off. I found her lying in bed in the big room I used as my study in the summer; it was the room she preferred when she spent a few days at La Roque without opening the whole house. I am almost sure she recognized me; but she did not have any clear idea of the time or the place or of herself or of the people about her; for she showed neither surprise nor pleasure at seeing me. Her face was not much changed, but her eyes were vague and her features so expressionless that it seemed as though her body no longer belonged to her and she had ceased to control it. It was so strange that I felt more amazement than pity. She was in a half-sitting position, propped up by pillows; her arms were outside the bed-clothes and she was trying to write in a large open account-book. Even now her restless desire to intervene, to advise, to persuade, was still troubling her; she seemed in great mental agitation, and the pencil she held in her hand ran over the blank sheet of paper, but without making any mark; and the uselessness of this supreme effort was inexpressibly distressing. I tried to speak to her, but my voice did not reach her; and when she tried to speak herself, it was impossible for me to make out what she wanted to say. I took away the paper in the hope she might be able to rest, but her hand continued to write on the sheets. At last she drowsed off and her features gradually relaxed; her hands ceased moving. . . . And suddenly, as I looked at the poor hands I had just seen laboring so desperately, I imagined them at the piano, and the thought that they too had tried in their unskillful way to express a little poetry, music, and beauty, flooded my heart with a great wave of respect and admiration, and falling on my knees at the foot of the bed, I buried my face in the bed-clothes to stifle my sobs.

It is not my personal sorrows that draw tears from me; however grief-stricken my heart, my eyes remain dry. There is always one part of me which hangs back, looks mockingly at the other and says, "Come! Come! You're not so unhappy as all that!" On the other hand, I have a great abundance of tears to shed over other people's griefs, which I often feel more keenly than my own; but I have even more for any manifestation of beauty, nobility, abnegation, devotion, gratitude, courage, or sometimes for a very ingenuous, very child-like expression of feeling. And any very vivid artistic emotion too is immediately watered with my tears, to the extreme astonishment of my neighbors, if I happen to be in a picture-gallery or concert-room. I remember the uncontrollable laughter of two English girls in Florence on seeing my streaming eyes in front of Fra Angelico's great fresco at San

Marco; my friend Ghéon, who was with me, wept in unison, and I admit that the sight of our two waterfalls must have been very ludicrous. In the same, there was once a time when the mere name of Agamemnon opened some secret floodgate in my heart, so great was the feeling of awe and mythological reverence with which the majesty of the King of kings filled me. So that now, it was not my loss that so greatly upset me (and to be quite sincere, I am obliged to confess that my loss afflicted me very little; or perhaps I should say the sight of my mother's suffering afflicted me, but not the idea of her leaving me). No, it was not grief that made me cry, but admiration for that heart that had never allowed anything vile to touch it, and that beat only for others, with an unfailing devotion to duty that was not virtue so much as natural inclination, and with a humility so great that my mother might have said like Malherbe, but how much more sincerely: *I have always held my service such a despicable offering that to whatever altar I bring it, it is with a heart ashamed and a trembling hand.* And above all I admired her for her life which had been one continual effort to draw a little nearer to what she thought lovely or worthy to be loved.

I was alone in the big room, alone with her, watching the solemn approach of death, and feeling the restless beatings of that unflagging heart re-echo in my own. How it still labored on! I had been present at other deathbeds, but I had not thought them so pathetic as this, either because they had seemed to put a more conclusive and natural end to a life, or simply because I had looked at them less fixedly. It was certain she would not recover consciousness, so that I felt no need to summon my aunts; I was jealous of watching by her side alone. Marie and I assisted her in her last moments, and when at last her heart ceased to beat, I felt myself sink into an overwhelming abyss of love, sorrow, and liberty.

It was then that I experienced the singular propensity of my mind to let itself be dazzled by the Sublime. I spent the first weeks of my bereavement, I remember, in a sort of moral intoxication which led me to commit the most ill-considered acts; provided I thought them noble, it was enough to ensure them the approval of my mind and heart. I began by distributing as souvenirs to distant relations, some of whom had scarcely known my mother, the trifling jewels and knick-knacks that had belonged to her, and which for that reason I specially prized. Out of exalted love, out of a strange longing for privation, I would have given away my whole fortune at the very moment I became possessed of it; I would have given myself too; the feeling of my inward wealth filled me to overflowing, inspired me with a sort of heady abnegation. The sole idea of keeping anything back would have seemed to me shameful and I lent an ear to nothing that did not help me to admire myself. The very liberty, which during my mother's lifetime I had so craved for, stunned me like a wind from the open, suffocated—perhaps, indeed, frightened me. I felt dazed, like a prisoner unexpectedly set free, like a kite whose string has been suddenly cut, like a boat broken loose from its moorings, like a drifting wreck, at the mercy of wind and tide.

If It Die . . . An Autobiography

Stephen Spender

He died when I was seventeen, certainly the age when sons react most strongly against their parents. Thus my portrait of him may be oversimplified by the fury of adolescence. To his contemporaries he may have seemed more a man of the world, more intuitive and understanding than he appears here. Nevertheless, for me his attitudes were both in a material and spiritual sense unreal. For it is no exaggeration to say that at the end his unreality terrified me. Just as Midas turned everything he touched to gold, so my father turned everything into rhetorical abstraction, in which there was no concreteness, no accuracy. It got to a stage when I was frightened of things because they were almost superseded in my mind by descriptive qualities which he applied to them. A game of football ceased to be just the kicking about of a leather ball by bare-kneed boys. It had become confused with the Battle of Life. Honor, Integrity, Discipline, Toughness, and a dozen other qualities haunted the field like ghostly footballers.

He impressed so much on me his achievement in having passed certain examinations, that to gain a First, a Scholarship, Honors or a Credit seemed as difficult as scaling some great height. Indeed, to climb a real Alp would have been easier, because it would have presented a tangible difficulty, whereas the difficulty contained within Examinations seemed impalpable. I knew only that those who passed them brilliantly were mysterious Victors with Double Firsts, Scholarships, and so forth. Even answering a question in class became a problem, for the idea of some insuperable Difficulty lurking within the question distracted me from the question itself. I meditated on the idea of Difficulty: what was Difficult could not be easy; but if I knew the answer that would be easy, therefore it could not be the correct answer, and the question must conceal some hidden trap. How often at school the boy next to me, or the one next to him, gave the right answer, which I had known, but could not believe to be correct, just because it had appeared easy.

The answers handed in at examinations, and so carefully sealed and taken away, often in boxes, never seemed to me just answers. There was something mysterious, unknown to me about them, like the confidences made in the confessional, or like specimens of cerebral fluid extracted by the examiner from the examinees by the operation of examining. I could not believe that the people who got brilliant Firsts,

Double Firsts, and so on, for their General Essays, were just writing papers which had something in common with, say, articles appearing in reviews on some specialized subject.

I remember lying awake at night and thinking about Work, Discipline, and Thought itself, just as though all these activities were divorced from objects, and were quite abstract functionings of the mind.

I think that if, when I was young, I had been told, "Go out on to that field and kick that ball" or "Sit at that desk and answer that question": in a word, if I had been committed to particular tasks on particular occasions, I would have escaped a good deal of confusion. But the abstract conception of Work and Duties was constantly being thrust on me, so that I saw beyond tasks themselves to pure qualities of moral and intellectual existence, quite emptied of things.

As Work was associated with Duty, I knew that it could have no connection with enjoyment. Thus when at school I enjoyed a subject, I felt that it had ceased to be Work for me, and had become a kind of self-indulgence. It was easy, and I therefore felt that I should turn to something Difficult. At the same time my whole being revolted against my own conception of Work. I did not have the courage to enjoy myself, nor the strength to force myself to act against my inclinations.

More serious than the effect of my father's rhetoric on my school work was its influences on my ideas of morality. Discipline, Purity, Duty, became abstract concepts for me, states of pure existence almost removed from particular actions. Thus they tended to seem absolute, and individual failures to work or behave well were not just separate acts which proved little or nothing about my character in general, but proofs that I could not achieve that pure goodness of existence which I sought.

My parents impressed on us the fear of being an inad-

missible, unrespectable, loveless kind of person, a moral out-
cast. They had a special kind of cowardice, which was a fear
of finding out out some final wickedness in ourselves, some
unspeakable shame of ultimate depravity. In all their relationships there was the sense of something which might turn
up and which could never be mentioned. Ours was a morality
based on a fear of discovering something horrible about others—or even about ourselves—not on a love sternly but pa-
tiently judging every separate action within its own sep-
arateness, a love sometimes confronted with pain and failure,
but never withholding forgiveness, never finally withdrawn.

My revolt against the attitude of my family led me to
rebel altogether against morality, work, and discipline.
Secretly I was fascinated by the worthless outcasts, the depraved, the lazy, the lost, and wanted to give them that love
which they were denied by respectable people. This reaction
was doubtless due to the fact that I wanted to love what I
judged to be the inadmissable worst qualities in myself. But
such a revolt confronted me with new problems, because
love, although not a discipline of fear, is also a discipline. If
it accepts the reality of evil, it nevertheless tries to melt it
into the wholeness of a creative purpose, and does not rest
contented with what mere conventionality has rejected.
Without this positive discipline, work and human relationships were no easier for me than they had been within the
negative discipline of fear.

World Within World

A. S. Neill

Nearly all children go through a stage during which they become very critical of their parents. This happens with the strengthening of a psychological urge to break free from the apron strings. I went through such a stage from about eighteen to twenty-four. At one time, I was ashamed of both my parents. My father embarrassed me because he had no "manners"; if we had a guest to dinner, [my sister] Clunie and I implored Mother not to have soup because of Father's loud method of supping it. I was ashamed of Mother because she talked too much, often irrelevantly. She was really a very bad listener, and always tried to edge in a word, even when the conversation dealt with subjects she knew nothing about. I recall one occasion when this infuriated me. A visitor was telling us about his adventures in China, and she kept interrupting him with silly remarks about her brother Sandy once having known a man there. I was impatient, arrogant; my father, on the contrary, had the patience of Job. He read his *Scotsman* every morning, while my mother always took up the paper about bedtime. "Listen to this, George," she would say and proceed to read out a whole column of news that he had already seen. Not once did he dare say, "I've read it, Mary."

My rather hateful, critical attitude toward my parents seemed to disappear after Clunie's death. Only then did I begin to have tender feelings about my father. No longer was I the Cinderella of the family; by this time, Father had accepted me as a son to be proud of—someone who had made good—though he still tried to look out for good jobs for me. When an old friend of Mother's came on a visit from Australia, where he had made good, my father spoke to him about my prospects out there. He said that he was a bosom friend of the Prime Minister, and would get me a job as inspector of schools if I said the word. I didn't say the word, but have sometimes wondered what would have become of me if I had gone out to Australia.

I was ashamed of my mother's garrulity, for she liked to make conversation a monologue. But all the time I hated myself for criticizing her. My parents gave up so much for us; they were so concerned about our health and happiness and future. They were really grand folk, but so very remote from us in every way that was of inherent moment.

As a grown man, I used to write home once a fortnight. Every letter took a long time. I sat and chewed my pen and wondered what to say. Most of the letters were about the weather. And when I went home as a young man, I found it difficult to talk to my parents. We had no common interests. Poor souls, they were so naive about us. When I was nineteen, on occasion I would come home late. Father asked where I had been, and I could not tell him I had been out with Liz Macdonald because one did not tell parents such things in the early days of the century. I did what all other sons and daughters did then—and may do now—I lied. I always got away with my lies, but my brother Willie made a bloomer when he said he had been having a chat with old Geordie Cable. Geordie had been dead for five years.

I am sure that most people carry throughout their lives a guilt feeling about their parents. My mother used to lecture us on our ingratitude. "We have done everything for you, fed you and clothed you, and what do we get? No gratitude. Mrs. Smith who half starved her children and treated them harshly, her children adore her now and would do anything for her." The sad feature was that the statement was true.

The gulf between Victorian parents and their children was unbridgeable. It is too often the same today. The fear a child acquires from angry adult voices and spankings in babyhood lives on for a lifetime. It was fear of our parents that made us strangers to them.

"Neill! Neill! Orange Peel!"

Richard Elman

People are always saying: WEREN'T YOU JUST A LITTLE AFRAID OF FREDI & SHIRL?
  OF MY FATHER . . . ?
  YES.
  MY LOVED ONES?
  YES.
  THOSE WHO WERE NEAR AND DEAR TO ME?
  THEM TOO . . .
  OF COURSE NOT. I WAS SCARED TO DEATH.

  RICHARD WHY ARE YOU ALWAYS FLINCHING? ARE YOU AFRAID OF US?
  I'M AFRAID NOT.
  DON'T BE AFRAID RICHARD. WE DON'T WANT TO HURT YOU . . .
  BUT YOU ALWAYS DO . . .
  THAT'S JUST AN ACCIDENT.
  WELL MAYBE YOU OUGHT TO BE MORE CAREFUL . . .
  Fredi says, LOOK AT BIG SHOT RICHARD GIVING ADVICE. LISTEN TO HIM . . .
  AFRAID SO.
  RICHALEH, says Shirl, CAN'T WE JUST LET BYGONES BE

BYGONES. IT'S NOT AS IF WE DIDN'T LOVE YOU.

I think about that one a minute. To Shirl letting bygones be bygones means I am not to remember all the times she gave me enemas and poured perfume on me and Fredi beat me with Mr. Strap because, after all, I must have provoked them somehow, and it's not as if they didn't love me. On the other hand, it seems to me it's not as if they ever did . . .

AFTER ALL WE'VE DONE FOR YOU, Shirl says.

I TOLD YOU RIGHT FROM THE START SHIRL THAT KID WAS NO GOOD . . .

YOU SEE, I tell her, SEE WHAT I MEAN ABOUT HIM.

RICHALEH PLEASE BEHAVE.

YOU TOO!

I'LL KILL HIM. I'LL KILL HIM SHIRL FOR TALKING TO US LIKE THAT . . .

NOW DO YOU SEE WHAT YOU'VE DONE, Shirl says. YOU'VE MADE YOUR FATHER LOSE HIS TEMPER AND IT'S ALL YOUR FAULT.

The thing about growing up in an enlightened twentieth century household like mine: if I was ever afraid of Fredi & Shirl I usually had good reasons.

Fredi & Shirl & The Kids:
The Autobiography in Fables of Richard M. Elman

Graham Greene

I think that my parents' was a very loving marriage; how far any marriage is happy is another matter and beyond an outsider's knowledge. Happiness can be ruined by children, by financial anxieties, by so many secret things; love too can be

ruined, but I think their love withstood the pressure of six
children and great anxieties. I was in Sierra Leone, running
ineffectually a one-man office of the Secret Service, when my
father died in 1943. The news came in two telegrams delivered in the wrong order—the first told me of his death; the
second, an hour later, of his serious illness. Suddenly, between the secret reports to be coded and decoded, I unexpectedly felt misery and remorse, remembering how as a young
man I had deliberately set out to shock his ideas which had
been unflinchingly liberal in politics and gently conservative
in morals. I had a Mass said for him by Father Mackie, the
Irish priest in Freetown. I thought that if my father could
know he would regard the gesture with his accustomed liber-
ality and kindly amusement—he had never disputed by so
much as a word my decision to become a Catholic. At least I
felt sure that my method of payment would have pleased
him. The priest asked me for a sack of rice for his poor Afri-
can parishioners, for rice was scarce and severely rationed,
and through my friendship with the Commissioner of Police I
was able to buy one clandestinely.

Both parents have known someone the children have
never known. My father had known the tall girl with the
tiny waist wearing a boater, and my mother the young dandy-
ish man who appeared in a tinted Oxford photograph on
their bathroom wall, with a well-trimmed mustache, wearing
evening dress with a blue waistcoat. More than ten years after his death my mother wrote to me. She had broken her hip
and she had dreamed unhappily that my father had not come
to see her in hospital or even written to her and she couldn't
understand it. Now, even when she was awake, she felt unhappy because of his silence. Oddly enough I too had
dreamed of him a few days before. My mother and I were
driving in a car and at a turn in the road my father had
signaled to us, and when we stopped he came running to

catch us up. He was happy, he had a joyful smile as he climbed into the back of the car, for he had been let out of hospital that morning. I wrote to my mother that perhaps there was some truth in the idea of purgatory, and this was the moment of release.

For me this dream was the end of a series which had recurred over the years after his death. In them my father was always shut away in hospital out of touch with his wife and children—though sometimes he returned home on a visit, a silent solitary man, not really cured, who would have to go back again into exile. The dreams remain vivid even today, so that sometimes it is an effort for me to realize that there was no hospital, no separation, and that he lived with my mother till he died. In his last years he had diabetes and always beside her place at table there stood a weighing machine to measure his diet, and it was she who daily gave him his injections of insulin. There was no truth at all in the idea of his loneliness and unhappiness, but perhaps the dreams show that I loved him more than I knew.

A Sort of Life

Alfred Kazin

Our cousin and her two friends were of my parents' generation, but I could never believe it—they seemed to enjoy life with such outspokenness. They were the first grown-up people I had ever met who used the word *love* without embarrassment. *"Libbe! Libbe!"* my mother would explode whenever one of them protested that she could not, after all, marry a man she did not love. "What is this love you make such a stew about? You do not like the way he holds his cigarette? Marry him first and it will all come out right in the end!" It astonished me to realize there was a world in which even unmarried women no longer young were simply individual human beings with lives of their own. *Our* parents, whatever affection might offhandedly be expressed between them, always had the look of being committed to something deeper than *mere* love. Their marriages were neither happy nor unhappy; they were arrangements. However they had met—whether in Russia or in the steerage or, like my parents, in an East Side boarding house—whatever they still thought of each other, *love* was not a word they used easily. Marriage was an institution people entered into—for all I could ever tell—only from immigrant loneliness, a need to be with one's own kind that mechanically resulted in the *family*. The *family* was a whole greater than all the individuals who made it up, yet made sense only in their untiring solidarity. I was perfectly sure that in my parents' minds *libbe* was something exotic and not wholly legitimate, reserved for the "educated" people like their children, who were the sole end of their existence. My father and mother worked in a rage to put us above their level; they had married to make *us* possible. We were the only conceivable end to all their striving; we were their America.

So far as I knew, love was not an element admissible in my parents' experience. Any open talk of it between themselves would have seemed ridiculous. It would have suggested a wicked self-indulgence, preposterous attention to one's own feelings, possible only to those who were free enough to choose. They did not consider themselves free. They were awed by us, as they were awed by their own imagined unworthiness, and looked on themselves only as instruments toward the ideal "American" future that would be lived by their children. As poor immigrants who had remained in Brownsville, painfully conscious of the *alrightniks* on Eastern Parkway—oh, those successes of whom I was always hearing so much, and whom we admired despite all our socialism!—everything in their lives combined to make them look down on love as something *they* had no time for. Of course there was a deep resentment in this, and when on those Friday evenings our cousin or her two friends openly mentioned the unheard-of collapse of someone's marriage—

"Sórelle and Berke? I don't believe it."

"But it's true."

"You must be joking!"

"No, it's true!"

"You're joking! You're joking!"

"No, it's true!"

I noticed that my parents' talk had an unnaturally hard edge to it, as if those who gave themselves up to love must inevitably come to grief. Love, they could have said, was not *serious*. Life was a battle to "make sure"; it had no place, as we had no time, for whims.

Love, in fact, was something for the movies, which my parents enjoyed, but a little ashamedly. They were the land of the impossible. On those few occasions when my mother closed her sewing machine in the evening and allowed herself a visit to the Supreme, or the Palace, or the Premier, she would return, her eyes gleaming with wonder and some distrust at the strangeness of it all, to report on erotic fanatics who were, thank God, like no one we knew. What heedlessness! What daring! What riches! To my mother riches alone were the gateway to romance, for only those who had money enough could afford the freedom, and the crazy boldness, to give themselves up to love.

A Walker in the City

Michael J. Arlen

I've often wondered how my mother and father were together in bed. Have wondered lately, I should say, because at
first I didn't think about it at all, except secretly, that sudden
wild thought, the image of two people on the bed, forcing
itself almost physically into the side edge of one's mind, ex-
ploding briefly, and then gone. And later, still not thinking
about it very much, I more or less assumed that they were
very good. Whatever that meant. They loved each other a
lot. They kept telling each other that they loved each other a
lot. They told me that they loved each other a lot. Oh, I
knew they had their arguments, their temperamental differences. They would display their disagreements sometimes, almost as an act, the sort of act a well-teamed husband and
wife might perform publicly together. Look now, we have
these differences. In actuality, they had few fights. Doubtless
they had some in private, or I would hope so anyway. But I
guess one learns that if husbands and wives fight much in
private, sooner or later they fight in public, or at any rate
"before the children," and there wasn't ever much of that.
My mother seemed affectionate and deferential toward my
father. My father seemed adoring and considerate toward her.
Friends would often compliment them on their marriage. I
see them together of a certain evening. The library. Curtains
drawn. A guest is there, talking to my father. The guest is
English, togged up in one of those steel-thick suits. He is enjoying, he keeps saying, one of his "last days of civilization"
before setting off on a lecture tour of South Dakota. My father sits in the green chair. Gray trousers. Beige Sulka shirt,
silky, open at the neck. An ascot around the neck. A brown-
checked, loose-hanging jacket. There is a rustling in the hall.
My mother comes into the room. Long flowing gown. Dark

hair, now very gray, piled high, swept high atop her head. She smiles. Gives her hand. My father and the visitor are standing. My father brings her a drink. She settles down into the couch. "Jocelyn was just telling us about ..." my father says. Conversation. It is all so lovely. It is a ballet. The little glasses in everyone's hand. The room so quiet, private, enfolding. The visitor makes more jokes about South Dakota. Another drink. The maid comes in to pass around bits of things upon a platter. "How simply marvelous," the visitor says. After a bit he leaves. We all have dinner, and then I go out, and then they have coffee in the library, read. Read. Drink. My mother drinks a lot, I know. At first I don't notice it, try not to. At first, long ago, I'd rather liked it—back in those first years in New York, coming down from school on holidays, I used to make her drinks. Old-Fashioneds they were then. Sugar. Bitters. Slice of orange. I never got it quite right about the bitters. Now it is mostly Scotch. Scotch and soda. Before dinner in a short glass. After dinner in a tall glass. Most evenings now she stays up very late, long after my father has gone to bed. "It's a good thing I always nurse my drinks," she says. One whole evening I watch her. Like a spy. Awful. She drinks a great deal in those days. Sometimes she erupts in sudden black rages. America. The Bloomingdale's credit department. Me. General Eisenhower. My father paces alone all afternoon inside that library. And all the while, this adoration ... *dearest ... my beauty ... beautiful.* My father is so gentle towards her, in his ways of telling her she is beautiful. He tells *me* she is beautiful. Your mother is a very beautiful woman, things like that. (My mother, what the hell. Annabelle French, who lived on the third floor, was beautiful. But still I know....) Gentleness. Consideration. Love. I have some of that in me, now grown, this gentleness, and much of it is false—false gentleness—and I wonder

how much of that was in him. Another speculation, unan-
swerable. But sometimes I read his books again, look into
them, catch momentary, almost thrown-aside flashes of him
from inside his writing. Real flashes. The flash of how he
looked at times. Alone. With other people. I wonder (one of
the many things I wonder) how all that nerve and passion
got so locked in, allowed itself to go underground. Fear? One
talks so facilely of fear these days. Indeed he must have been
fearful of so much, and how I can imagine him detesting that
sentence, and how I can imagine the people who knew
him reading that and becoming angry. Fear? Why, he
had all the nerve in the world. Do you not remember how he
first came on to London? Do you not remember how he won
your mother? Do you not remember that time when Goebbels
was staying at the Imperial, on the floor below, and stepped
onto his balcony, and your father went to the sideboard,
mixed a Martini, very exquisitely called down to Goebbels,
and poured it on his upturned face? Do you not remember? I
think I do, or partly so anyway. I remember a lot, because the
two of them, this man and woman, were vividly drawn, and
in the foreground, and I paid (it seems) attention more to
figures than to landscape. Still I wonder about them in bed,
because although "bed" doesn't tell you everything about
anybody, what it does tell seems true to itself, inescapably
true to itself; and maybe the history on many people's faces
has at least a good deal to do with trying to escape what is
told at night, in those odd moments. I think sometimes of my
father when he was young (and out of sight to me). I try to
imagine how he must have been—the afternoon he first
heard from Heinemann's of their enthusiasm for *The Green
Hat*. (He told me that on his way back home he stopped in
at Cartier and bought himself a jeweled stickpin; my mother
gave it to me after his death, a little duck, blue and white on
gold; a jaunty thing.) And later. All the photographs. They

were a very striking pair. Much love. There are all these photographs remaining, often of the two of them looking at each other. I really wonder what they saw. The other night I brought some of them out, laid them on the floor. I was looking for one for this book. It is quite haunting to look at photographs of any two people, young, *connected*, beginning one of those mythic, meshed, knowing, unknowing journeys. Austria. Golf at Antibes. In-front-of-the-Savoy. I thought of him, his family, spinning, whirling, spinning away from them (the old lady in rimless glasses in the room in Lancashire), the ambition, driving forward, momentum, momentum, success, reaching out now for all the shiny things he'd dreamed about, *reaching* (and now the woman beside him, the marvelous woman, golf at Antibes), catching— catching what? Warmth? Beauty? Children in English clothes? Sometimes (one guesses) the air must have been as stifling as death. And she, the girl in the new golfing jacket, quiet looking, beautiful, hanging back a little in the picture, a slightly "foreign" look, a not quite gentle smile, the girl who worried over what to say to Mr. Maugham, or what to write in a thank-you note to Lady Mendl, who embraced her children (sometimes) like a peasant, who surely needed (those deep eyes) more than being made love to, or wrapped in endearments and adorations, to be fucked—there is no other word now, is there? What of her? Golf at Antibes. Death. Things in between. I picked up the photographs and stashed them away. There is a place I keep them in the basement, an old suitcase.

Exiles

Edward Dahlberg

My life was a heavy affliction to me at this time; the chasm between my mother and me had widened. I blamed her for everything; whom else could I find fault with except my sole protector? Why had she not provided me with a family? Could the bastard issue of a lady barber with dyed, frizzled hair amount to anything? Why had not my mother given up that common trade? Was I to stumble in the winds too? No matter how we begin our lives it is a misfortune. One has to overcome the best as well as the worst of circumstances. But thinking this did not help me; my grievous childhood stuck in my gizzard, and I recalled how Captain Henry Smith had persuaded my mother to send me to an orphanage.

Now the sight of a suitor in loose, acid pants and slept-in suspenders made me prudish. How could my mother stomach such men? How immoral was her sensual hymn of flesh and sweat to me. It is everybody's folly to judge others; did we not do so there would be no morals at all. Lizzie always tried to keep me from seeing what went on between herself and her admirers. They were of use, though swill to her imagination. Nor could I bear any longer that cranny at 16 East 8th Street; when I saw the cuspidors bespattered with tobacco juice and watched one of the barber girls step away from her chair to cast her phlegm into one of them, I ran out of the shop.

I had acquired airs and prejudices that I believed were natural. How much difference is there between the educated and the commoner sort except in the way they spit and rasp their throats? It takes no more than a single adage from Lord Chesterfield to make a debonair fop: "Do not look into your handkerchief after you blow your nose."

Who is my father? was my continual liturgy. Was I got upon the knop of a little hillock, like Gargantua? It did not matter. Not where or how, but who? Has not the pismire a sire? Eber was born unto Shem, and Cush begat Nimrod, but who begot me? In an old midrash it is told that birds are fashioned out of marshy ground saturated with water. Was my origin similar, or did I come out of the loins of the maggot? We live in an unfilial age, and though the son curse the father, he ranges the whole earth looking for the Cave of Machpelah, where lie Abraham, Isaac, and Jacob.

Had I no progenitor? Christ can revivify mouldy Lazarus, but who can raise the living from the grave? I wanted to feel, but had no emotions, and I sighed for thoughts and had no conceptions. My sleep spoke to me, but it was slack and shoaly, and it came up only as far as my ankles, and I could not drink it. I was a dark root of nothing, and my own emptiness groaned. . . .

Moving around listlessly in our sitting room, I looked at my childhood. All my kin were in this room: there was my aunt, the mahogany oval-shaped table; the cut-glass bowl in the center of the table was my sister; in the corner of the parlor was an avuncular oak table, and the settee, which was for company, was my cousin. What an orphan I would have been without this familied room. My fingers would have been waifs in the world, and my hands no part of my body, if my mother moved away from the 8th Street flat. I had been begotten in Boston, but this was my borning-room; here I had hoped and dwindled and now I died every hour.

I had forgotten that my mother was in the parlor with me. Then I looked at that woman, less than five feet of relentless will. Oh God, her stockings were sick and raveled again. Could I have come out of such wild rags? She was still sitting in the rocker, the upper part of her torso covered by the newspaper. My neck was hard. She rocked slow and sly, peering at me, I knew. How could I wrest from her the knowledge of my beginnings?

When I turned toward her, all my interred bones groaned: "I am a man, and there are ghosts of trees and a ravine howling within me, and at the root of a mountain sits a man. Who is he? You have always talked to me about your father, sisters and brothers, but I never saw one of them. What relations have I ever had or touched or smelled? In what city are my father's footprints? Does he walk, does he breathe, and is he suckled by the winds? See, I am a shade emptied of ancestors; I am twenty-three years old and grown into full sorrow."

The rocker was mute, and I stood there filled with a fatherless emptiness. Stepping backward, I slipped on a tattered, woolly rug and I shouted, "O heaven, these rags, all our hopes have been moth-eaten rags."

Then I caught sight of the rusty tin rack of stale postcards on the wall. What paternal finger had grazed that faded brown wallpaper? For a moment I stood bowed in front of these holy relics: there were three scenic views of Swope Park, one of Fairmount Park, one of Cliff Drive, another of Swift's packing house. There was the Grand Opera House where Chauncey Alcott had sung so many times, and the Willis Woods Theater where I had seen Anna Held when I was eight. There were the photographs of the old-timers; Lizzie never threw anything away, not even a reminder of her most wretched experiences.

I studied a card that showed Lizzie when her hair was still brown and tender and her face had a meditative contour. Next, the U.S. Major, bald, with a stylish military mustache, and in uniform, stared at me—but he had been too pallid for my mother's bed. I passed him to glance at skinny Birdie, then Gladys from Tulsa, and Blanche Beasley, for whose stupendous buttocks a cashier for the M-K-T had stolen ten

thousand dollars. What a victual was Ruby du Parr, but des-
tined for the public stews, and there was the dear, fetching
figure of Emma Moneysmith. Such a big-trousered man was
Hagen. Popkin had a spruce, carroty mustache, with tidy
fringes of hair around his ears and neck, but he looked so
quick and tailored. And old Cromwell, wearing spectacles,
who was now in his grave; he would never let anyone give
him a chin-scrape except Lizzie.

My origins were still unriddled. The rocker was creaking;
the newspaper lay on my mother's crumpled kitchen apron.
When I contemplated her untied shoelaces, I moaned, "You
sent me to an orphanage because Henry was fat and I leaned
on him; before that I was in a Catholic home, and then in a
parochial school where the boys beat me every day because I
was a Jew."

The woman, so distant from my anguish and the bitterness of my days, now replied, "My son, when I went under
the knife, what could I do? I sent you to the Jewish home in
Cleveland because I could not manage you. You were in the
streets all day, and sick and puking, and I had the scissors
and comb in my hands. I could not give you regular meals or
control you. What could I accomplish with a widow's ten
fingers, and who was there to help me? Do you think I could
find money in the gutter? I wanted you to be high-tone; you
have the aristocratic face, my son, of my brother Ignatz, may
he rest in peace."

"Don't mention a brother or sister to me; even a worm
has a parent, but nobody begat me. I am nothing, and I came
out of nowhere," and I was filled with gall, and layers of
grief lay over it. I heard Job on his muckheap: "The ox
knoweth his owner, and the ass his master's crib."

I crossed the front room, returning to the tin rack of
postcards, for these sepulchral memories bound my mother
and me together. On a sudden, I was gazing at a hand-tinted

picture of a man with the curls of a dandy; he wore the dude's chestnut-colored vest with the usual fob, gold chain and watch. He was showing the teeth of the fox that spoils the vines. It was Saul! Whenever business was slow or her bladder gave her that desponding, dragging feeling, Lizzie would often exclaim, "May Saul burn in hell," and then breaking off into German, she would let out a blasphemy: "*Verdammter Saul!*"

I pulled the tintype out of the rack and leaning against the cemetery of postcards, I roared, "It is Saul! Who else could my father be? I know it is Saul. My blood is ruined; a thousand lusts boil in his skin and in his tumored brain. But where is he? You must know. He is my father. Tell me, I must know . . . or live and die unborn . . . for I will wail all the hours of my flesh if I am unfilled by a father!"

She sat immovable. No grave was more silent than she, and no matter what words and sounds I made, she did not move. I stared at her helplessly, for she was a terrible headstone without an epitaph, from which no secret could be wrung.

Because I Was Flesh

James Dickey

Long deathwatch with my father. Nothing in his wasted and lovable life has ever become him so much as when he moved close to death. It is astonishing to understand that one's father is a brave man: very brave. The only thing he worried about was my seeing him in that condition. He cannot ever understand, whether he lives or whether he dies, how much better he looked with his arms full of tubes, with one of those plastic hospital things in his nose, and the rest of it, than at any time I have ever seen him before. He was a man up against an absolute limit, and he was giving as well as he got and he was afraid of nothing in this world or out of it. God bless that man. No matter how I came from him, I hope that it was in joy. For the end is courage.

Journals

Edmund Wilson

I have found among my father's papers a speech on the Homestead strike, in which he sharply takes the strikers to task. This, in the early nineties, was of course the correct Republican line. Having read the Fabian Essays and other socialist writings, I always assumed through my college days that my father was as reactionary as I was advanced, and I did not dare discuss my ideas with him; but I had failed, as I realized later, to understand his real point of view. One of his favorite cronies in Red Bank was the socialist editor of a local paper, and, since my mother would not allow him to invite this man to dinner—she objected to his deliberately unmodish clothes and asserted that he did not wash—they were obliged to take long walks together. It was only after the war when I came back from France, and felt quite independent, that I ventured to talk to my father about socialism in Europe and Russia. To my surprise he was not disapproving, but spoke of it with moderation as something they went in for abroad which had no relevance to the United States. "The main merit of socialism," he said—he was thinking of our local variety—"is to emphasize the brotherhood of man." I was by that time no longer afraid of him, and only then did I get to know him. My first meeting with him on my return unexpectedly made me feel proud of him. I had been waiting for my discharge all too many days in a Long Island army camp, and he came to see me there. He was always impatient of delay, and he complained with his usual peremptoriness to a bureaucratic officer who had failed to produce me at once. The officer had retorted that he'd better be careful, he couldn't talk to the army like that, there were penalities for that kind of talk. "You're no doubt thinking," my father replied, "of the Espionage Act and the Sedition Act. Neither of them has any application to what I've been saying to you nor to what I'm about to say. The inefficiency of you army people is an outrage against the tax-paying citizens." I was gratified when—still fuming—he told me about this interview: I had had almost two years of the army, and a story I had written in France about the dismal side of army life had recently been held up by the censor when I had tried to send it to the United States, and had brought upon me a bawling-out. When I got home, I was rather surprised—knowing how little my father could sympathize with the aims of the Communists and Anarchists—to find that he was indignant over the arrests without warrant and the indiscriminate expulsion of radicals. I had been so full of Wells and Shaw and Barbusse and the Russian Revolution that I was only learning now from my father what the principles of American justice were.

He enormously admired Lincoln—his allegiance to the Republican party had undoubtedly been partly inspired by this. He collected a whole library of Lincolniana, and he liked to deliver a popular speech called *Lincoln the Great Commoner.* I made, automatically, a point of knowing as little as possible about Lincoln. I could see that my father in some way identified himself with the Great Commoner, and this seemed to me purely a pose, which verged upon demogoguery. I have said that he was quite without snobbery, but though he dealt with people strictly on their merits, it was always to some extent *de haut en bas*. When he died, I was struck by the criticism in one of the local papers that, in spite of his distinguished qualities, he had either not the desire or the ability to meet people on a democratic level. Both at home and in his office, he was constantly sought by persons who wanted to ask his advice on every conceivable subject, and when he died, many people we had never seen—sometimes poor farmers and their wives—came from miles around to his funeral; yet it was true, I remembered, when I read his obituary, that he had always told people what to do on a dictatorial tone and with a certain restrained impatience, for which, however, he would try to compensate by dismissing them at the end of the interview with an exaggerated courtesy and sweetness. Where, I wondered, was the kinship with Lincoln? It was only after his death that I understood. Now for the first time I read up Lincoln, and I realized that the biographies he had recommended were always the least sentimental ones. I remembered his saying at a time when he was reading one of the books about Lincoln by Nathaniel Wright Stephenson that it was more realistic than most; and he was always trying to get me to read Herndon—which I never did till after his death. Then, in Herndon's portrait of Lincoln, I at last found the explanation of my father's great interest in him: a great lawyer who was deeply neurotic, who had to struggle through spells of depression, and who—as it followed from his portrait—had managed, in spite of this handicap, to bring through his own nightmares and the crisis of society—somewhat battered—the American Republic.

A Piece of My Mind:
Reflections At Sixty

Jack Kerouac

Last night my Father was back in Lowell—O Lord, O haunted life—and he wasnt interested in anything much— He keeps coming back in this dream, to Lowell, has no shop, no job even—a few ghostly friends are rumored to be help- ing him, looking for connections, he has many especially among the quiet misanthropic old men—but he's feeble and he aint supposed to live long anyway so it doesn't matter— He has departed from the living so much his once—excite- ment, tears, argufying, it's all gone, just paleness, he doesnt care any more—has a lost and distant air—We saw him in a cafeteria, across street from Paige's but not Waldorf's—he hardly talks to me—it's mostly my mother talking to me about him—"Ah well, ah bien, he vivra pas longtemps ce foi *icit*!"—"he wont live long *this* time!"—she hasnt changed—tho she too mourns to see his change—but God Oh God this haunted life I keep hoping against hope against hope he's going to live anyway even tho I not only know he's sick but that it's a dream and he did die in real life—ANY- WAY—I worry myself ... (When writing *Town and the City* I wanted to say "Peter worried himself white"—for the haunted sadness that I feel in these dreams is white—) May- be Pop is very quietly sitting in a chair while we talk—he happened to come home from downtown to sit awhile but not because it's home so much as he has no other place to go at the moment—in fact he hangs out in the poolhall all day— reads the paper a little—he himself doesnt want to live much longer—that's the point—He's so different than he was in real life—in haunted life I think I see now his true soul— which is like mine—life means nothing to him—or, I'm my father myself and this is me (especially the Frisco dreams)—but it *is* Pa, the big fat man, but frail and pale, but so mysterious and un-Kerouac—but is that me? Haunted life, haunted life—and all this takes place within inches of the ironclouds dream of 1946 that saved my soul (the bridge across the Y, ten blocks up from 'cafeteria'—) Oh Dammit God—

Book of Dreams

2. Lovers

Eugène Ionesco

I am with my father again, in a room, not at the house we live in. We have gone to visit my mother who is lying in a bed. A gray light, a yellow wall, the vague presence of my father. His dark silhouette: all he ever wore was black over-coats. People had bought apples and brought them to her. She adored apples. She takes one and bites into it.

My mother must be sick. I am sorry for her, I am anxious about her, but all this is mingled with a sort of repulsion. There is something that is a little dirty. My mother and he speak, I see my mother's lips move. (I now realize that this must have been when my little brother was born.)

Present Past Past Present:
A Personal Memoir

Julian Green

My mother bathed me herself, running a heavy cake of yel-low soap over my shoulders and down my back, a soap that she never lost the habit of using. This operation over, she got up and, moving away from the bathtub, looked at me disap-provingly. At this point, words might betray me, and others should be invented to describe what took place in the eyes of a woman I loved so much. I felt that she was both displeased and attentive. "The neck," she said, "and then the ears and behind the ears." I obeyed. "And now the body.... Under the arms and then the front. . . ." She said the word *body* in such a way that until I was fifteen or sixteen, I hesitated to use it, as though it referred to something shameful.

In a silence scarcely broken by the splashing of water, a mysterious thought passed from my mother to me, a thought that fixed itself I cannot tell where, to reappear in my consciousness many years later. Because of the way she looked at me, lovingly to be sure, but with an indefinable mistrust, I now understand that human nakedness aroused her suspicion. A sentence once escaped her that I remembered precisely because it was incomprehensible to me and at the same time it had such a strange sound that it was impossible for me ever to forget it. I lay in the warm water and, a few steps away, my mother was drying her hands with a worried air when suddenly she glanced down at a very precise part of my person. As though she were talking to herself, she murmured, "Oh, how ugly that is!" And she turned her head with a kind of shiver. I said nothing, but felt myself blush without knowing why. Something in me had been affected in an incomprehensible manner. I must have been eleven and profoundly innocent. My mother looked at me sadly, as one would look at a culprit too much loved to be punished, and once I was dressed, she hugged me. . . .

To Leave Before Dawn

William Gibson

My mother was comforted that I lay thus in her company of angels, but it was only above the bed, I would lie underneath it when more mundane company heaped it with coats so I could study the ladies' legs. My image of the female anatomy was derived altogether from manikins in storewindows;

though my sister and I inhabited one room, sleeping with our hands clasped across the gap between our beds, my mother was indefatigable in steering us out of each other's sight at clothes time; and my first glimpse of a young nude the summer I was thirteen—she was two, in somebody's yard—was a shock. I worried about that frontal cleft for years, believing my angle of erection was malformed. I saw each of my parents unclothed only once, on their deathbeds: my father was near comatose when, lifting his pelvis to change his pajamas, I averted my eyes from the modest digit that had sired me, for in the earlier weeks he "didn't want Billy to see" him and one of my mother's last breaths, as I ministered to her fleshless flank with a hypodermic needle, was of regret that I had to "see everything." The law was bodily reticence.

Yet under it I had no boyhood rights, my mother scrubbed at me in the bath every Saturday night until I was pubescent, and when I was on my belly to practice my swimming stroke she blurted, "What are you doing?" in alarm that I was copulating with the bathtub. My parents each had a hollow try at preparing me for the other sex. In my eleventh year my mother told me posthaste that girls lacked a weewee, which corroborated the manikins; later, prone with schoolmates in the weeds of the Harlem bluffs, I spied on a couple parked in a car below, but could not see why, and in the excited aftertalk of beholding her "cop a feel of his and boy him with his hand on hers" it was on the tip of my tongue to cry out in a triumph of news, "She hasn't got one!" This datum was more than I gleaned from my father, who sat me down, advised me he "hadn't missed a thing," ran out of other advice, was inspired to suggest I bring him my questions, and assured my mother I "probably knew more than he did." I brought him no questions, though my ignorance was pansexual: I was into my teens when I walked by a policeman on a mount with a meaty dangler, and only my timidity saved me from warning him the horse had a dangerous leakage of entrails.

A Mass For the Dead

John Updike

In crucial matters, the town was evasive. Sex was an unlikely, though persistent, rumor. My father slapped my mother's bottom and made a throaty noise and I thought it was a petty form of sadism. The major sexual experience of my boyhood was a section of a newsreel showing some women wrestling in a pit of mud. The mud covered their bathing suits so they seemed naked. Thick, interlocking, faceless bodies, they strove and fell. The sight was so disturbingly resonant that afterward, in any movie, two women pulling each other's hair or slapping each other—there was a good deal of this in movies of the early forties; Ida Lupino was usually one of the women—gave me a tense, watery, drawn-out feeling below the belt. Thenceforth my imaginings about girls moved through mud. In one recurrent scene I staged in my bed, the girl and I, dressed in our underpants and wrapped around with ropes, had been plunged from an immense cliff into a secret pond of mud, by a villain who resembled Peg-Leg Pete. I usually got my hands free and rescued her; sometimes she rescued me; in any case there hovered over our spattered, elastic-clad bodies the idea that these were the last minutes of our lives, and all our shames and reservations were put behind us. It turned out that she had loved me all along. We climbed out, into the light. The ropes had hurt our wrists; yet the sweet kernel of the fantasy lay somehow in the sensations of being tightly bound, before we rescued each other.

The Dogwood Tree: A Boyhood

Havelock Ellis

I have said that probably in childhood I was sexually normal. But I think I can trace a slight fiber of what, if possibly normal in childhood, is commonly held—though this I doubt since I have found it so common—not to be so when it persists or even develops after puberty. I mean a slight strain of what I may call urolagnia, which never developed into a real perversity nor ever became a dominant interest and formed no distinguishable part of the chief love-interests of my life. It was not a recognizable emotional interest in childhood, but the clearness with which several small incidents from that period stand out in memory seems to indicate that it was of some interest to me. To this in later childhood a more scientific interest, possibly my earliest scientific interest, was added when I observed the differences in vesical energy among my schoolfellows, my own being below the average, and began to measure it exactly as private opportunities offered. Many years afterward I continued these observations and published the results in a paper on "The Bladder as a Dynamometer" in the *American Journal of Dermatology*, May 1902. Later my vision of this function became in some degree attached to my feeling of tenderness toward women—I was surprised how often women responded to it sympathetically—and to my conception of beauty, for it was never to me a vulgar interest, but rather an ideal interest, a part of the yet unrecognized loveliness of the world, which we already recognize in fountains, though fountains, it is now asserted, have here had their origin. It would be easy to overrate the importance of this interest. But it is necessary to note it.

In later years, I would now further note, it has seemed to me that I may have inherited this trait from my mother, whose early love of water I have already referred to. Once she took me at the age of twelve to spend the day at the London Zoological Gardens. In the afternoon, as we were walking side by side along a gravelled path, in a solitary part of the Gardens, she stood still, and soon I heard a very audible stream falling to the ground. When she moved on I instinctively glanced behind at the pool on the path, and my mother evidently watching my movements, remarked shyly, "I did not mean you to see that." I accepted the incident simply and naturally. Much later in life, recalling the incident—I remembered it clearly so it must have made an impression on my mind—I realized that my mother's remark could not be taken at its face value. Nothing would have been easier than to step on the grass, where detection might possibly have been avoided, or to find a pretext for sending me a few yards off, or to enter a Ladies' Room. Her action said clearly, "I meant you to see that." Today I probably understand it better than she herself could. No doubt there was a shy alarm as to what her now tall, serious boy would think of this new experience with his mother, but there was also the impulse to heighten a pleasurable experience by blending it with the excitement of sharing with her son. There was evidently a touch of exhibitionism, the added pleasure of mixing a private and slightly improper enjoyment with the presence of a beloved male person, for a woman is always a little in love with her first-born and only son. Every woman who has a streak of what I call Undinism will understand the fascination of this emotion on the threshold of intimacy. Her real feeling would have been better stated: "I loved you to see, but I didn't want you to see if you would have been disgusted." On the next occasion, some time later, there was no longer any shyness and she confided in me beforehand. We had just had dinner at an exhibition, and, as there were people strolling about, this time she really took some precautions. She stood on the grass, and, before she had finished, walked on a few paces and then copiously recommenced, while I spontaneously played a protective part and watched to see that no one was approaching. When in much later life I mentioned this experience to my sister Louie, she told me that our mother had always been extremely reserved with the girls in regard to this function, and remarked, after consideration, "She was flirting with you!"

I could add various significant details which confirm the presence in my mother of this trait, such as the habit of urinating on her hand, which, she said, was good for the skin, but really, I doubt not, found pleasurable. I should add that there was never, on my part at any time, the slightest impulse of curiosity such as young boys sometimes manifest with regard to their mothers; there was an awe in my affection for her which would have prevented even the feeling of curiousity; it seems significant, however, that I remember clearly these as well as other incidents, earlier in life, when the same subject was presented to me in connection with women, the earliest being at the age of four when the nurse, wheeling my baby sister, stood still to perform this function, with no word either on her part or mine, though I still remember the spot in the Morland Road. It was not until the age of sixteen that this trait became a conscious and active, though always subordinate, element in my mind. It can hardly, therefore, be considered either the persistence of an infantile impulse or a regression. It proved of immense intellectual benefit to me, for it was the germ of a perversion and enabled me to understand the nature of perversions. On the emotional side, also, it has been a more or less latent element in that tender sympathy for women which, as I have come to realize, they so greatly appreciate.

Love comes normally to a child through what we call the soul rather than through the body. In this and indeed throughout—with whatever wide variations from the most common types—I was normal. The young boy's love is a spiritual passion generated within by any stray spark from the real world, and so far as his own consciousness extends, even without any sensory, still less any sensual, elements whatever, easy as it might be to detect such elements. A chance encounter of life sets free within him a vision which has danced within the brains of his ancestors to remote generations and has no relation whatever to the careless girl whose playful hand opens the dark casement that reveals the universe.

My Life

Salvador Dali

Adolescence is the birth of the body hairs. In my case this phenomenon seemed to occur all at once, one summer morning, on the Bay of Rosas. I had been swimming naked with some other children, and I was drying myself in the sun. Suddenly, on looking at my body with my habitual narcissistic complacency, I saw some hairs unevenly covering the very white and delicate skin of my pubic parts. These hairs were very slender and widely scattered, though they had grown to their full length, and they rose in a straight line toward my navel. One of these, which was much longer than the rest, had grown on the very edge of my navel.

I took this hair between my thumb and forefinger and tried to pull it out. It resisted, painfully. I pulled harder and when I at last succeeded, I was able to contemplate and to marvel at the length of my hair.

How had it been able to grow without my realizing it on my adored body, so often observed that it seemed as though it could never hide any secret from me?

A sweet and imperceptible feeling of jealousy began to bud all around that hair. I looked at it against the sky, and brought it close to the rays of the sun; it then appeared as if gilded, edged with all the colors, just as when, half shutting my eyelids, I saw multitudes of rainbows from between the hairs of my gleaming eyelashes.

While my mind flew elsewhere, I began automatically to play a game forming a little ring with my hair. This little ring had a tail which I formed by means of the two ends of the hair curled together into a single stem which I used to hold my ring. I then wet this ring, carefully introducing it into my mouth and taking it out with my saliva clinging to it like a transparent membrane and adapting itself perfectly to the empty circle of my ring, which thus resembled a lorgnette, with my pubic hair as the frame and my saliva as the crystal. Through my hair thus transformed I would look with delight at the beach and the distant landscape. From time to time I would play a different game. With the hand which remained free I would take hold of another of my pubic hairs in such a way that the end of it could be used as the pricking point of a needle. Then I would slowly lower the ring with my saliva stretched across it till it touched the point of my pubic hair. The lorgnette would break, disappear and an infinitesimal drop would land with a splash on my belly.

I kept repeating this performance indefinitely, but the pleasure which I derived from the explosion of the fabric of my saliva stretched across the ring of my hair did not wear off—quite the contrary. For without knowing it the anxiety of my incipient adolescence had already caused me to explore obscurely the very enigma of the semblance of virginity in the accomplishment of this perforation of my transparent saliva in which, as we have just seen, shone all the summer sunlight.

The Secret Life of Salvador Dali

William Golding

This chestnut tree was my escape. Here, neither the darkness of the churchyard nor this vast pattern of work and career and importance could get at me. The texture of bark, the heraldic shapes of stick buds, these were private, were an innocent reality, were in fact nothing but themselves. Here, stirring the leaves aside, I could look down at the strangers in that world from which we were cut off and reflect on their nature. Safe from skeletons, from Latin and the proper requirements of growing up, I could ponder over or snigger at the snatches of conversation from passers-by underneath. There were two little girls who came along, patter, patter, through a deserted churchyard and a bright afternoon. One was thin and dark and awe-stricken and excited. The other was fair, a little bigger, giggling and self-appalled. She was leaning down sideways, explaining. As she passed, her voice came into tune.

"They gets you down and pulls off your clothes."

Giggle away under the trees. Gone. What a fierce and dramatic life these girls must lead in their own place, I thought! How cruelly inhuman their treatment of each other! Then the old bookie passed. He was short, gray, and square as a sarsen stone. He came from the pubs at three o'clock in the afternoon. He inched along the path, with shuffling steps each no more than a span, or less. He inched along, swearing to himself, inscrutably angry, muttering. He would stop, strike at the stone walls with his stick and inch on. There was that other pair too, a man and a woman. They stopped below me one evening when the late light of summer and a full moon had encouraged me to brave the shadows and stay in my tree until night. Even the moonlight was hot, molten moonlight, a great dollop of white moon stirred by the twigs and leaves into a shower of moving drops. These two, the man and woman, stood by the wall under me, she against it, he pressing her hard, and they wrestled and murmured gently. She would take her mouth away from his face and say, "No, no, no," and put it back again. His moony hand was in her neck. Then he began to undo something near her neck and she said, "No, no, no," more earnestly and laughed and giggled. But his hand went into her chest and she gave a gasp of pain like being pricked with a pin or having something raw touched, and the branch I was holding aside flicked back with a swish. They started apart and stood looking up at me, or at the covering leaves only a yard away. She said, "What was that?" He said: "It was a bird"—and his voice had a lot of heart-beat and phlegm in it. But there were footsteps coming past St. Mary's now. The man and woman hurried away.

The Ladder And The Tree

Floyd Dell

I had now much companionship with boys of my own age, but still no acquaintance at all with girls. The girl problem, however, from which I endeavored to escape into books, pressed upon me from the outside world. It was something which I earnestly and uncomfortably tried not to think about. During the period from five to twelve, I somehow managed not even to know what the almost universal auto-erotic pleasure-habit of childhood was—I took the constant references to it to be a silly and meaningless joke. But the world in which I lived was full of disquieting hints and rumors about sex; not restricted by any means to adult behavior.

I walked to school one day with a boy younger than myself, whom I did not know very well, but who confided to me, with very convincing details, what he and a little girl who lived near by had been doing together, of which he was very proud, taking for granted that it proved in my eyes, as in those of all his peers, that he was graduated satisfactorily from being a child. He asked me if his hips showed it—he insisted that it made the hips larger.

Now this was not the first time I had heard stories of such a kind. Its importance lay in the fact that this boy was one who in clothes, language, and manners was one whom my mother would have picked out as a nice boy, a wholly desirable friend and playmate for me; and the little girl who had been his partner in these exploits was shown by some of the details of his story to be one whom his mother approved—a nice little girl.

A good boy who belongs to a poor family knows what to think when stories like this are told by boys whose language is rough and whose manners are tough. The invitations which I, if my ears had not deceived me, had received from time to time to come along and take part in these exploits, were easy to decline—or rather, casually evade, since tough little boys were sensitive to any airs of moral superiority on the part of others, and it was best to pass off with a laugh these appeals for companionship.

But the case was different when it was a well-dressed boy with refined manners and good language who, with all the satisfaction of a young scholar who had successfully passed on his examination in arithmetic, recounted such achievements as these—and not with the washerwoman's little girl, either. It was difficult to import any ready-made moral attitudes into the consideration of the misbehavior of perfectly respectable little boys and girls among themselves.

But, after all, it did not concern me, their behavior; they might have their own laws, and I still abide by mine. I need not judge them; and what I did was to build another moral universe, beside my own. I stayed in mine; and that little boy and girl could stay in theirs.

It sprang up overnight, this new moral universe, like a palace built by a genie in the Arabian Nights, pieced together out of scraps of things seen and heard, out of jokes and observations, out of a thousand bits of truth which did not fit into a maternally-constructed moral universe. There it stood, for all to dwell in who chose, secure from maternal judgment. That was its purpose, to make it unnecessary for me as a good little boy to think evil of those who lived by different laws—particularly nice little girls, whom it pained me to judge harshly. Their freedom did not concern me otherwise; though I pressed my nose against the glass sides of that new universe of moral freedom, and contemplated its treasures thoughtfully, I was a window-shopper only—I was not going inside, I did not want anything that was there for myself, I would just look and then go on about my business.

Meanwhile, that little girl whom the well-dressed boy had told me about—she went to this school, was one of the little girls who romped on the little girls' playground. I didn't know, would never know, which one she was; she might be *any* of these little girls! A good little boy couldn't help but wonder. . . .

Homecoming: An Autobiography

Tommy Trantino

about a month after being shipped to j h s 50 i just so happened to be going down the down staircase one day and i see these three crazy chicks who are in the ninth grade and who wear makeup and all of that *and more*   they are smoking coming up the down staircase and they all got big tits and tight skirts and nice asses   i'm late for class and i say excuse me please they all start giggling and one says *hey he cute hey hey hey he curly   hey*   one says he donny's cousin and another says *younger* cousin tee hee hee hee hee tee hee   and i say *shit* and they come closer   i say excuse me please i've got to go to class   my cheeks are hot and so am i and they come closer saying *hey hey youre cute* do you know how to make fucky and i say *fucky?*   i am hot my cheeks are red and i'm wondering do they know i piss the bed?   *fucky* do you know how to make *fucky* you so cute *hey hey hey* and they are laughing and now one says hey let me feel your *cocky*   and i say *cocky? cocky?*

cocky makes fucky one says grabbing on my swipe hard enough to make my nose bleed and i say OOH! and they are

pissing in their pants laughing and pulling on my swipe and
i'm going OOH! OOH! OOH! and they are all laughing saying fucky fucky fucky and i say *ooooooooooh!* RAPE! but it
wasn't a cry for help   it was a suggestion.

Lock The Lock

Bertrand Russell

My childhood was, on the whole, happy and straightforward,
and I felt affection for most of the grown-ups with whom I
was brought in contact. I remember a very definite change
when I reached what in modern child psychology is called
the "latency period." At this stage, I began to enjoy using
slang, pretending to have no feelings, and being generally
"manly." I began to despise my people, chiefly because of
their extreme horror of slang and their absurd notion that it
was dangerous to climb trees. So many things were forbidden
me that I acquired the habit of deceit, in which I persisted up
to the age of twenty-one. It became second nature to me to
think that whatever I was doing had better be kept to myself,
and I have never quite overcome the impulse to concealment
which was thus generated. I still have an impulse to hide
what I am reading when anybody comes into the room, and
to hold my tongue generally as to where I have been, and
what I have done. It is only by a certain effort of will that
I can overcome this impulse, which was generated by the
years during which I had to find my way among a set of
foolish prohibitions.

The years of adolescence were to me very lonely and very
unhappy. Both in the life of the emotions and in the life of

the intellect, I was obliged to preserve an impenetrable secrecy towards my people. My interests were divided between sex, religion, and mathematics. I find the recollection of my sexual preoccupation in adolescence unpleasant. I do not like to remember how I felt in those years, but I will do my best to relate things as they were and not as I could wish them to have been. The facts of sex first became known to me when I was twelve years old, through a boy named Ernest Logan who had been one of my kindergarten companions at an earlier age. He and I slept in the same room one night, and he explained the nature of copulation and its part in the generation of children, illustrating his remarks by funny stories. I found what he said extremely interesting, although I had as yet no physical response. It appeared to me at the same time self-evident that free love was the only rational system, and that marriage was bound up with Christian superstition. (I am sure this reflection occurred to me only a very short time after I first knew the facts.) When I was fourteen, my tutor mentioned to me that I should shortly undergo an important physical change. By this time I was more or less able to understand what he meant. I had at that time another boy, Jimmie Baillie, staying with me, the same whom I met at Vancouver in 1929, and he and I used to talk things over, not only with each other, but with the page-boy, who was about our own age or perhaps a year older, and rather more knowing than we were. When it was discovered that we had spent a certain afternoon in doubtful conversation with the page-boy, we were spoken to in tones of deep sorrow, sent to bed, and kept on bread and water. Strange to say, this treatment did not destroy my interest in sex. We spent a great deal of time in the sort of conversation that is considered improper, and in endeavoring to find out things of which we were ignorant. For this purpose I found the medical dictionary very useful. At fifteen, I began to have sexual passions, of almost intolerable intensity. While I was sitting at work, endeavouring to concentrate, I would be continually distracted by erections, and I fell into the practice of masturbating, in which, however, I always remained moderate. I was much ashamed of this practice, and endeavored to discontinue it. I persisted in it, nevertheless, until the age of twenty, when I dropped it suddenly because I was in love.

The Autobiography of Bertrand Russell: 1872–1914

Theodore Dreiser

About this time it was that, because of my growing sex interest as well as my contact with the baker's daughter and at the same time my inability to front the elusive subtlety of the more attractive girls of the town, I fell into the ridiculous and unsatisfactory practice of masturbation, which finally became a habit that endured—broken, of course, by occasional normal sex relations with passing women and girls—until I married.

One hot summer day, alone in my room after a bath, I sat down on the side of my bed thinking of what I would do if Gusta Phillipson or Stella Davenant or Nata Weyler, as opposed to my baker girl, were in my arms. To me at least they were such torrid flames of beauty! And, in this state of emotion, I suddenly and quite unexpectedly brought on a sensation which, as in the case of my contact with the baker's daughter, thrilled and yet quite terrified me. For I had not intended any such result and had not even assumed that in this case it would occur. When it did, I jumped up fearful lest I had injured myself. I dressed quickly, resolved not to trifle with myself in this fashion again nor to think the thoughts which our local priest was always telling me were evil.

Following this came several days of strenuous effort to remain pure in mind and body. But this decision lasted only some three or four days. The physical beauty of girls as well as the delight and relief of the process I had discovered—the only substitute for the sex contact I so much craved—came back to me with overwhelming force. I forgot my good resolutions. No harm had come to me, apparently from either this or my preceding single relationship with a woman. Subsequently I longed, of course, and with flaming eagerness, to find some girl other than the one mentioned with whom I

could continue, but in lieu of that, this other, this something
that stung and thrilled, must serve. I ran to my room and indulged in the act again. A heavy reaction of mood again
followed, but a few days served to efface the memory of anything save the intense delight. For weeks and months, every
two or three days at the utmost, I now indulged myself in a
kind of fury of passion I would run to my room or any
secret place I had appointed, and there in a kind of excess of
passion and delight, give myself over to this form of self-
abuse. At the same time, I would combine it with passional
thoughts of one of the girls whom I most admired: Carrie
Tuttle, Stella Davenant, or Nata Weyler. It has always been
a matter of curiosity to me that the personality of Myrtle
Trego was never visualized in this connection. It never occurred to me that I could satisfy myself with her in this fashion.

The natural result of this was, first, a radical change in
point of view, and, second, and to a lesser extent, a change in
my physical condition. For one thing, temporarily my face
became blotched and marred by pimples, which caused Harry
Croxton to exclaim one day: "What are you doing to yourself, Ted? Your face is all covered with pimples!" Abashed at
the thought that my face was advertising my secret, I
resolved to quit. But I could not. The pleasure and relief to
my desires were too great. Besides, now that Croxton had indicated this facial condition as a sure sign, I noted other boys
and girls to be in the same state. Better, though, I came to
talk more freely of all this (sex) with Croxton, McNutt, and
others and to learn of seemingly endless variations of it. Jud-
son Morris, the hunchback son of the book-store man, had secured a number of immoral, fly-by-night pamphlets, which in
those days were allowed to pass through the mails undetected
and which for the price of ten cents retailed all the delights
of the wedding night. John and George Shoup, Gavin

McNutt, Beachey Reid, and others—quite a circle of the youths of the school—used to gather to read them at Jud's father's corner book store. A Rabelaisian, immoral business, but so it was. Not a morbid crowd either, if I except myself, but rather of a laughing, jesting, jovial turn. And incidentally, and coeval with this—very likely because of it—I came to know of books that dealt with sex in a revelatory if more or less classic way: *Tom Jones, Joseph Andrews, Moll Flanders*; also passages from Dryden, Pope, Shakespeare's sonnets. For several years after that my main concern with old or famous books was to find the portions which dealt with sex, though the merit of a conservative work was by no means beyond me.

But after a time—due to my morbidity in connection with it all—a nervous depression. I was sitting one night at the dinner table some three or four months after I had begun this practice, when all of a sudden I was taken with a whirring in my head and ringing in my ears, which frightened me nearly out of my wits. For a few moments I thought I was going to die. Nature's way, apparently, when an internal physical adjustment is to be made, is not to give warning beforehand but to keep up an appearance of normal health until it can no longer possibly be maintained. In this case I cannot even suggest, I fear, the ominous portents of physical change or readjustment that seemed suddenly to play about my mental horizon. If you can imagine a black landscape with a yellow storm in the offing, or a fever victim pursued by spying, lurking devils, or an inferno glimpsed in half light and quaking with strange and hitherto unimagined sights and sounds, you may arrive at some idea of what I endured. If I had not been sitting, I would have fallen. As it was, I put down my knife and fork, placed my hands on the table to steady myself, and closed my eyes. In my brain was spinning a whirligig of spectral lights: yellow, red, green, blue, gray, white. In place of my normal heart-beat was a feeble fluttering, which alternated with a heavy thumping which seemed to spell instantaneous collapse. I tried to get up, but could not. Then after, say, thirty seconds—by which time I was nearly exhausted—the uproar in my ears ceased, my heart beat less feebly, the grinding and clanking in my brain subsided, and I arose and went upstairs, saying I had forgotten something.

In my room, though, I sat and meditated on all this. Sickness! Brain trouble! Total physical collapse, no doubt! The truth was, I was really thinking of those innumerable advertisements addressed to "Weak Men" or "Victims of Self-Abuse," as the advertisements of those days ran, which Croxton and others by their talks had called to my attention and concerning which we used to jest. But now no more. The emaciated, sunken-eyed victims of youthful excess always illustrated by them haunted me. For now was I not one of these? If not as yet, then obviously I was to become one, emaciated, with hair and teeth falling out, eyes sunken, and no hope of any future of any kind save in the particular pills or nostrums advertised or such periods of treatment as could be procured from "Old Dr. Grindle" of Buffalo, New York, or "Old Dr. Grey," of Scranton, Pennsylvania. The particular "swamp root" or tannic acid pills or electric belt or "Neurophag" prescribed by these was all that was left. I shook in terror, for I had no money. My mother would not be able to afford sufficient money to permit me to undergo any one of these saving treatments, even though I had sufficient courage to tell her what had befallen me. And then what?

And worse, the whirrings and interior disturbances returned and at seemingly regular intervals for at least a month or two. Also I had the most terrifying dreams, in which ghosts or skeletons walked and threatened imminent destruction. At two in the morning—the zero hour at which the earth seems to suffer a change or period of inhalation or exhalation—I was wont to awake, feeling as though I were about to expire. A peculiar whistling in my ears would begin and might continue for several hours. I had, or imagined I had, all the symptoms of prolonged insomnia, only with this difference: that when I became exhausted, I would fall into a heavy sleep. After much thought, I hit upon the idea of copying out a prescription which I found in somebody's *Family Medical Guide* and asking the most friendly of the two local druggists—the one who was not Myrtle Trego's father—to fill it and charge it for a month. He did so, but with true rural sagacity, mailed the bill to my mother: a bill for $4.25. Now I know, as I half suspected then, that the medicine (like ninety percent of all medicine) was worthless. It brought me merely a few days' hope, then greater despair, because the night sweats, etc., continued, and there was the necessity of explaining, or attempting to explain, the matter of the bill to my mother. Curiously enough, that strangely sympathetic woman did not press the mystery of the purchase too far. When she saw I was confused and distressed, she let the matter rest.

"If you think something is the matter with you that you don't want to tell me about, why don't you go and see Dr. Woolley?" she said. Her voice was as soft and pleasing as that of a sweetheart.

But one service the author of *The Family Guide* rendered me was to point out the efficacy of cold baths, exercise, sleeping with the windows open, on a hard bed, etc. All this, coupled with the gradual realization that I was not to die at once, gradually led to a modified view of my condition. Perhaps I was only to be crippled sexually for life, as the advertisements I had been reading by the ton invariably asserted. That was bad enough, of course, but after all it was not insanity or death.

Poor, ignorant humanity! I wish that all of the religious and moral piffle and nonsense from which I suffered in connection with this matter could be undone completely for the rest of the world by merely writing about it. What tons of rot have been written and published concerning the spiritual and moral degradation of this practice! Old wives' tales, for the most part. Quacks and thieves printing lying advertisements to sell nostrums to the ignorant, and so terrifying poor fools who stand in no more real physical or mental danger than a man with a taste for green plums! Doctors, more religionistic than medical, writing endless silly books on hearsay or because of early asinine terrors of their own! I have often wished that the pagan or Hebraic view of things had prevailed in my own family and that at this age I had been taken in hand and introduced to a bagnio, or that I had possessed sufficient courage to persuade a girl to have physical relations with me. I was of the temperament that required it. As it was, for four or five years I was thrown into the most, at times, gloomy mental state, that is, whenever I thought of my assumed condition, and yet there was no more the matter with me than there is with any healthy, normal boy who takes to this exotic practice.

Dawn: A History of Myself

Norman Mailer

Q. Do you think you're something of a puritan when it comes to masturbation?

A. I think masturbation is bad.

Q. In relation to heterosexual fulfillment?

A. In relation to everything—orgasm, heterosexuality, to style, to stance, to be able to fight the good fight. I think masturbation cripples people. It doesn't cripple them altogether, but it turns them askew, it sets up a bad and often enduring tension. I mean has anyone ever studied the correlation between cigarette smoking and masturbation? Anybody who spends his adolescence masturbating, generally enters his young manhood with no sense of being a man. The answer—I don't know what the answer is—sex for adolescents may be the answer, it may not. I really don't know.

An Impolite Interview With Paul Krassner

Charles Mingus

Charles had never heard this kind of talk before or any kind of talk at all from a grown man, though he was now sixteen years old. His father never told him anything and it was flattering to have Buddy's father treating him just like another fella. Charles began to frequent the Collette house and the youthful-seeming father now and then gave little lectures to the boys on the art of making love.

He told them sex was important and not meant to be dirty. "Don't waste your youth," he said. "Don't masturbate. Learn to control yourself. Find out about girls. It's a lifetime tease if you let them go on fooling you. Listen to me and you'll see they want you more than you want them. This is the whole art of sex between a man and a woman. They'll pay for this understanding kind of a man because most men think a woman don't like sweets the way he do, that she thinks it's nasty what he wants to do to her. So when she accept it in the end, he treat her like she's a receptacle, a come machine. He don't even pat her on the head when he's finished. There was a wise old man told me a story once. He said, 'If you try what I'm going to tell you, every woman you touch will come back for more of your sweets and she'll tell you these same words: she'll tell you she ain't never had nothing like that done to her in her life before.' That's what the old man said, and I should charge you boys for this advice. Someday you gonna walk right in and hand me some money and say, 'You sure was right, Collette.'

"What this old man told me was, for those who don't have the natural talent, here's some good rules for fucking. Kiss her. Play with her awhile. Then insert your peppermint stick, just the knob, the head of it. Rub it all up her split for a long time over the clitoris, in just a little bit and out, from bottom to top and around until she's warming up to you. You gonna make love like this for hours, kissing, playing, sucking her breasts and fingering that good pussy till she's begging for you. Then you don't just ram it in. You put the head in sorta gentle and easy."

All this was shocking coming from an adult. Charles was blushing but Buddy was smiling, he'd heard it all before. He and Charles discuss those lectures sometimes now in their manhood.

Pop went on, "After it's good and moist, seeping all

through the sheets, you don't give her all that white-folk freaky stuff. Just plain old good fucking. The best position that old man found was on one side with her on her back, 'cause he was a big man. She's about dying from waiting now, but you're just teasing, gradually giving it to her. Stay in for just a little while to let her know what kind of sweets you got but pull back if she reaches up for it, all the way out and around the edges of the lips. Then all of a sudden you hit it hard and deep as you can and hold it there firm and tight and rock from side to side. Then draw back, almost out. Tease. Move every which way but so easy she can barely feel it move. Tighten and loosen its muscles. That gives her a throbbing sensation. She'll start reaching for it again. Pull away. Just when she gives up and settles on her ass hit it in hard and deep as you can, draw it out fast and hit it quick again. Don't move for an instant after it's all the way in. Hold it tight and rock, then draw it out again easy. This time let her soft flesh cling to you—she'll try to follow and keep it up inside her. Now she starts to beg you and everything to hit it for her like you just did. Don't do it. Just play and tease some more. If she ain't never done anything like this, she'll start getting frantic, crying and begging. Then—*when you make up your mind to*—let her have it again hard, fast and deep. Hit it and hold it in there and rock from side to side, kiss her and hold her in your steady rock. Then ease it back and pretend you're gonna quit. Take it out. And if she don't grab you and plead and beg you to please fuck her *your* way then you can have one of them Cadillacs sitting out there! . . . Now, Charles, you try that on the next little girl you get. Watch the difference to her response. See if she don't tell you these very words: 'Charles, I never had it done to me like that in my life!' And see if you don't want to pay me fifty to one hundred dollars for the results you get."

Beneath The Underdog

Chester Himes

My father had the use of the school Ford, and each Sunday he drove us early to the Baptist church, where he taught Sunday school and served as a deacon. After Sunday school I would skip church if I could and go out and sit in the Ford in the shade of a tree and entertain my sycophants. I was a big shot to all the other little black children who went to Sunday school because I was from the college and drove the school tractor during the week, and sometimes the school Ford on Sundays. The little black girls offered their bodies. In the South, black girl children reach puberty at nine or ten years old and at thirteen they are mating like rabbits. They are not a bit ashamed of lying on their backs and opening their legs and offering their nappy pussies. They don't care who knows as long as it's kept from their parents and the "old folks." Church picnics were the best occasions for them to go off in the woods with the boys. The boys would return and show how "greasy" their penises were to prove their manhood. The girls would name each boy she had lain with. Strangely enough, it was not that summer I lost my virginity. Their shamelessness repulsed me; I felt disgusted by their casual fornication. I must have been a puritan all my life. Then as now, I consider the sexual act private. I do not want my sexual experiences to be made public. I do not care for women who discuss the sexual behavior of men in public, or vice versa. I don't want to hear about it.

The Quality of Hurt

A. S. Neill

Snobbery also had its way in my idealization of women, which commenced at this period. I did not idealize common girls; I aimed higher. The girl I loved was always quite unattainable, always in a rank of society far above mine. Forfar, like every other town in the world, had its social structure, with very definite lines of demarcation between classes. If a girl went to Miss Smith's private school she was a superior being, and naturally, at my stage of lowly occupation, I found my objects of worship among the Miss Smith clientele. I say *objects,* for the admired one was never a constant. Today it might be Cis Craik; tomorrow, Jean Gray.

There was nothing consciously sexual about this. Even in imagination, I never thought of kissing them. I was satisfied to have seen them pass in the street; and if the adored one happened to glance in my direction, my joy was complete. Sometimes I made detours round by the Lour Road when delivering my parcels, hoping to get one glance at Jean Gray. One day when I met her, she looked absolutely beautiful in a large sun hat, with her little tilted nose and her bright eyes. My face must have paled with excitement.

Of course, this idealization was the result of the beatings I had received for what might be called sex in the raw; but even at this period, I was having quite earthly adventures with village girls whose feet did not turn the daisies into roses. The two interests never met; they existed in separate compartments, or rather, they were parallel lines that never met.

"Neill! Neill! Orange Peel!"

John Wain

At the very moment when I was preparing the seed-bed of my emotions, getting everything ready for a grand passion, my father made the acquaintance of a man who worked for one of the big insurance companies. This man's home was in some genteel Surrey suburb, and his work usually took him into London, but—whether in consequence of the bombing or not, I do not know—he had been moved up to Stoke-on-Trent for the rest of the war, and was in the process of finding a house so as to send for his wife and daughter to follow him. This he mentioned on a visit to our house, and at the word *daughter* I pricked up my ears. A girl from Surrey, from that "south" towards which we all felt ingrained feelings of envy, a girl with stylish London associations, would be an improvement on the local girls whatever she was like. This, I realized, might be the Big Thing.

After that, it could hardly help being the Big Thing. The house was found, the wife and daughter appeared, introductions were performed, and I marched into my self-constructed cell and slammed the door behind me. There was no key. The door was not made to open. I rotted in that emotional dungeon until the door rusted off its hinges; some eighteen months, in fact.

There is no point in describing the tensions, the daydreams, the sleepless nights, the agonies and exaltations triggered off by microscopic incidents, the pleas, declarations, self-abasements, and general doglike devotion. Everyone has had them. There was nothing unusual about my case except that it lasted unusually long and was unusually virulent.

The power of women to inflict suffering is known and feared by all men; but in this case I cannot honestly say that the girl did inflict any suffering. I wounded myself, and ruined my chances of impressing her in the process. Looking back, I see it all. The family had arrived, full of misgiving, in this strange barbaric region of smoking chimneys and unintelligible accents. There was a shortage of "people to know," to say nothing of suitable escorts for the girl. Our family, as one of the leading families of the district, obviously had a head start; if I had simply played it cool I should probably have aroused the girl's curiosity, won the approval of her parents, and quite possibly got her to fall in love with me without firing a shot. Instead, I rushed headlong in, proffering my undying devotion, and reduced the whole thing to smoking ruins. The girl, who was just at the point where she had the mind of a child in the body of a woman, was frightened back into childhood instead of being drawn smoothly forward into womanhood; the father, a good-natured man, was dubious and worried; the mother, who had the sort of "social" pretensions that go naturally with outer-suburban life, decided definitely that I was *not* suitable and for the whole eighteen months snubbed and humiliated me incessantly. Everything capable of giving pain was present, nothing to give joy—except where my imagination could seize on some small hint of encouragement, bred of compassion, and magnify it into a cause of rapture. So help me God, if I was allowed to hold her hand as we sat in the bus, I was drunk for three days. Sweet and touching! The innocence of first love! Let us admit the truth, that it was emotionally overheated, unbalanced, and harmful. From beginning to end, my emotions were essentially self-regarding. Even when she was present, the poor girl hardly existed in her own right; she was a dream figure, on to which I hung fantasies. These fantasies, of course, were wonderfully "pure"; I was too preoccupied with other emotions to feel physical desire for her. Sometimes, in the long burning hours of those sleepless nights, I used to ask myself, What do I want? And I came to the conclusion, I remember, that the ideal would be to hold her in my arms, sleeping and waking—just that and nothing more.

If I *had* held her in my arms, of course, it would only have been a matter of time, and not much time, before normal needs asserted themselves. But that was a stage my imagination never reached. It climbed up the steep slope as far as the thought of holding her in my arms, and then fell back, like a beetle trying to get out of a bath. And to complete the image I should add that the bottom of the bath was full of slime.

That, in fact, was the worst of the consequences that flowed from this unhappy fixation. That I was unhappy for eighteen months is no particular tragedy; most boys of sixteen and seventeen are unhappy in one way and another; what matters is the amount of permanent damage. In my case the damage consisted of a dualism in my emotions. Like all boys of that age I thought of sex, physical sex, pretty continually; my body, bursting with its new-found powers, saw to that. But this driving force was not directed, even in imagination, towards the girl I was in love with. It was driven into a desert, where it proceeded to breed a race of misshapen demons. I was, throughout the whole of this crucial period, alternately kneeling at the shrine of an impossibly "pure" devotion, and subsiding into a disgusting dirty-mindedness.

The consequences can easily be imagined. I became hypocritical, a prig, and an emotional liar. Confronted with sexual recklessness, I conveniently forgot about my own unhealthy fantasies and assumed a holier-than-thou attitude. Most of the boys I associated with were as innocent as lambs with regard to the other sex, but one or two were not, and I left these fellows in no doubt that I looked down on them from a great height. One, who left school at sixteen and plunged fairly steeply into promiscuity, seems to have really shocked

me. My diary entries are almost incredible, even to me. I write about him as if I were the silver-haired vicar and he the errant son of a parishioner. As long as he had been prepared merely to talk about it, I accepted him as a companion; the minute he translated our talk into action, I raised hands and eyes to heaven. At such moments my passion seemed beautifully refined and exalted, almost satisfying. I did not see it, with the eye of honesty, as a merely undignified affair of pointless nagging and scene-making.

But hypocrisy can be cured. What was even more damaging was that the experience of being so persistently rejected helped to make permanent my early sense of defeatism. From childhood—babyhood, almost—I had found the world a place in which such as I were, at best, only tolerated. The prizes, the comforts, were not for us. All we could do was to get by without being persecuted or destroyed. And now that sex assumed a central position in my life, all this sense of discouragement, of impossible difficulty, hooked itself on to sexual instinct. This is what I mean by saying that if this one affair had worked out differently, my life would have been different. Once I had decided that sexual fulfillment was one more of the things that were not for me, I was damaged in the really vital recesses of my being.

Sprightly Running: Part of an Autobiography

Graham Greene

The younger children, Elisabeth and Hugh, had grown too old for a nurse, and so my kissing instructress had not been replaced, but instead a governess had been appointed, a young woman of about twenty-nine or thirty—ten years or more older than myself. During the first days at Sheringham she made little impression—my daydreams were still of my cousin and of the waitress at the George. My brother and sister were happy, I noticed, with her, and she joined cheerfully in our games of cricket on the sands. The first time I looked at her with any interest was at the same instant the *coup de foudre*. She was lying on the beach and her skirt had worked up high and showed a long length of naked thigh. Suddenly at that moment I fell in love, body and mind. There was no romantic haze around this love, no make-believe: I couldn't share it like calf love with a waitress at the George.

It is strange how vivid the memory has remained, so that I can see the stretch of beach, my mother reading, the angle from which I examined her body, and yet I cannot even remember the first time I kissed her or the hesitations and timidities which surely must have preceded the kiss. For her it was a flirtation which at first, before she scented danger, must have helped the passage of the boring hours, alone in the big nursery at Berkhamsted with two children as companions. For me it was an obsessive passion: I lived only for the moments with her. She began soon to be a little scared of what was happening; every evening of the winter vacation I would go upstairs to the nursery where she sat alone and the slow fire consumed the coals behind an iron guard. My parents must have heard my footsteps night by night as they crossed the floor, just as when I sat below I could hear her movements on the ceiling while I pretended to read. Sometimes during the day she would enlist my sister's aid to hide from me. I took dancing lessons in order to please her, and on Saturday nights we would go together to what were called hops at the King's Arms. To keep up appearances I would have to dance occasionally with some boring wife of a master at the school and surrender her to other arms. Sometimes in the dark schoolroom out of term, on the excuse of teaching my brother and sister to waltz and foxtrot, we had dances of our own when half-kisses could be exchanged without the children seeing.

But the fear set in. She told me how she was engaged to be married to a man working for Cables & Wireless in the Azores. She had not seen him for over a year, and he had become like a stranger to her. Soon he would be returning, and she would have to leave Berkhamsted to marry him. Once when she talked to me of her marriage, she wept a little. I was too inexperienced to press her for more than kisses; marriage for me seemed then to be years out of reach and there was the great difference in our ages. All I could do was urge her to break her promise and I had nothing to offer in exchange. We wrote to each other every week when I returned to Oxford, and her handwriting became so fixed in my memory that when, more than thirty years after we had ceased to write, I received a letter asking me to get her seats for my first play, *The Living Room,* I recognized her hand on the envelope and my heart beat faster until I remembered that I was a man of over fifty and she, by now, well into her cruel sixties.

A Sort of Life

Richard Elman

On the eve of the Jewish New Year I am in such a hurry to be home for supper after playing basketball, else I never would have allowed myself to be picked up in front of the schoolyard by this man in the black Buick sedan.

He has steel teeth, and when he smiles at me and calls me Sonny, I have the feeling that he is being slightly more

than just obliging. It is dark outside. I am all alone. I was expected home for supper and services a half an hour ago.

Up Bedford Avenue with a sudden burst of speed: CALL
ME JEFFERY. . . .

A hand drops onto my lap.

SAY, YOU'RE A BIG FELLA AREN'T YOU? HOW OLD ARE
YOU?

FOURTEEN. . . .

WHATA BIG FELLA. . . .

We swerve onto a side street.

Jeffery has his radio on. It only seems to receive police
and fire calls.

I'm in trouble.

Jeffery says he wants to stop off at his place to get something to eat; I tell him I'm in an awful hurry to be home.

MAYBE YOU SHOULD LET ME OFF HERE. . . .

O NO . . . I WOULDN'T THINK OF IT. . . .

Jeffery's hand twitches against my lap.

DO YOU PLAY LOTS OF BALL?

A LOT. . . .

I'D LIKE TO PLAY WITH YOUR LITTLE BALLS SOME-
TIME.

I'm in big trouble.

Jeffery has his big hand inside my fly.

O SAY A BIG FELLA LIKE YOU SURE HAS A BIG FELLA.

I'm in really big trouble.

Under the shade of a large elm we have pulled to a stop,
near one of those big old frame houses on Albemarle Avenue.

Jeffery says, I WON'T HURT YOU HONEST. LET'S JUST
PULL OVER A MINUTE.

Already he has his lips around my cock.

MY PARENTS WILL BE WORRIED ABOUT ME ... MIS-
TER. ....

YOU'LL LIKE IT. HONEST. I WON'T HURT YOU HONEST.
PLEASE ... PLEASE. ....

Jeffery is licking me.

He looks up. SORRY BUT I GOT TO LEAVE THE RADIO
ON. ....

Jeffery is throbbing against my hand.

PULL IT KIDDO. PULL IT FOR ME PLEASE. ....

Jeffery hands me a Kleenex.

YOU'RE A NICE BIG FELLA. I BET YOU LIKED THAT
DIDN'T YOU?

The car radio starts up another time.

I HAVE TO GO HOME NOW MISTER.

OF COURSE.

Jeffery starts to whistle.

YOU LITTLE JEWISH BOYS ARE CUTE.

MISTER I'M REALLY PUERTO RICAN.

I give Jeffery a false name and telephone number. He
leaves me three blocks from where I live. I tell him,

THIS IS WHERE I LIVE MISTER.

I'LL LOOK FOR YOU AGAIN IN THE SCHOOLYARD.
JESUS. . . .
I DON'T USUALLY PLAY THERE. . . .
I'LL LOOK FOR YOU ANYWAY. . . .

Fredi & Shirl are celebrating the Jewish New Year by
going off to services angry at me. That's no big deal. They're
always that way.

When I open the door that drops you down into their
sunken living room, Edna emerges from their bathroom in a
white uniform, newly pressed, very very pretty too, just like a
servant in the movies, or maybe a spy. Ilona Massey in black-
face.

YOUR PARENTS HAVE SOME FOLKS COMIN' OVER AF-
TER TEMPLE. I'M S'POSED TO DO THE SERVING.
THAT'S NICE. . . .
IT'S A LIVING. . . .
THAT'S NICE. . . .
Edna takes note of my disarray. She gives me her hardest
look. Right against my cock.
WHAT KINDA HOLIDAY IS THIS ANYHOW?
A SAD HOLIDAY. . . .
I THOUGHT SO.
She takes note of my rumpled face.
WHERE YOU BEEN?
OUT. . . .
YOU FEELING OKAY?
I WANT TO TAKE A SHOWER. . . .
RICHARD. . . .
WERE THEY VERY MAD?

A few minutes later I am drying myself off good *down
there* with a towel. Sort of inspecting the damage.

A knock on the bathroom door.
RICHARD. . . .
WHAT. . . .
ANYTHING SPECIAL I CAN FIX YOU. . . .
DON'T BOTHER PLEASE. . . .
I'M HERE. I'M BEING PAID. I MIGHT JUST AS WELL. . . .
I'M NOT TOO HUNGRY. . . .
MAYBE THERE'S SOMETHING ELSE YOU WANT FIXED?
The pearl doorknob begins to wiggle.

How I was initiated as both a homo- and a heterosexual
in a matter of half an hour was finally an act of mutual
compassion.
Edna said, RICHARD. . . .
I said, I'LL PAY YOU. HONEST. TELL ME HOW MUCH. . . .
YOU POOR KID, she said. COME HERE.

Later we are both crammed inside the bathtub.
Edna rides me just like a Johnny-on-a-pony.
I'm sobbing because I've never wrestled with a naked
woman in all my life.
Abruptly we are upended.
I'm all over Edna like a great white centipede.
She has propped herself up by the elbows.
RICHARD, STOP THAT RIGHT NOW. I REALLY LIKE YOU
AND IF YOU WANT US TO TAKE CARE OF BUSINESS THAT'S
OK WITH ME BUT FIRST YOU GOT TO ACT LIKE A MAN.
PLEASE SHUT THE DOOR.

I grew up thinking compassion was a politeness for rape.

Fredi & Shirl & The Kids:
The Autobiography in Fables of Richard M. Elman

Dan Greenburg

Danville, Illinois, is (or was—I haven't been there in more than fifteen years) a depressing, low-income, one-industry town less than an hour's drive from the U. of I. campus. Its one industry, as far as anyone from the university could tell, was prostitution, which is, I suppose, better than no industry at all.

Since my arrival on campus two years before, I had been extended invitations on the average of twice each week to join some of the hornier residents of my rooming house on an expedition to Danville "to get our rocks off." I always politely begged off. For one thing, I wasn't anxious to lose my cherry in such an unaesthetic manner. For another, since I expected to marry a virgin and did not believe in any double standard, I was more or less Saving Myself for my future wife. But mainly, I was chicken—of disease, of a police raid, of not being able to get it up and being laughed at by the prostitute.

However, after my breakup with Jennifer (the Disillusioned Lover Giving Himself Over to a Life of Sin), I decided to accept the invitation and go to Danville. Accordingly, one night in early spring, I and my similarly virginal roommate Buck and a jolly Navy vet named Willy borrowed a car, divested ourselves of all valuables (lest we be robbed), and all identification (lest we be raided), and all money except the three-dollar going price of a straight lay, and the three of us set out for Danville.

Willy, who was engaged to a Nice Girl on campus, was not coming with us to get laid (he had embarked on a brief period of celibacy in honor of his impending marriage) but was only going along to guide us as a tribal elder into the initiation of manhood.

We got to Danville about ten-thirty in the evening with no precise idea of where it was we were going, and after several frantic phone calls back to campus for an address or at least a street name, and after much cruising down streets lined with darkened, shabby, single-family frame dwellings, we stopped the car and got out.

What did one do now—walk up to any house at random, ring the bell, and cheerily inquire if it was a whorehouse?

But then, a stroke of luck: a tiny flickering red light in the front window of the nearest house. With Willy leading the way for moral support, we climbed the sagging wooden steps of the unlit porch and pressed the buzzer.

In a moment a presence materialized on the other side of the screen door and a tired Negro madam's voice said, "Just one girl workin' tonight, boys."

At the precise moment I had made the decision to beg out of the whole operation, Willy yelled, "Go get her, Greenburg!" and shoved me through the now open screen door and into the unlit living room.

The possibility that the first sexual experience of my life was to be not only with a whore but with a Negro whore filled my liberal Jewish brain with an ambivalence that would never have been resolved had I not been immediately pushed into a bedroom adjoining the room I'd entered and then heard the door snapped shut behind me.

In the light of a 10-watt blue bulb on a bedside table I beheld my first woman. She was not Negro but white, with dark hair and a tired expression on her nondescript face and a dark nondescript dress on her short, stocky, nondescript body.

I had no idea what small talk or greeting was appropriate in such a situation, but fortunately the whore got the conversational ball rolling herself.

"Let's see it, honey," she said.

At first I didn't understand, and brought out my crumpled ball of dollar bills, but she shook her head impatiently.

"Let's see *it*" she said. "Your little thing."

True, I hadn't expected to be invited to sit down and engage in idle chitchat about the cold war or the stock market, but this request still struck me as being somewhat abrupt.

I've always been a cooperative sort, however, even when asked to do embarrassing things like taking off my clothes in front of young nurses or providing female lab technicians in hospitals with stool samples in little round white pasteboard boxes, so I was equally cooperative in this situation. I unzipped my fly and dug out my little thing and handed it to her.

With a dexterity bred of long professional practice, she examined it thoroughly for venereal disease, then dusted it with a little germicidal powder and gave it back to me. That the "little thing" I'd handed her was limp rather than stiff I viewed with considerable relief, so impersonal and nurselike her attitude. She instructed me to undress and, in keeping with this nursy attitude, stepped into an adjoining bathroom while I did.

I started to take off my clothes and then I found myself wondering how much or how little she expected me to take off. I thought maybe, just as in a doctor's office, you were only supposed to get down to your undershorts.

"Listen," I called to her over the sound of running water in the next room, "what do you want me to take off here—everything, or what?"

"Just your pants and shorts," she called back.

Somehow I couldn't visualize myself dressed like that for my first sexual experience, so I took off my shirt and T-shirt too. When she came back into the room all I had on, for some idiot reason, were my watch and my socks. I don't know what reaction I expected from her, but there wasn't one. She just asked me whether I wanted the straight three-dollar lay or the five-dollar round-the-world. Although I only had three dollars with me, I pretended to weigh the pros and cons of each in my mind, like any conscientious consumer, and finally settled on the three-dollar job. I fished around in my clothes for the money, found it, and handed it to her.

She took it with a little darting motion, then grabbed the hem of her dress with both hands and whipped it over her head. She was out of her bra and panties so fast it wasn't till she'd lain down on the bed, with her knees up and her thighs spread, that I realized her whirlwind strip had been at least perfunctorily intended to excite me.

I stood there in my watch and socks, pondering the naked person on the bed in front of me and I tried to relate to the odd tableau of which I seemed somehow to be a part. Finally, with some impatience, she motioned to me and said, "Hop on."

I hopped gingerly on, not at all sure where to put my knees, elbows, head, and so on, and not a little embarrassed at having my naked body touching that of a perfect stranger. I was feeling a lot of things by then—curiosity, embarrassment, absurdity, unreality—feeling, in fact, almost everything in the world except aroused.

"What's the matter with your little thing?" said the whore, vainly trying to stuff its flaccidity into herself. "Is he shy of strangers?"

"Yes," I said, "I guess he must be shy."

We both examined my little thing as one might examine a moderately rare species of mollusk which has retreated into its shell. Finally deciding that direct stimulation was the ticket, she grabbed it and began rolling and patting it briskly between her palms like a tortilla. Neither it nor I found this

technique terribly erotic, and the continued rolling and patting and kneading and slapping were beginning to alarm me.

"Listen," I said with barely disguised impatience, "why
don't you let *me* have a try at it?"

Reluctantly, she surrendered it to me. And then, in the
presence of a total stranger, driven by the growing panic that
I was going to leave the whorehouse still a virgin *and* waste
three dollars, I commenced to masturbate.

Presently there was a pounding on the door, and the
madam yelled, "Hurry up in there!" The whore bounded out
of bed and started scrambling into her clothes, just as signs of
life began stirring in my hand.

"Wait!" I exclaimed. "I think I've got it!"

"I've got other customers, honey," she said, smoothing
out her dress. "I think you better put on your things and go."

"But I can *do* it now," I insisted. "Please—I'm ready to
come."

She darted into the bathroom and re-emerged with a wad
of toilet paper. "Use this," she said. Unhappily, I had no
choice.

"Get dressed now, honey," she said. "And hurry, because
the old lady's getting mad."

I was really depressed, as much about the three dollars as
about my humiliation. "Listen," I said, "can I come back later
tonight if I'm more in the mood?"

"Don't worry," she said, "you won't be."

There was more pounding on the door. I slowly walked
across the room, still loath to leave.

"Listen," I said, "what am I going to tell my friends?"

"Why tell them anything?" she sensibly replied.

But I did. I told them the whole grisly story. Buck was so
depressed he decided to hang onto his virginity awhile
longer. But Willy, unaccountably aroused by any talk of sex

at all, excused himself and hustled into the whorehouse for a quickie.

When we returned to campus, our story was that Buck and I got laid and that Willy remained in the car. But once inside the rooming house I raced Willy to the showers, and afterward we shared two antibiotics I had left over from a recent bout of flu.

Scoring: A Sexual Memoir

Frank Conroy

I paused in the aisle, unsure which of my two favorite techniques to use. I could sit in the row in front of her, drape my arm over the back of the seat next to me and attempt to contact her knee with my hand, or I could sit next to her, with one empty seat between us, and play footsie. The small balcony was almost empty. I entered her row and sat down. From the corner of my eye I could see her white raincoat going on and off in the reflected light from the screen below. I watched the movie for half an hour before making my move. Shifting around in my seat, I extended my legs in the darkness until my foot almost touched hers. After a while I raised my toe and applied a gentle pressure to the side of her foot. To my astonishment she answered immediately, giving me three firm, unmistakable taps. I moved into the seat next to her and she turned her head for the first time.

"It's you!" I said. I'd picked her up in another theater a few weeks before.

"Didn't you know?" Her accent was heavy. She was Belgian, nineteen, and she had a job looking after two children.

"No. Of course not."

"I hoped I should see you again."

I put my arm around her. "Me too." Congratulating my-self on my luck, I kissed her cheek. She turned and I kissed her mouth. She wasn't very pretty, and there was an odd bloodless quality to her, almost as if she was undernourished, but she was a girl, the most cooperative girl I'd ever met. I slipped my free hand over her breast.

"The movie is bad," she said.

Fifteen minutes later, my leg up on the seat in front to screen us off, I had my hand between her legs, slipping my finger in and out of her wet sex.

"There," she whispered. "No, there. Yes. That's right."

She reached out and grabbed me through my trousers. Her fingers touched and pressed. She unzipped my fly. She pulled me out into the cool air and squeezed. I couldn't be-lieve what was happening. She struggled to get her hand all the way inside. "That's what I want," she said as her hand closed over me.

"Let's go somewhere," I said after awhile.

"Where?"

"We'll find someplace." My mind was racing. If I could get her alone she would let me fuck her. Under the stairs in the service entrance to my house. In the alley. In the park. Anyplace dark. "Let's go."

"We better not."

"Why?"

"You know why."

"No, I don't. It isn't wrong." I stared at her profile. Her mouth was set in a faint smile, barely perceptible. I pulled her shoulder gently. "Come on. It's all right."

She leaned forward, sitting on the edge of her seat, and stared out over my shoulder into the darkness. For a moment I thought she was going to leave me—simply walk out on her own and go home—but then she looked at me, nodded, and stood up. I followed her down the aisle, my eyes locked on her back.

As we emerged from the theater I turned toward the park. "This way." The marquee lights threw our shadows on the sidewalk in front of us, long, thin shadows stretching away up the block, growing longer and fainter as we walked.

"You're going too fast," she said.

"I'm sorry." As we passed my house I gave up the idea of the alley or the service stairs. We continued toward the park in silence. I was conscious only of movement, of the girl beside me, and of the blood roaring in my head.

At the corner of Madison Avenue she said, "I'm scared."

"Why?"

She didn't answer.

"What is there to be scared of?" I helped her over the curb. She shook her head, watching the sidewalk moving under us. Suddenly I understood. "You mean you're scared of having a baby."

"Yes."

"Don't worry. We'll take care of that." It flashed through my mind that I could buy a prophylactic at the drugstore on the corner. Then I remembered I'd spent the last of my money for the theater ticket.

We went into the park through the same entrance I had used as a child. After a few steps I led her off the path into the darkness. There was a place I remembered from years ago—a little hollow between the footpath and the sunken roadway to the West Side. Leading her by the hand, I found it quickly.

"Let's put your coat on the ground," I said.

She took it off slowly and gave it to me. I spread it over the rough grass and went down on my knees. We remained motionless as someone walked along the path on the other side of the bushes. Light from a distant lamppost filtered through the trees and played over her shoulders and neck. When the footsteps died away she came down into the darkness and lay beside me.

She lifted her hips as I raised her skirt, and again as I pulled her panties to her ankles. Opening my clothes I looked down at her white belly glowing in the shadows.

"Do it," she said. "Before someone comes."

I got on top of her and, after a moment of blind fumbling, drove myself into her. She cried out in pain and threw her head to one side.

"What's the matter?" I asked, pausing, but she didn't answer and I began to move again. I found myself thrusting hard once more, and when she didn't flinch I got up on my elbows and quickened the pace. She lay motionless, her head averted.

As I fucked her, a certain moment arrived when I realized her body had changed. Her sex was no longer simply the entrance way one penetrated in search of deeper, more intangible mysteries. It had become, all at once, *slippery*—a lush blossom beyond which there was no need to go.

Afterward, I lay still, dazzled. Coming out of her was a shock. I seemed to be floating weightless in space. On my hands and knees I paused to feel the earth and orient myself. A noisy bus went past in the sunken roadway. I looked up and she was on her feet, waiting.

"Hurry," she said. "I am so late."

We walked to the subway without talking. At the top of the stairs she turned to me. "Goodbye."

"I'll look for you," I said, aware of how feeble it sounded, knowing we would never meet again. "We'll see each other."

She started down.

"Goodbye," I said.

She turned, holding the rail. "What is your name?"

"Frank." I said quickly. "Frank Conroy."

She turned again and went down the stairs into the roar of an arriving train.

Stop-Time

Sherwood Anderson

I thought I had got into something like a new strange world. It was paradise. I had become a man. I was one who had been singled out by a strange new kind of girl. She wasn't at all like that other one, the daughter of the whale man. Surely this one had not been as that one was.

That one had been free to all. She was a little rather tired silent one. She just laid herself down.

This one was firm of flesh. There was a certain freshness. She was strong. She did not just submit. She came to you.

She had taken my hand in one of her hands and had put it on one of her breasts.

"Don't you like to feel there? I like you to." She smiled boldly at me.

"Shall we do it here or shall we go somewhere else?"

Her words were like bells ringing. Was I in a dream?

Here were doors being thrown open to me. Life was suddenly becoming wonderful, glorious.

She thought perhaps we had better go out and walk.

"We will find some nice place."

The grandmother or the grandfather might awaken. There was that aunt who lived downstairs. It would be just like her to poke her nose in.

We went together out of the house, walked along a street, crossed a bridge over a creek, climbed over a fence and went across a field. It was a moonlit night. It was a night I would remember all of my life.

There was this new strange aliveness. Something in me had swept away my timidity. It seemed to me that night that every leaf on every tree in a strip of woods into which we went stood out separate and apart from every other leaf, that every blade of grass, in the meadow we crossed, separate and apart from every other blade.

We were there, in the little strip of woods, for what seemed to me a long time. We were lying quietly there.

We were walking again. We went into a graveyard. She said she wanted to lie with me on a grave.

The idea did not shock me. There was something about her that was all youth and life, defying old age and death.

She plucked a flower off the grave on which we had been lying and put it in the lapel of my coat.

We went back to the house of the teamster. We sat on the wooden stairs. There was a little garden back of the house with a grassy path. We went to lie there.

There was dew on the grass but she did not mind.

We were exhausted. We talked softly. The little back yard, back of the brick house, with its vegetable garden and the grassy path that led to an outhouse at the end of the garden, was, no doubt, in the daytime or when seen under ordinary circumstances, commonplace enough but on that night it was to me utterly lovely.

I wanted to sleep, to lie with her arms about me and sleep. I spoke of it to her.

"It would be nice if we could do that, if we could lie here together like this, forever."

Was it love? I was with her on the next night, and the next and the next. There was a night when it rained.

It did not matter. We were on the couch in the room upstairs. We were on the floor. I could hear the snoring of her grandfather and her grandmother. I could hear the aunt, that tall strong looking woman, moving about downstairs in the house. She went away, to that other town where she lived with another old grandfather and grandmother, and I worked and saved money to hire a horse and buggy and go there too.

When I was with her I was happy, in a kind of paradise, but when I had left her, in the daytime, when I was going about with other boys and girls, when I was with my brothers and my sister I said nothing of my adventure.

I became afraid.

"She will be having a child and I will have to marry her."

There were times when I was with her when I thought I wanted that. There was a night when we were sitting together and there was a little rumbling sound in her body.

She took my hand in one of hers. She put my hand on her little belly.

"Did you hear him?" she asked, laughing.

"It is your son, down in there, trying to call to you. He wants to call you 'Daddy.' "

The words had sent a little thrill of fear through me. I had made such great plans for my life.

I was going to be a businessman and grow rich. I lived with my father and mother, my brothers and my sister in a little yellow house on one of the poorest streets of the town.

I wanted to build a great house for my mother. She was not strong and worked too hard. I wanted to buy her beautiful clothes. There was in the town a certain woman whose husband had invested money in the enterprises of a man named Rockefeller and who, every year, while doing nothing, grew richer and richer. She had got two beautiful horses and in the afternoon rode about in her carriage.

I wanted such a team and such a carriage for my mother.

I wanted to become a driver of race horses. Sometimes I thought, I will become a businessman and get rich, and again I thought, No, I will become a famous race horse driver.

There was a man in town who owned a stable of race horses and who, at certain times of the year, went away to the races and I went often to his stables. There was a fair ground at the edge of town with a race track where the horses were trained and I went there.

The horses were going at speed and oh how beautiful they were. How I longed to be sitting in the little cart back of the horse, holding the reins, guiding, directing all of the beautiful creatures.

I was in the town. I was on the streets, was with boy friends, I was at a party at the house of some nice girl.

She who had been so free with me would be free with others.

There was that aunt and it was said that, when her husband was away from town, at his job on the railroad. . . .

But she had been so generous to me, so wonderful.

And yet. . . .

I grew more and more afraid.

"No, I must not go to her. I must not. I must not."

One day I was walking in the street and there was her aunt. She stopped me on the street.

"Have you been to see her again?

"When are you going again?

"You had better look out," she said and laughed.

She went away laughing along the street and I grew white with fright.

"I must not. I mustn't any more."

If it happened my mother would have to know, my sister, my brothers. I came at last to the taking of a resolution.

"I'll cut it out. Now I am going to cut it out."

I waited, in fear. She was in my dreams. She had become a terror to me but nothing happened and when a month, two months, three months had passed and there was no word from her I began to be proud.

I became the conquering one. I walked proudly. The other boys of the town might talk but who among them had known, had been privileged to know such an adventure as that of my own?

Memoirs

Max Frisch

QUESTIONNAIRE

1. Are you sorry for women?

2. Why? (Why not?)

3. When a woman's hands and eyes and lips betray excitement, desire, etc., because you touch them, do you take this personally?

4. What do you feel about other men:
a. when you are the successor?
b. when you are the predecessor?
c. when you are both in love with the same woman at the same time?

5. Did you choose the woman who shares your life?

6. When years later you meet (on friendly terms) women with whom you used to live, can you understand your previ-

ous relationship or does it puzzle you? In other words, do you have the impression that your job and your political opinions must once really have interested them, or does it now seem to you that you could have spared yourselves all those arguments?

7. Are you disconcerted by an intelligent lesbian?

8. Do you profess to know how to win the love of a woman, and, if you eventually find out what it really was that won you a particular woman's love, do you doubt her love?

9. How do you define *masculine*?

10. Have you any convincing proof that women are particularly suited to certain jobs a man feels to be beneath his dignity?

11. Which of these has most frequently seduced you:
a. motherliness?
b. the feeling of being admired?
c. alcohol?
d. the fear that you are not a man?
e. beauty?
f. the overhasty assumption that you will be the dominant partner however lovingly protective?

12. Who invented the castration complex?

13. In which of these cases do you speak more fondly about a past relationship; when you have left the woman or when she has left you?

14. Do you learn from one love affair things of use in the next?

15. If with women you are always having the same experience, do you think this is due to the woman? That is to say, do you in consequence consider yourself a connoisseur of women?

16. Would you care to be your own wife?

17. What has taught you more about intimate relationships between the sexes; conversations with other men or conversations with women? Or have you learned most without the use of words; from women's reactions—that is to say, by noting what women are used to and what not, what they expect from or fear in a man, etc.?

18. When a conversation with a woman stimulates you, how long can you keep the conversation going before you start thinking of things that you keep to yourself because they have nothing to do with the subject?

19. Can you imagine a woman's world?

20. What do you find a woman incapable of:
a. philosophy?
b. organization?
c. art?
d. technology?
e. politics?
and do you in consequence feel a woman who does not conform to your male prejudices to be unwomanly?

21. What do you admire in women?

22. Would you care to be kept by a woman:
a. on money she has inherited?
b. on money she has earned?

23. And why not?

24. Do you believe in biology? In other words, do you feel
that the existing relationship between man and woman is
immutable, or is it, for example, the result of a historical development covering thousands of years that woman have no
language of their own for their thought processes, but have
to make do with the male vocabulary, and thus remain sub-
servient?

25. Why must we not understand women?

Sketchbook 1966–1971

James Dickey

In sexual experience, one has the answer to a very great deal
of human anxiety and uncertainty. For one thing, sex *is* certain: it is a quick clean and total release, and as therapy for a
very great many human conditions, it has the utmost possible
importance. There is no mystery in this, and I see no reason
for the complicating of the essentially very clear issue that
goes on in all minds: of psychoanalysts, of commentators on
sex of any and all kinds. The thing itself is so basic that all
these intellectualizations about it and around it seem laugh-
able, and do the marvelous, primitive cleansing action of the
thing a great deal of disservice.

Journals

John Dos Passos

TO RUMSEY MARVIN

Camp Crane Allentown
Oct 20 {1918}

Rummy—

Still stationary—foaming at the mouth, gnashing my teeth, swearing, squirming, raging, pacing up and down in the cadenced monotony of utter boredom—bored as a polar bear in a cage—Golly.

They seem to be keeping you busy—at least they give you the illusion of activity—I wish I had it. I wonder that the U.S. army hasn't yet found a way of polishing the moon—they will soon, don't worry.

They are sane about sex in the army, aren't they? It is a comfort not to have the sacred phallus surrounded by an aura of mystery and cant, but one sometimes wonders if man is a selective animal at all in matters of sex. Yet I think he is. The fact remains though that the majority of men—allowing for the fact that they talk bigger than they act—think rather of a piece of tail than of a woman. It means to them the frequent stimulation of a certain part of the anatomy and nothing else. Perhaps I overrate the mating instinct, but I think it is susceptible of slightly higher development. Maybe it isn't. Still I think that the piece of tail attitude is partly caused by the stupid conventional morality that makes copulation wrong in itself, and only licenses it grudgingly through a marriage ceremony. The result is that people degrade their everyday habits to a sexual stupidity hardly shared by animals.

I *almost* think that Europeans have a higher—less promiscuous view of sex than Anglo Saxons. The Frenchmen goes out *pour faire l'amour* instead of to have a piece of tail. Maybe the difference is mainly in superior phraseology, but I think not. *Amour* postulates reciprocity, a human relation. A piece of tail might be got off the bunghole of a cider barrel—And the American hates with a righteous hatred born only of outraged morality the goddam' whore who gives him his piece of tail—or rather sells it.

Excuse me for inflicting this ethical disquisition, but it is a subject that interests me hugely—almost in a scientific way. One has no data to go on, as the moralizers have falsified everything; so one has to find out for oneself—and it is so shrouded in the mists of conflicting conventions that research is fascinatingly difficult.

One peels off layers of conventions like skins off an onion.

First there is the family convention that man is a monogamous animal swiving few times a year for the production of offspring.

Then there is the sporty young man convention that a man should want to swive everything in skirts.

Then there is the convention of the god dam' whore as opposed to the real nice girl who'll go just so far but no further—and how many others?

It does seem to me that we of the present day have managed to bring sex to a pitch of ugliness never before reached. We have so muddied the waters that it is hardly possible to see clearly even with the greatest effort.

(To be continued)

The departing of a section for Hoboken and the front is nearly killing me. I had counted on getting into it, but Head-

quarters refuses to hurry itself in deciding my status. I'd like
to dynamite them from Colonels to office boys———
    And we are still under quarantine for the floo———
    Write lots to the Prisoner of Camp Crane
    Talk about the Bastille!

love
Jack

The Fourteenth Chronicle

Henry De Montherlant

From the age of seventeen onward when I started going to
parties, I used to feel very strongly that: "The bodies make up
for it all."

After arriving at this conclusion, you can be as misanthropic as you like. But an odd sort of misanthrope whose
sole reason for existing is to caress another being and then
possess that being. Humanity may, at the same time, be the
shame of the earth (or more accurately, the poisoner of the
earth), what does this matter? The point is to protect oneself
against it in that capacity while enjoying it, and giving it enjoyment in the other.

When you reflect that among all the bloody fools around
you there is not one who was not desirable, for one fleeting
moment in youth, who, in other words, did not have a reason for existing even if no one took advantage of it. . . .

The act of carnal possession gives me the strongest
possible conception of what is called the Absolute. I am sure
of my pleasure and sure of my partner's. I experience no
misgivings, no questionings, uneasiness, or remorse. The act

is simple and whole, as definite and definitive as a circle in geometry.

You may ask: "Why the sexual act in particular? A good meal also is something quite definite."

Because of the human material: because of the respect you feel for your partner, and the friendship, tenderness, confidence, and protectiveness, in short all the kind feelings one creature can experience with regard to another. And then there is pride in the pleasure you can arouse and sometimes pride in having taught your partner the pleasures of love, so that the gradual apprenticeship in sensual delight is as much your creation as your literary work.

And is it not a wonderful thing, when some new creature falls within your grasp, that your whole thought should be concentrated on the pleasure you are going to give, on the art of enjoyment you are going to teach, rather than on the satisfaction you yourself are going to enjoy?

(I have shaped my literary works and my love-partners with an eye to pleasure, theirs no less than mine. I have never achieved anything else—trained no minds, souls, or characters.)

I have often quoted Jean-Jacques Rousseau's remark: "Sensations are merely what the heart makes them." This is an exaggeration of course, but it is quite true that sensation is multiplied tenfold when it has behind it such human fellow-feeling. This is a feeling which is always ready to flow abundantly in me. Since I have little or no liking for creatures who arouse no desire in me, I am left with plenty of love for those who do—in fact, much more than the average man has to give.

In short, adapting the famous phrase, I may say that I have never experienced any sorrow that half an hour's affectionate copulation has not enabled me, or could not have enabled me, to forget. And since I am quoting figures, I may add, adapting another famous phrase (Goethe's reference to his three weeks of happiness), that if I wished to work out the sum of all the happy hours I have enjoyed in my life, it would be quite enough to add up the hours of affectionate copulation, which would make a total of several years of happiness.

It follows that nothing is more important than the happy equilibrium which results from the regular practice of affectionate copulation. The foundation of life is tranquil sexual satisfaction. When the——is all right, everything else is all right. Everybody knows this, but the knowledge is not sufficiently applied in practice.

The Notebooks

Joe Willie Namath

Women are the best thing going in the world. I've got nothing against guys. They're great to drink with and to play cards with and to laugh with, and I like to have them blocking for me on the football field.

But, if I have to, I can go a week or two or even three without seeing a guy. I don't want to go a day without seeing a woman.

I like women. I prefer tall blondes but, shoot, I really like them all, tall, short, experienced, innocent, amateurs, pros, blondes, brunettes, just about everything there is, except redheads. I don't know what it is, but redheads don't turn me on. It's got to be my fault, not theirs. I guess I just haven't met the right redheads yet.

I have my own golden rule that I apply to women: Make

her happy, and she'll make you happy; look after her, and she'll look after you. I really believe that. Hell, it's got to be a two-way street. I know some guys who look at women just like objects, just like something they can use, and I think that's plain sick. Women are just too good to be treated like that.

I've got respect for women, all kinds of women. There are some girls I meet who I know are not going to be easy. I mean, sometimes I'm a genuine eighteen-point underdog. They like me and they like my company, but they don't want a guided tour of my apartment. I can understand that. Well, no, I can't really understand it. I can't imagine anyone who doesn't enjoy sex, who doesn't want sex all the time. It's the best thing ever invented. But if I meet a girl and I like her, and she's just interested in conversation, well, hell I can still enjoy being with her. And, sometimes, it turns out that the point spread was wrong, that I should have been a favorite all along. I remember one chick who was just so cool, proper and poised and everything, a tall Southern belle. Goldang, she almost killed me later on. I thought Ben Davidson, that Oakland end who broke my jaw, had caught up to me again. She was damn near as big as Davidson. The only way I knew it wasn't Davidson was that she didn't have a mustache.

You never know how an evening's going to turn out. Once I was in Las Vegas, and some guy put a hooker on me, like a present or something. She owed him some favors. We had a few drinks and went up to my room, and we started talking, and it turned out she was from Freedom, Pennsylvania, just a few miles from my hometown. I thought that was funny as hell, going all the way to Las Vegas to find a prostitute from home. She was a nice girl—I mean, she knew her business, but she was still a nice girl—and I don't put her down at all for her line of work. All I know is that she was good to me, and that's how I judge people. We talked for hours, about football—where I come from, even the hookers are football fans—and about her game. I was really interested in what she had to say. I wanted to know what it was like for her to be with a seventy-year-old guy, whether she could do him any good, things like that. Hell, I'm going to be seventy myself someday.

I Can't Wait Until Tomorrow . . .
'Cause I Get Better-Looking Every Day

Andrew Bihaly

I just came down from Arthur's, Alfred's next door neighbor. He'd asked me a simple question: "When was the last time you got yourself a piece of tail?" It's been a long time, I told him.

So I take a shave, a nice warm bath and put on something decent and go out to get myself a chick. Like in the old times before I picked up Mignone. Full scale ahead. Cut and dried. Straight. Let's get hot, woman.

It isn't like it used to be . . . I went out but was kind of lost, did not know where to go. I went to the Engage, a coffeehouse I like to frequent because I do not feel it is a commercial enterprise.

The woman who owns the Engage asked, "What will you have?" When I said I had eaten, she told me, "You will have to leave. Tonight we have a rule: only those who will eat supper may stay here before nine."

So I left but felt rejected because I had repaired that broken window this past Monday and it wasn't right for her to treat me as a stranger.

I picked the Gallery Gwen, on East Fourth Street, as my most likely place to find tail and found it closed.

As I wandered, I saw two young girls go into a downstairs coffeehouse. I followed them and stood at the stairway waiting for them to choose a place to sit. I wanted to sit at their table, but they walked over to the only occupied one where three young boys were sitting.

The blonde, who looked more mature than the slim brunette, asked in an innocent and naive tone, "Would any of you have some dope on him by any chance?" The boys were flabbergasted and embarrassed. But they liked the girls and when they pointed to me, standing on the steps, warning. "That man there might be a cop," the blonde said, "No, I never get into any trouble. I have all the luck in the world. Even if someone pointed to me and said to a cop. 'Look she is carrying a pound of opium in her pocketbook,' I would just keep walking and nothing would happen to me because I was born under a lucky star."

I, in the meanwhile, sat down at the next table and listened silently, brazenly gazing over where the five were sitting. One of the boys said, "We do have something on us." The blonde asked him to show it to her.

One of them, a youth with a pimply face and angular, manneristic movements and programmatic questions, invited me to come sit at their table and asked what I was doing. I told him I was walking around the Village because my girlfriend and I broke up yesterday and I was looking for a new friendship. I had seen the girls go into the coffee shop and followed them because I thought they were beautiful. He seemed to be satisfied with the simple explanation, and I, for my part, kept silent from then on.

The boys finally invited the girls and me to their apartment on Fifth Street to smoke some pot. Before we got up from the table, however, the blonde asked, "Do you fellows have any other motives besides turning us on?" and the fellow in the middle said, "If you come at me and rape me, or pull me into the other room, I shall not resist; but otherwise we shall not want to have anything further to do about making out with you."

So we went to the apartment, smoked pot and I went home alone.

The Journal of Andrew Bihaly

Jack Kerouac

SEX DREAM—Marie Fitzpatrick or somebody, and I, hot, go down the cellar stairs holding each other's organs—I have hers, she mine, as we descend steps slowly—We're gonna look for a place to work—It's the basement of the Fortier Hugehouse on Salem—I pick a little sidecellar coal room, gray with ashes, dank, and stand her against the wall as we wake up—Just sweet immediate wanting—she's slicking up breath in her hiss hot teeth—I'm grinding my molars in the bighard girlholding grash—r-r-o-p!—We're gonna find a place to gnash our hot and juicy parts pole into hole in some hideout craphole of the great cellar, no one'll know, we'll have bare thighs and write on chalk on the wall and smack goosy flesh and have hot jumping juices in the ecstatic secret liplicking lollswallowing lip-lolling suckcellar hole, droop—I'll grab her bare rumps and squeeze and dump in, standing, the straight pole, up her roamous slit, deep, she'll part warm breath to huff—I'll grang her—spew spill flood her inside belly womb—flutter my knees—tickle her top—accidentally plop in, God.

Book of Dreams

Seymour Krim

Sex I say sex is the red open mouth which has eaten into all American life during my brief earthtime! Sex is the honey and the hangup and the sob and the dollar and the fist and the vaseline which has savaged through my small literary life and your Plymouth-hustling life and your IBM-punching life, O respectable-looking roasting-alive pleasure-lappers in Cleveland and Dayton and Norwich Conn! Sex sex sex sex has roared out of its lion-cage O brother-beasts and sister-moaners and I see it everywhere raging loose on our American dream-scene slitting my eyes and yours with its killer scent bombing every thought with its thousand many-pricked possibilities! I am crazy with sex and my America and yours is hourly inflaming my mental crotch with its ceaseless barrage of legs tits asses stockings panties Tampax garterbelts perfumes highheels—the entire arsenal of girl that Yankee dollar has provoked into the boldest display of suggestion and fever ever known to man! O I know—I know too well believe me!—that the American volcano of cunt and whipdream and going-down and blow and three-of-us-making-it-together and dog-style and suck and 69 87 Christ 736 is the doing of no single being is the explosion of all our being is the helpless multiple boom-boom release of spermgusheries commensurate with blistering U.S. dream! I say it is our mythic rocket-pace of more lavish new eat taste sip try grip clutch devour quick new more NOW NOW that has driven us beyond the dwindling square planet of happiness, that has made us joystoned with sex as the very source of private dream of heaven 5 times a day for our breathless breed! I say sex is our mortalest bang of being here now in these headless young-giant states and at this moment in our unreal moon-bound history it alone is the frantic message wolfed down by every ear! I cry we have sex on the head in the pants in the street waking sleeping reading writing thinking dying—and I have seen me and seen you wince and jerk with the heat of it beat of it meat of it and I swear to you there is no relief in sight!

The Magical Underwear Panty
(With Detachable Garters)

Cesare Pavese

23rd December 1937

The child who passes his days and nights among men and women, knowing vaguely but not believing that this is reality, troubled, in short, that sex should exist at all, does he not foreshadow the man who spends his time among men and women, knowing, believing that this is the only reality, suffering atrociously from his own mutilation? This feeling that my heart is being torn out and plunged into the depths, this giddiness that rends my breast and shatters me, is something I did not experience even when I was befooled in April.

The fate reserved for me (like the rat, my boy!) was to let the scar heal over, and then (with a breath, a caress, a sigh) to have it torn open again and a new infection added.

Neither deception nor jealousy have ever given me this *vertigo of the blood.* It took impotence, the conviction that no woman ever finds pleasure with me, or ever would. We are as we are; hence this anguish. If nothing else, I can suffer without feeling ashamed: my pangs are no longer those of love. But this, in very truth, is pain that destroys all energy:

if one is not really a man, if one must mix with women without being able to think of possessing them, how can one sustain one's spirits and vital power? Could a suicide be better justified?

To accord with such a dreadful thought, it is right that I should have this terrible sensation of being crushed, annihilated, in my breast, my muscles, my inmost heart. So far, it lasts only for an instant, but what of the day when it will last longer? When it will endure for an hour or all day long?

25th December

With love or with hate, but always with violence.

Going to prison is nothing: coming back from it is frightful.

The average man ought to be well disciplined, not a street-loafer. I am neither the one nor the other.

There is something sadder than growing old—remaining a child.

If screwing was not the most important thing in life, Genesis would not have started with it.

Naturally, everybody says to you, "What does it matter? That's not the only thing. Life is full of variety. A man can be good for something else," but no one, not even the men, will look at you unless you radiate that power. And the women say to you: "What does it matter," and so on, but they marry someone else. And to marry means building a whole life, a thing you will never do. Which shows you have remained a child too long.

If you got on so badly with her, who was everything you dreamed of, with whom could you ever get on well?

The Burning Brand: Diaries 1935–1950

Nelson Algren

Q: How important is sex to you?

ALGREN: Well, I think sex is part of everything. I don't think of sex as just something that happens now and then. I can't imagine writing without the feel of sex. I mean sex is a diffuse feeling. It diffuses everything and only once in a while would it be called sex. Sex is diffused with love and affection and only once in a while it comes to the hard-on point. The feeling is always there, but there isn't necessarily always an erection. I mean I don't think you can make things like that happen. It has to start the other way. Otherwise it's pretty meaningless. Once in Paris I was driving around with a pretty attractive girl who was a little on the loose, a good-looking girl about twenty-eight, took me out to a swimming pool and she drove me home. She talked very frankly about sex. She had the afternoon free and I would have liked to have gone to bed with her but I said, "The trouble with it is I'm leaving Paris—how are you going to start something and then finish it? You can't just say, you know, let me use your cunt and I'll give you my cock and we'll just go at it." She said, "What's the matter with *that?*" I said, "I don't know *what* the hell's the matter with it. I got no heart for it. I don't know, I don't know. I just want to do something more than just *go at it*. I can do without it if that's all there is." I just didn't have the heart, you know. It wasn't hard to do, but the feeling went out. I thought, Oh what the hell, and I said, "Drop me off here." I didn't feel any regret about that. I think I was right. It's got to be the other way around. It's got to be the big thing first and then this other thing is just incidental. When you start planning it and being deliberate about it, it goes wrong. It's usually just when you're both

thinking about something else, or rather you're just preoccupied with one another as people, and *boing!* That's when it's
all right. But you can't make that happen. You can't say,
"Now let's have a big sex deal." That spoils it right away. At
first I couldn't figure something out, but it's really very
simple, that women who come around looking very persistently for sex, usually married women looking for sex, I
thought that this meant that they're sexy. But it means that
they are sexless. The worst lay I ever had was a woman who
came voluntarily, unsolicited, a married woman showed up
and you'd think that was a big thing. But it was just the opposite—quite sexless. It took me a while to put that together.
The woman didn't realize that the lack was in herself. So
she's shopping all around for this thing that isn't going to
happen. And it's sexlessness, not sex, which I think is the big
thing at *Playboy*—something of the same sort of search. I
think it's basically a sexless thing. I think the people who
like sex stay home. I mean I don't think they make a big
thing out of it.

Conversations With Nelson Algren

James Blake

The affair with young Sandy was something I didn't seek,
couldn't foresee, and never regretted. As Willie the band-
leader diagnosed it, Sandy needed only a little attention to
bring him out of his alienated state. After I began taking him
down to the band hall with me in the afternoons and had an
opportunity to talk to him alone, it seemed to me that he also
needed love. That it was homosexual love was, in my

opinion, of no importance. It was the only variety available and the need was crucial.

So we became lovers. Our being alone in the band hall so much brought a lot of comment from the other musicians, and from other convicts. Willie asked me about it, and I told him the truth. His answer was merely that I should be careful to protect myself and Sandy.

Sandy's cell partner was a glib, sinister con artist, a Jew who had become a converted Baptist and posed as a Bible-toting evangelist. A type convicts called *Bible-Back*.

Sandy told me that this charlatan terrorized him with threats of perdition, quoted Scripture at him, and at night in the cell sodomized him.

If I was performing fellatio, it was because Sandy wanted it, enjoyed it—there was never any question of duress. In time Sandy became the dominant one in our relationship. It was of little importance to me, and I felt that it gave him confidence. In the matter of music, I remained his teacher and required him to learn.

When the band supervisor told me that he was getting anonymous letters about Sandy and me (and because he liked me and I was useful to him, his attitude was one of amused tolerance), I knew they were coming from Sandy's cell partner.

The population of the prison was huge (3,000); the bureaucratic confusion was formidable. Under cover of this confusion, it was possible for alert convicts to operate to a remarkable degree. So I went to a friend of mine who worked as a secretary in the custodial office and made a deal with him. On the street he had been a church organist and had ambitions to succeed me in my job as chapel organist.

In return for letting him use the chapel organ and recommending him to the chaplain as my successor, he agreed to extract the folder (*rap sheet*) of Sandy's cell partner from the master file and place it in the road-transfer file. This was the list of inmates marked for transfer from the main prison to one of the state road camps.

Accordingly, one morning at daybreak, Sandy's cellmate was called out and placed on a bus for transportation to a road camp.

It was tough for me to leave Sandy when the time came for my discharge, but I was proud of the change in him, and Willie promised me that he would look after him.

Much later, I heard that Sandy had done what I had always told him he would do—returned to the small town he came from, married, and started a family. Happy, or reasonably happy, ending.

The Joint

Orson Bean

One night we lay in each other's arms and we found the courage not to fantasize or pretend, not to think of anyone or anything, not even to think, Here we are, it's us. We hadn't planned it; as a matter of fact, it was a night when we were rather tired and distracted and had thought of nothing except sleep. But suddenly our eyes met and something in us melted. We reached out to each other and touched and it was as if layers of us fell away. We moved closer and it was like two separate energy fields fusing into one. There was a wonder about it, a wonder about how we felt different to each other than we had before, physically different, an actual difference to the skin tone. And our eyes felt different and the touch of our lips caused a wave of excitement and pleasure that traveled up and down and around and through us. And a touch of hand to body was almost more than could be borne, every place touched awakened another place. And through it all, there was a sense of differentness, that we were different than we had been before and that we were different from other people. But there was a sense of sameness too, a feeling of belonging, of experiencing what someone in a meadow in Asia or on a hill in California might be experiencing and of making contact with everyone else at the very moment that we felt unique and separate. We felt totally come together, with the universe fallen away from us and yet we felt more a part of it than ever before.

The sheer wonder of it simply amazed us, the wonder of the pleasure—we knew that we had never known what pleasure was before—and the awesomeness of the feelings we felt, the deepness of them, the tenderness and the horniness coming all together. To be able to feel deep, deep, tender love and almost unbearable horniness all at the same time was like everything we had ever wished for in the most private recesses of our minds. Finally to come together in ourselves, to bring the two separate halves together and not to feel guilty because it's right and we know it in every fiber and in every secret, terrible part of us. Deeper and deeper we melted into each other and how can you think about a breast and a planet and a universe and all the vibrant life in it at the same time as you are laughing and crying because you never, never knew what love was before, you only had an inkling?

We clung to each other for a long time then, so close, so tight with our tears on her cheeks and our eyes deep into each other and then one of us, I don't remember which, said, "So that's what it's all about." And suddenly it was so simple, the meaning of life. The dumb jokes—"Life is like a well,"—and all the wars and the territorial imperative and

the Third Reich and Cadillacs and split-level ranchhouses
and the Spanish Inquisition and Jesus of Nazareth and Nietz-
sche and Kant and Marx and all of the madness fell into
perspective. We fell asleep holding each other close.

Me *And The Orgone*

Jakov Lind

To feel . . . I didn't like this verb; I didn't like the idea; I
didn't like the reference. Feel it! I feel it. Can you feel it?
What do you feel? Does it feel nice? Do you like the feeling?
Feel, don't think! I liked to think about *it*, not "feelings"—or
rather I didn't, when I felt something, like to like feelings. I
felt limp. My right side ached as if a bone had been removed
and not replaced. With one woman I felt complete. Two
people are a powerful presence—a right partner is added
strength, to both woman and man. I sincerely believed that
only the two that make one are a perfect human being. The
real problem was a philosophical one. How can one be complete and do something of interest if one has a permanent
erection? Unthinkable, because the best part is the erection;
as soon as you are rid of it you must get up and work. Therefore it is wanting the erection and not losing it by fucking
one must strive after. In order to have peace and erection
one has to have one right woman only, for life; best for this
purpose is a loving and understanding sister and friend,
which of course has the considerable disadvantage of being
less exciting. It is one woman for one man for a man who
loves his work and wants to keep his erection. To waste it on
a great variety of not sisterly and not friendly but stimu-
lating females and yet to keep it, is a philosophical prob-

lem—and certainly not a matter of feelings. It was hard enough to keep us excited without more feelings than it needed to play demented father and lesbian daughter, grandmother and aged sister, first cousins at the age of twelve, two strangers in a country jail, two lesbians in a car, and games of that kind.

Numbers: A Further Autobiography

Ned Rorem

*I've often thought that I would like
To be the saddle of a bike.*
　　　　　　　—AUDEN

Zeus and Hera quarreled, each claiming the other's sex was more capable of gratification. To prove the point they called in the hermaphrodite Teresias.

"Who has more fun in bed, Teresias, man or woman?"
"Woman."

In fury Hera struck Teresias blind. In compassion Zeus bestowed foresight upon him.

*For so hard I think on man the
thought crumbles into absolute
unnature. . . .*
　　　　　　　—PAUL GOODMAN

The bachelor, simply because he's used to it, will confront oncoming solitude with more felicity and circumspection than the widower. Now the confirmed bachelor is probably pederastical, since the sexuality of 99 out of 100 un-married men over forty is suspect, and the 100th is no Casanova but a hermit. Of course it doesn't follow that a ho-mosexual is more circumspect and felicitous than a hetero (we know better), but then again it's not sure he's *less* so. But he *is* more versed in loneliness, thanks to his dubious talent for promiscuity.

> *I speak of it as a thing with a future*
> *as yet badly done by amateurs neglecting*
> *the opportunity to be discriminating.*
> —KAY BOYLE

A turkish bath, like the Quaker service, is a place of silent meeting. The silence is shared solely by men, men who come uniquely together not to speak but to act. More even than the army, the bath is by definition a male, if not a masculine, domain. (Though in Paris, whimsically, it's a lady who presents you your *billet d'entrée,* robe, and towel.) There are as many varieties of bath as of motel, from the scorpion-ridden hammams of Marrakech, where like Rim-baud in a boxcar you'll be systematically violated by a regi-ment, to the carpeted saunas of Frisco, where like a corpse in a glossy morgue you'll be a slab of flab on marble with Musak. There is no variety, however, in the purpose served: anonymous carnality. As in a whorehouse, you check inter-personal responsibility at the door; but unlike the whore-house, here a *ménage* might accidentally meet in mutual infidelity. The ethical value too is like prostitution's: the con-solation that no one can prove you are not more fulfilled by a stranger (precisely because there's no responsibility to de-flect your fantasies—fantasies which now are real) than by the mate you dearly love, and the realization that Good Sex is not in performing as the other person wants but as you want. You will reconfirm this as you retreat into time through every bath of history.

For decades there has existed in central Manhattan one such establishment, notorious throughout the planet but never written about. Certainly this one seeks no publicity: word of mouth seems sufficient to promote its million-dollar business. Located in the heart of a wholesale floral district, there's small chance that an unsuspecting salesman might happen in for a simple rubdown, the nearest hotel being the Martha Washington—for women only. The customers do constitute as heterogeneous a cross section as you'll ever find. (There are only two uncategorizable phenomena: the care and feeding of so-called creative artists, and the nature of a Turkish bath's clientele.) Minors and majors, beatniks and bartenders, all ages and proclivities of the married and single, the famous and tough, so *many* from Jersey! but curiously few mad queens because it's hard to maintain a style stark naked. To run across your friends is less embarrassing than cumbersome: who wants gossip now?

You enter at any age, in any condition, any time of night or week, pay dearly for a fetid cubicle, and are given a torn gown and a pair of mismated slippers (insufficient against the grime that remains in your toes for days.) You penetrate an obscure world, disrobe in private while reading graffiti, emerge rerobed into the public of gray wanderers so often compared to the lost souls of Dante, although this geography is not built of seven circles but of four square stories each capable of housing some eighty mortals. Once, you are told, this was a synagogue; today it's a brothel lit like *Guernica* by one nude bulb. The top floor is a suite of squalid rooms giving onto a corridor from *The Blood of a Poet* with background music of a constant pitty-pat, whips and whispers, slurps and groans. The second floor, more of same, plus massive dormitory. On the ground floor, are cubicles, a television room, a monastic refectory. The basement contains fringe benefits: a dryer, a massage room, a large dirty pool, and the famous steam-room wherein *partouzes* are not discouraged.

The personnel, working in shifts, comprises at any given time some ten people, including two masseurs and a uniformed policeman. Each of these appears dull-witted due to years of inhaling the gloomy disinfectant of locker room and hamburger grease.

There are feast and fast days, rough Spanish mornings and sneaky afternoons, even Embryo Night at the Baths. Eternal motion, never action (meaning production): despite a daily ocean of orgasm the ceaseless efforts at cross-breeding could hardly make a mule. Not from want of trying: at any time you may witness couplings of white with black, beauty with horror, aardvark with dinosaur, panda with pachyderm, skinny-old-slate-gray-potbelly-bald with chubby-old-slate-gray-potbelly-bald, heartbreakingly gentle with stimulatingly rugged—but always, paradoxically, like with like. Your pupils widen as a faun mounts that stevedore, or when a mountain descends on Mohammed. Some cluster forever together in a throbbing Medusa's head; others disentangle themselves to squat in foggy corners, immobile as carnivorous orchids, waiting to "go up" on whatever passes. There's one! on his knees, praying with tongue more active than a windmill in a hurricane, neck thrown back like Mata Hari's and smeared with tears nobody notices mingling with steam. All are centered on the spasm that in a fraction switches from sublime to ridiculous, the sickening spasm sought by poets and peasants, and which, like great love, makes the great seem silly. . . . Yet if at those suburban wife-swapping gang-bangs there's risk of pregnancy, these mirthless matings stay sterile—not because the sexes aren't mixed but because the species *are*.

If you don't believe me, says Maldoror, go see for yourself. You won't believe it *of* yourself, the money and months you've passed, a cultured person lurking in shadows governed by groin! Did you *honestly* spend the night? Can't you, with your splitting head, manage it down the hall to pee, through shafts of black sunlight and idiot eyes and churning mouths that never say die, and crunched on the floor those tropical roaches you hadn't noticed last evening? Don't slip in the sperm while retching at the fact that it's 8 A.M. and there's still a dull moan and a sound of belts (they've really no sense of proportion). So leave, descend while cackling still rends the ear, reclaim that responsibility checked with your wallet. Hate all those bad people; or, if you will, feel lightened and purged. Allow the sounds to dim—the anticlimatic puffing and shooting and slippery striving, the friendless hasty jerkings that could fertilize a universe in the dirty dark (*quel embarras de richesses!*). Quit the baths to go home and bathe, but make clear to yourself that such uncommitted hilarity doesn't necessarily preclude a throbbing heart. For three times there you found eternal love.

The New York Diary

Paul Gauguin

I should like to be a pig: man alone can be ridiculous.

Once upon a time the wild animals, the big ones, used to roar; today they are stuffed. Yesterday I belonged to the nineteenth century; today I belong to the twentieth and I assure you that you and I are not going to see the twenty-first. Life being what it is, one dreams of revenge—and has to

content oneself with dreaming. Yet I am not one of those who speak ill of life. You suffer, but you also remember. I like the philosophers, except when they bore me or when they are pedantic. I like women too, when they are fat and vicious; their intelligence annoys me; it's too spiritual for me. I have always wanted a mistress who was fat and I have never found one. To make a fool of me, they are always pregnant.

This does not mean that I am not susceptible to beauty, but simply that my senses will have none of it. As you perceive, I do not know love. To say "I love you" would break all my teeth. So much to show you that I am anything but a poet. A poet without love! Women, who are shrewd, divine this, and for this reason I repel them.

I have no complaint to make. Like Jesus I say, The flesh is the flesh, the spirit is the spirit. Thanks to this, a small sum of money satisfies my flesh and my spirit is left in peace.

Here I am, then, offered to the public like an animal, stripped of all sentiment, incapable of selling his soul for any Gretchen. I have not been a Werther, and I shall not be a Faust. Who knows? The syphlitic and the alcoholic will perhaps be the men of the future. It looks to me as if morality, like the sciences and all the rest, were on its way toward a quite new morality which will perhaps be the opposite of that of today. Marriage, the family, and ever so many good things which they din into my ears, seem to be dashing off at full speed in an automobile.

Do you expect me to agree with you?

Intimate Journals

Waldo Frank

My own sex life was full of trouble. I could not carry on the mental posture common to the West, particularly the Latin lands, toward the sex act as *la bagatelle,* making it a game like tennis. I had encountered it, of course, in Paris and elsewhere, and I had more than once tried it. Literally it made me sick. There was a deeper pagan concept of sex as mystery and ritual. I accepted it. The Hindu cult of Tantrism, which ennobles the act as the archetypal union of two into the One, attracted me. My sex partner had to play a conscious drama of fusion and of union with my *idea.* Of course, this caused trouble. It was a burden for the woman to find her body exalted as an allegory and ignored as a fact. If they are honest with themselves, women do not like it. My second wife, for instance, who was a blue-eyed, golden-haired Yankee from New Hampshire found that her "accepting" me meant (to me) Anglo-America's acceptance of the dark Mediterranean "outsider." We did not know each other, not physically, not emotionally. My image of her was a barrier between us. And while for a term the myth flourished, love, which *is* knowing, agonized.

In the twenties and thirties the invitation to sexual experiment and experience prevailed wherever youths and girls emerged from their cocoons and buzzed about like newborn flies. Like every presentable young man, I was constantly being tempted to play the game of *la bagatelle* and constantly failing. And when I did not fail, I suffered more. I recall a typical encounter with a lusty woman who adored the play of sex as a ravenous child loved food. We dined over two bottles of wine; we went to my apartment, and the embrace began. It was highly creditable to the male ego. The woman responded and responded. I was a good instrument.

Sated, the woman got up, dressed, and left. I lay in a violent tremor that lasted twenty-four hours; and when the woman next day again offered me her superb body, I was nauseous.

I recall another typical episode with a very modern daughter of the "earth." It was October, and I was alone in my Cape Cod house. The ocean beach was empty, and I went in naked. A woman came out of the surf, and I saw that she was also nude. There was no embarrassment between us. We dressed silently and drove to her home. There, still without words, we undressed again. I achieved the detachment she desired and became what is known as a good lover. From that day I could not bear this woman. Alone with her I succumbed to the devotions of sheer sex she wanted. I was enslaved. Since I could not avoid her otherwise, I ran away from the Cape.

There were ignoble passages.... In the third floor hall room of my lodging house on Washington Place lived a girl whom I occasionally crossed on the way to and from the floor's common bathroom. She was a homely little mouse with small scared eyes. I had noticed her smile and was aware of what it meant. One evening I passed her in the hall, but turned and went with her. She locked the door; and I saw her meager home, barely wide enough for the cot, the bureau, and the chair. I helped her undress, for she was trembling; and I embraced her to combat her chill; and this desire to impart my warmth was the nearest I got to union between us. As if I were in a hurry with an engagement elsewhere, I entered her dry little body and ejaculated almost at once. Then I threw on my clothes, not even kissing her goodbye, and left her.

Returned to my large room, I pulled a small notebook from my pocket. It contained the list of names of women I had gone to bed with. I realized then that I did not know the girl's name.

This episode also is misleading. I refused many an invitation to the feast of sex after I had won it, overcome by a sense of disharmony with the woman. Often I was like a virgin whose desire takes the form of freezing fear because it is too great to bear. I found as I passed thirty that I was trading on my gifts. I don't think I was an unusually attractive man; and there were several types of women who looked through me as I were not there, so little did what *was* there interest them. But there were others who were romantically thrilled by the poet, the rebel. Women of this ilk climbed the five flights to my attic in Paris or came to my room in New York. I found I was exploiting my talents to ready women for bed. I would read a poem or a chapter of my own to thrill them. My intellectual and aesthetic powers became secondary sexual characteristics. In the hush and heat of the room, I could not resist this dishonesty. I resolved not to permit it, again and again.

Memoirs

J. R. Ackerley

How much of all this did I enjoy, this long pursuit of love through sex, out of which, in the end, I emerged as lonely as I began? The moods of the past are difficult to recapture. The orgasm itself is a pleasure of course—had I not always placed it first among the pleasures?—but its pleasure has degrees. When things suited me and I felt relaxed I enjoyed it. But I was seldom quite suited or relaxed. If my prejudices were gradually ditched, my anxieties remained; experience, from which we are said to learn, has no effect upon the inner nature. A new form of anxiety, a maddening impotence, began to afflict me. I can put no date to it, it emerged in the company of my old stand-bys, my few steadies. I believe it had nothing to do with increasing age, nothing to do with sexual exhaustion; although so many boys had passed through my hands I lived with none of them, they came and went, sometimes to return, at no point in this journey did I have a feeling of stability, of more than momentary satisfaction. Indeed when, some time in the thirties, a friend asked me if I had any notion how many boys I'd taken to bed, I was astonished to find that those I managed to recollect got into three figures, for I never had any sense of riches, only of poverty, and at last of dire poverty. The impotence that started to defeat me was neurotic. I was still close to incontinence with new experiences—becoming rarer and rarer— with that deserter, for instance, that last, long emotional affair, who had not yet flashed upon my sexual scene; with old friends things began to go "wrong," and with him also when he became an old friend. I looked forward eagerly in my poverty to seeing them when they could get away from their various units, to having their hands upon me and the use of their bodies; they knew what I wanted though they seldom wanted it themselves, and this hitherto I had not minded so long as I got my own comfortable satisfaction. Now I began to mind. Like the irksome, unsmotherable pea beneath the princess's mattresses, some fret would enter my head. In spite of my theories about sex, I had always found it hard to impose my wishes (further evidence of guilt no doubt), to go straight for the thing I most desired, and since these boys were normal they either had no such wishes to impose or left it all to me. The Welsh boy alone sometimes took the initiative, though; being newly married, he wanted nothing for himself. Excepting for him, and throughout my life now that I come to think of it, no one whom I wanted, from my sailor onward, even when mutual desires were involved, ever took the physical initiative; it was always left to me who found it difficult to take, and this, no doubt, was a situation I myself had created—and because of its frustration, perhaps desired. I seemed always to be pretending not to have an erection, not to be impatient and that the quid that usually passed between us at once (the boys were always short of cash) was not a *quid pro quo* but a gift. Now it began to defeat me, this situation with old friends who did not desire me and whom I myself no longer desired so much as the thing they had to give, if only I could get it. The fret would enter.... Why had I taken him to the pub first? it was getting late, I must hurry.... Why had I not taken him to the pub first? he was bored, I must hurry.... Why had I let him have his own satisfaction first? he was tired, I must hurry.... I was taking too long, he was only being obliging and my sweat and the weight of my body must be disagreeable to him, I must hurry, hurry.... Then the slow collapse, and nothing that he could do, or I could do in the way of furious masturbation, could retrieve the wretched failure.

My Father And Myself

Frank Harris

I had often heard of sixty-three as being "the grand climacteric" of a man's life, but what that really meant I had no idea till I had well passed that age.

Alphonse Daudet has written somewhere that every man of forty has tried at some time or another to have a woman and failed (*fit faux coup*). He even went so far as to assert that the man who denied this, was boasting, or rather lying.

I can honestly say that I had no such experience up to sixty. I had become long before, as I shall tell, a mediocre performer in the lists of love, but had never been shamed by failure. Like the proverbial Scot, I had no lack of vigor, but I too "was nae sae frequent" as I had been. Desire seemed nearly as keen in me at sixty as at forty, but more and more, as I shall relate, it ramped in me at sight of the nudities of girlhood.

I remember one summer afternoon in New York, it seems to me just when short dresses began to come in. A girl of fourteen or fifteen, as I came into the room, hastily sat up on a sofa, while pulling down her dress that had rucked up well above her knees. She was exquisitely made, beautiful limbs in black silk showing a margin of thighs shining like alabaster. I can still feel how my mouth parched at the sight of her bare thighs and how difficult it was for me to speak of ordinary things as if unconcerned. She was still half asleep and I hope I got complete control of my voice before she had smoothed down the bobbed unruly hair that set off her flaming cheeks and angry confused glances.

Time and again in the street I turned to fix in my memory some young girl's legs, trying to trace the subtle hesitating line of budding hips, seeing all the while the gracious triangle in front outlined by soft down of hair just revealing the full lips of the *fica*. Even at forty, earlier still, indeed, as I have related, I had come to love small breasts, like half-ripe apples and was put off by every appearance of ripe maturity in a woman. But I found from time to time that this woman or that whom I cared for could give me as keen a thrill as any girl of them all, perhaps indeed keener and more prolonged, the pleasure depending chiefly upon mutual passion. But I'm speaking now of desire and not of the delights of passion, and desire became rampant in me only at the sight of slight half-fledged girlhood. . . .

Now to my experience. In the early summer of 1920, having passed my sixty-fifth birthday, I was intent on finishing a book of *Portraits* before making a long deferred visit to Chicago. Before leaving New York, a girl called on me to know if I could employ her. I had no need of her, yet she was pretty, provocative, even, but for the first time in my life, I was not moved.

As her slight, graceful figure disappeared, suddenly I realized the wretchedness of my condition in an overwhelming, suffocating wave of bitterness. So this was the end; desire was there but not the driving power. There were ways, I knew, of whipping desire to the standing point, but I didn't care for them. The end of my life had come. God, what a catastrophe! What irremediable, shameful defeat! Then for the first time I began to envy the lot of a woman; after all, she could give herself to the end, on her deathbed if she wished, whereas a man went about looking like a man, feeling like a man, but powerless, impotent, disgraced in the very pride and purpose of his manhood.

And then the thought of my work struck me. No new stories had come to me lately: the shaping spirit of imagination had left me with the virile power. Better death than such barrenness of outlook, such a dreadful monotonous desert. Suddenly some lines came to me:

Dear as remembered kisses after Death,
Deep as true love and wild with all regret
Oh, Death in life, the days that are no more!

As I sat there in the darkening office, tears poured from my eyes. So this is the end!

My Life And Loves

Edmund Wilson

To one who has passed sixty, the exercise of the sexual functions can hardly be made a cult or the longing for it give
rise to extravagant idealization. The attainment of this satisfaction can no longer present itself as a supremely desired
end, as it sometimes does in youth—when, however, we may
not be aware that what we are aiming at is offspring more
viable than we are. We have not yet arrived, at sixty, at the
state of the aged Sophocles, who is made to say, in Plato's
Republic, that he is glad to have escaped at last from a mad
and cruel master. We still may desire, touch rapture, we still
may be left as if drunken with the aftermath of love. We
may even feel occasional symptoms of falling in love again,
as we do those of some old ailment—gout or a sneezing
from roses—to which we have become accustomed and
which by this time we know how to cure. Yet sex has come
to seem more irrelevant to the other things that occupy our
minds, and we may sometimes push it away with impatience
when we are busy with something else. We do not now
want any more children. It is as much as we can do to give
adequate attention to those we already have. And at this
time of life, in this state of mind, we can just begin to catch
a glimpse of a world in which what we call love would be
demoted to a place less important than it has occupied for
our part of the world in the past.

A Piece of My Mind: Reflections at Sixty

3. Husbands

Franz Kafka

The unhappiness of the bachelor, whether seeming or actual, is so easily guessed at by the world around him that he will curse his decision, at least if he has remained a bachelor because of the delight he takes in secrecy. He walks around with his coat buttoned, his hands in the upper pockets of his jacket, his arms akimbo, his hat pulled down over his eyes, a false smile that has become natural to him is supposed to shield his mouth as his glasses do his eyes, his trousers are tighter than seem proper for his thin legs. But everyone knows his condition, can detail his sufferings. A cold breeze breathes upon him from within and he gazes inward with the even sadder half of his double face. He moves incessantly, but with predictable regularity, from one apartment to another. The farther he moves away from the living, for whom he must still—and this is the worst mockery—work like a conscious slave who dare not express his consciousness, so much the smaller a space is considered sufficient for him. While it is death that must still strike down the others, though they may have spent all their lives in a sickbed—for even though they would have gone down by themselves long ago from their own weakness, they nevertheless hold fast to their loving, very healthy relatives by blood and marriage—he, this bachelor, still in the midst of life, apparently of his own free will resigns himself to an even smaller space, and when he dies the coffin is exactly right for him.

The Diaries of Franz Kafka 1910–1913

Cyril Connolly

Two fears alternate in marriage, the one of loneliness and the other of bondage. The dread of loneliness is greater than the fear of bondage, so we get married. For one person who fears being so tied there are three who dread being set free. Yet the love of liberty is a noble passion and one to which most married people secretly aspire—in moments when they are not neurotically dependent—but by then it is too late; the ox does not become a bull, nor the hen a falcon.

The fear of loneliness can be overcome, for it springs from weakness; human beings are intended to be free, and to be free is to be lonely, but the fear of bondage is the apprehension of a real danger, and so I find it all the more pathetic that it should be young men who dread loneliness and get married, and beautiful girls who worry most about becoming old maids.

The Unquiet Grave

A. S. Neill

I call myself normal sexually, even though I fancy I have sublimated sex to ambition. In my student days, I had the usual unedifying adventures with girls. As mentioned earlier, the nice girls were taboo: "Who touches me, marries me." So we students picked up shopgirls—girls from the working classes. I never once went to a prostitute, maybe because so many enthusiastic amateurs were around. But it was all wrong, all degrading. Once, after intercourse with a shopgirl on Blackford Hill, she began to cry. I asked her why. "It isn't fair," she sobbed. "You students take us out and we like your manners and educated speech, but you never marry us. I'll have to marry some workman who can only talk about football and beer." That was the end of my picking up shopgirls.

Twice I nearly got married. Both girls, like myself, were of the lower middle class. I hesitated. I was in love, but reason crept in: you want to do something important in life; will she be able to keep up with you? Stupidly, I tried in both cases to educate these girls, gave them books, talked of Shaw and Wells and Chesterton, of Hardy and Meredith. I think it was the old snob complex my mother had given me, now transformed from social to cultural climbing.

Also, there was the economic factor. I did not earn enough to support a wife and family, which would have meant settling down for a lifetime as a country headmaster, far from an urban intellectual life and a career in literature. Emotionally I was wrong, but I could not act in any other way, not with my grandiose plans.

"Neill! Neill! Orange Peel!"

Huey P. Newton

When I was very young, I accepted the institution of marriage. As I grew older and saw my father struggling to take care of a wife and seven children, having to work at three jobs at once, I began to see that the bourgeois family can be an imprisoning, enslaving, and suffocating experience. Even though my mother and father loved each other deeply and were happy together, I felt that I could not survive this kind of binding commitment with all its worries and material insecurity. Among the poor, social conditions and economic hardship frequently change marriage into a troubled and fragile relationship. A strong love between husband and wife can survive outside pressures, but that is rare. Marriage usually becomes one more imprisoning experience within the general prison of society.

My doubts about marriage were reinforced when I met Richard Thorne. His theory of nonpossessiveness in the love relationship was appealing to me. The idea that one person possesses the other, as in bourgeois marriage, where "she's my woman and he's my man," was unacceptable. It was too restrictive, too binding, and ultimately destructive to the union itself. Often it absorbed all of a man's energies and did not leave him free to develop potential talents, to be creative, or make a contribution in other areas of life. This argument—that a family is a burden to a man—is developed in Bertrand Russell's critique of marriage and the family. His observations impressed me and strengthened my convictions about the drawbacks of conventional marriage.

As a result of thinking and reading, I decided to remain unmarried. This is a decision I do not regret, although it has caused me pain and conflict from time to time and brought unhappiness to me and some of the women whom I have loved.

Revolutionary Suicide

Floyd Dell

In this Bohemia I saw something of love without marriage from the outside, and learned things about it that I had never known—things which had not been written in any of

the learned books that I had read. First of all, girls wanted
to be married, not only for conventional reasons, but also because sexual relations outside of marriage aroused in them
feelings of guilt which made them miserable. There were
three ways in which these feelings of guilt were commonly
exorcised—first, and most completely of all, by the emotions
of self-sacrifice. If a girl were moved to pity and compassion
for her lover, she would gladly sacrifice herself to give him
happiness, and find her happiness in that sacrifice. One saw a
good deal of that. Any tenth-rate free-verse poet could find a
capable and efficient girl stenographer to type his
manuscripts, buy his meals and his clothes, pay his rent, and
sleep with him; the maternal emotion sufficed instead of a
marriage ceremony. There was one poet in Greenwich Village, an ugly, dirty youth, who was a malignant caricature of
a human being, with a heart full of venom against all who
befriended him, of whom it was said that he worked Pity as
a racket, ruthlessly exploiting every person within his reach;
and the astonishing thing was that girls of whom one would
have expected more spirit and intelligence were helplessly
the victims of their feelings of compassion for such cry-ba-
bies. Being something of a Nietzschean myself, I despised
pity, and did not like it to be mixed up with love. I certainly
did not wish to be pitied by any girl. The other spiritual ho-
cus-pocus which sufficed instead of a wedding ring to give a
girl a good conscience, seemed to consist in quotations and
arguments from Edward Carpenter, Havelock Ellis, and
other modern prophets, arguments designed to show that
love without marriage was infinitely superior to the other
kind, and that its immediate indulgence brought the world,
night by night, a little nearer to freedom and Utopia; I had
once believed something like that, and had been sufficiently
eloquent along that line, at twenty, but I just didn't believe
it any more. All I had to offer to salve any girl's conscience

in what would be to me a trial marriage, was companion-ship, talk, laughter, poetry, picnic suppers beside a bonfire, the beauty of the countryside—I had a little house in New Jersey—and the music of the phonograph. There was a third very popular way of reconciling a girl's conscience to a love affair, and that was by giving her a lot to drink; but I didn't like to have alcohol mixed up with love, any more than pity. If a love affair couldn't get along without alcohol, pity, or Utopian theory, I would have to get along without the love affair.

Friendly talk between a lonely and unhappy youth and a lonely and unhappy girl might easily lead to lovemaking, without even the illusion of permanency. A few such incidents opened up to me the vista of a life spent like that. But there was something too profoundly important about the sexual relation for my emotions to accept it as a natural part of the process of getting acquainted with a girl; it involved for me emotions absurdly incongruous with my rational attitudes in such a passing relationship—the wish for self-sacrifice, for lifelong devotion, violently romantic feelings, which were defeated and made rather ridiculous by the mere facts of the case. However mismated we obviously were, in these two or three instances, however impossible it was that our relationship should continue, it had seemed to me strangely like a marriage; and when we had had breakfast at a Village restaurant and kissed each other goodbye on the street-corner before going our separate ways to work, with no expectation of continuing with what had so accidentally and impulsively begun, it was like a strange divorce, bewildering and distressing to me.

Homecoming

Vincent Van Gogh

I do not intend to ask Father and Mother for their advice and opinions as I did last year. Look you, Theo, Father and Mother are not the people who understand me—neither in my mistakes nor in my good qualities. They cannot realize my feelings. This is my plea: I hope to be able to manage so that I can save ten or fifteen guilders next month; then I shall beg Father to repeat his trip here at my expense, and to come and stay a few days with me. I wish Father could get a fresh and clear impression of a new future for me, and might have good courage; and that he could be quite reassured about my feeling for him. See, Theo, I know of no shorter, no more honest way or means to redress quickly and practically the good understanding between us.

I shall show him Sien and her little baby, which he does not expect, and the neat house and studio full of things I am working on. In a few words I shall tell him how Sien and I struggled through the hard time of her pregnancy this winter; how you helped us faithfully; how she is invaluable to me, first by the love and affection which circumstances established between us, and secondly because she has devoted herself with much good-will and common sense to helping me in my work. So that she and I heartily hope that Father will approve my taking her to wife.

I cannot say otherwise than "taking her"; for the ceremony of marriage is not what makes her my wife; we are bound together by a strong bond of mutual affection and by the help we mutually give each other. I have told you that I want to marry Sien, and this as soon as possible. About marrying, you said: Do not marry her; and you thought Sien fooled me. I did not want to contradict you flatly, because I believed, and still believe, that in time you would grow to like Sien. Only I said this much: There is a promise of marriage between her and me, and I do not want you to consider her as a mistress, or as somebody with whom I have a liaison without caring for the consequences. This promise of marriage is two-fold: first, a promise of civil marriage; secondly, a promise meanwhile to help each other, by sharing everything. Now, for the family the civil marriage is probably the most important; for her and for me it is secondary.

I propose to let the whole question of civil marriage rest for an indefinite time, or until I shall be earning one hundred and fifty francs a month by selling my work, when your help will no longer be necessary. With you, but only with you, I will thus agree for the time being not to have a civil marriage. I only hope, Theo, that what I tell you will show you that I do not want to have my own will in everything, that as far as I can I shall give in to your wishes. What I want is to save Sien's life and that of her two children. I do not want her to fall back into that terrible state of illness and misery in which I found her. I do not want her ever to feel again that she is deserted and alone. This I undertook, and this I must continue.

I have a feeling of being at home when I am with Sien, a feeling that she gives me my own hearth, that our lives are interwoven. This is a heartfelt, deep feeling, serious, and not without a dark shadow of her gloomy past and mine, as if some evil threatened us, against which we should have to struggle all our lives. At the same time, I feel a great calm and brightness and cheerfulness at the thought of her, and the straight path that is lying before me.

It is hard, very hard, ay, quite impossible to consider my love of last year as an illusion, as Father and Mother do, but I say: *"Though it will never be, it might have been."* Illusion it was not, but our points of view differed. I wish I could only understand why K. acted so, and how it was that my parents and hers were so decidedly and ominously against it, less in their words than in their complete lack of warm, living sympathy. Now, as things are, it has become a deep wound which has healed, but remains always sensitive.

Then could I immediately feel a new "love" this winter? Quite certainly not. But that these human feelings within me were not extinguished or deadened, that my sorrow awoke a need of sympathy for others, is that wrong? So at first Sien was for me only a fellow-creature, as lonesome and unhappy as myself. However, as I myself was not discouraged, I was able to give her some practical support; and this was at the same time an incentive for me to remain above water.

But by and by, and slowly, our feeling changed to that of a need for each other, so that we could not bear to be separated—and then it was love. The feeling between Sien and me is *real;* it is no dream, it is reality. When you come you will not find me discouraged or melancholy, but will enter an atmosphere that will appeal to you—a new studio, a young home in full swing; no mystical or mysterious studio, but one that is rooted in real life, a studio with a cradle, a baby's high chair, where there is no stagnation, but where everything stirs one to activity. It has cost what it has cost, and even now I cannot do without your help, but your money has not been thrown away. It is going to produce more and more drawings.

A little time in the hospital, and then I set to work again, the woman with the baby posing for me. To me it is clear as day that one must live in the reality of family life if one wishes to express that family life intimately—a mother with her child, a washer-woman, a seamstress, whatever it may be. By constant practice the hand must learn to obey this feeling for a household of one's own. To try to kill that feeling would be suicide. That the studio and the family life mingle as one is no drawback, especially for a painter of the figure. I remember perfectly interiors of studios by Ostade, small pen drawings, probably corners of his own house, which show well enough that his studio resembled very little those where one finds Oriental weapons and vases and Persian rugs. Therefore I say, "Forward," notwithstanding dark shadows, cares, difficulties—often caused, alas, by meddling gossip.

Dear Theo: The Autobiography of Vincent Van Gogh

Stephen Spender

There was perhaps another reason for the failure of our relationship. We had come against the difficulty which confronts two men who endeavor to set up house together. Because they are of the same sex, they arrive at a point where they know everything about each other and it therefore seems impossible for the relationship to develop beyond this. Further development being impossible, all they can do is to keep their friendship static and not revert to a stage of ignorance or indifference. This meant in our case that loyalty demanded, since the relationship itself could not develop, that neither of us should develop his own individuality in a way that excluded the other. Thus a kind of sterility was the result of the loyalty of each to the other; or rather of his loyalty to the relationship itself which he did not wish to grow beyond. . . .

My relationship with Jimmy had therefore made me realize that if I were to live with anyone it could not be with a man. Through this very relationship I began to discover a need for women, to think about them, to look for them. At the same time I did not lose my fundamental need for the friendship of a man with whom I could identify my own work and development, even the need for women. But I did not now need this friendship on the same terms as before. Then, when I thought I had arrived at a goal, I was only at an early stage of a difficult journey.

The things I am now writing of are difficult to explain. Very few people dare to have a clear view of their own complexity. They would prefer to simplify themselves even at the expense of condemning their way of life rather than maintain complex and perhaps contradictory attitudes toward it, from which a harmony might finally be achieved.

At this time, then, I became vividly aware of an ambivalence in my attitudes toward men and women. Love for a friend expressed a need for self-identification. Love for a woman, the need for a relationship with someone different, indeed opposite, to myself. I realized that self-identification leads to frustration if it be not realized; destruction, perhaps, if it be half-realized; a certain sterility if it be realized. The relationship of a man with the "otherness" of a woman is a relationship of opposite poles. They complete, yet never become one another, never reach a static situation where everything which is possible to be known between two people is known, every gesture a repetition of one already performed, where little development, except the loss of youth, seems possible beyond this. As I understand Goethe, he defined creative human energy as the action of male force, energizing, intelligent, constructive, upon the receptive body of that which is outside it—*das Ewigweibliche*—the eternally feminine. I could not develop beyond a certain point unless I were able to enter a stream of nature through human contacts, that is to say, through experience of women. Yet I never lost the need for camaraderie also, my desire to share

my creative and intellectual adventures with a man, whose search was the same as mine.

The two needs, while existing side by side, seemed to some extent to be mutually exclusive, so that whilst I was with a friend it might seem that I had renounced a whole world, of marriage, of responsibilities, and I had been received into another where everything was understood, where work, ideas, play, and physical beauty corresponded in the friend's life with my own. On the other hand, when I was with a woman, it was as though I had shed my other personality, left it in some other room, and that instead of reflecting and being reflected by my physical-spiritual comrade, I had entered into the wholeness of a life outside me, giving to the woman that in myself which was not contained in her, and taking from her what was not in me. At the same time, I was afraid of losing too much by this exchange, afraid of becoming something different from what I was.

World Within World

Sherwood Anderson

WOMAN AT NIGHT

The night can never be quite gorgeous, to its full possibilities, without the woman and I cannot understand those men who do not want marriage or the men and women who, being married, do not sleep together.

There are the nights that come when you are excessively alive. Now, for this one night, you do not want or need the ultimate intimacy. There is the woman beside you asleep.

How quietly and softly she breathes. How excessively alive you are. Now the mind and the fancy both race. You seem to feel and hear, with her breathing, the breathing of the earth under your house, breathing of trees. There is a river just down a short hill from the house. It also breathes softly.

Now the moon is breathing, the stars breathing.

Woman, woman.

How nice to run the hand softly down over your hips, along your legs. You get out of bed and light a candle. An electric light or a lamp would make too much light. You do not want to awaken her.

What you want now is a new way of entering in. You are the male. Now she has become for you all life outside self, become quiet and very beautiful.

I remember once climbing a little hill, above a dark and dense pine forest. It was evening and the light was soft. I threw myself down on the grass. There was a soft gray sky and a new life, a new world was born. The pine forests seemed to hang suspended, downward. Airplane drivers who do stunts, loop the loop, etc., must see the world so.

The hair of the woman in bed is like the tops of dark pine trees in a soft evening light. She has got her head into an uncomfortable position and you go and change it.

Very gently now.

Very very gently.

You do not want to disturb her dreams. You want to enter in a new way, thrust your dreams into her dreams.

Dreams thrust into skies, rivers, mountains, into Mother Earth.

"Woman, you are earth beautiful.

"Now I am a farmer thrusting down seed. Source of life is in you woman."

The dream passes. The night stays. Sometimes terror comes. You have blown out the candle and crept back into bed. In her sleep she draws close to you. There is now a small woman's hand on your hips. How softly touching, softly drawing dreams into self, taking night terrors away.

What fools are men who do not search and search until they find a woman with whom they may lie thus.

Memoirs

James Agee

TO FATHER FLYE

New York City
January 3, 1933
Friday

Dear Father Flye:
A very happy New Year to you and to Mrs. Flye—and wish us one. Via Saunders and I will be married about the end of the month. I've meant for days to let you know—there's been the worst pressure yet at the office, to keep me from it. That has at least let up to some extent, leaving me, as you can easily enough see, thoroughly stupid and inert, with the Small Talk all leaked away and no brains or energy to write or even think any of the things I wish I could. I notice a good many things about becoming engaged and moving toward marriage that are sometimes tough to realize, but not really surprising. One is that you're no more subject to high feelings, gaiety, good cheer, or sustained ecstasy about it than you'd be in becoming a priest or in writing a poem. From the outside it looks like a very simple and entirely pleasing matter, with no room for anything except Grade A hap-

piness. It is, as a matter of fact, a definitely Serious Estate, and I couldn't enter into it lightly no matter how much I tried. The same goes for Via. My own misfortune is that Seriousness means Gloom to me, about half the time. Which God knows is hard on her. Another thing I notice is, that when you talk about it you talk about this as the gloomy side of it. The other side you understand better, and know other people do, and to put down We're-the-Happiest-People-in-the-World seems not only probably untrue but rather a private matter. It makes no difference what I notice, and I'd be glad not to notice things. The dirty part of it is that you write such a note as this and give people a fine impression of being really and consistently *un*happy about it. Which Heaven knows we are not.

We've already found an apartment, down near Uncle Hugh's, and Via's living in it now. A nice and unusually old house. We have two large basement rooms (this in case it's of any interest), a kitchen somewhat more roomy than they're likely to be in this hideous town, a broad and sheltered back porch, and a large yard with pool, large trees, incipient grass, flower beds and ivy. We'll be married Saturday, January 28th, in a church in Utica. Via wants to be confirmed. I'm advising her (and she prefers, I think very rightly) to take her time with that—that is, to be converted and really very fully convinced in herself, rather than simply marrying into the church. We'd both be very grateful, as you know, if you'll remember us in your Mass that day.

Much love to you both,
Rufus

Letters of James Agee to Father Flye

Eugène Ionesco

When I had told my mother that I was going to get married, she went to see my fiancée, and when the latter opened the door to her, my mother looked at her for a moment, although she had known her for quite a long time, as though she had an unfamiliar person in front of her; she looked at her with different eyes, as when one gazes at a landscape from a fresh angle which makes it seem like a strange landscape; a friend, the daughter of a friend, who was also a stranger, was becoming in some unexpected fashion her closest relative, as it were a daughter, as it were another myself, as it were another herself, someone she had been expecting from the beginning, whom she had foreknown, whom she did not recognize, and at the same time whom she seemed to have known since the beginning of time: the person appointed by fate, whom she was compelled to accept and yet had chosen. This was the princess, her heiress, soon to become queen in her stead. My future wife returned my mother's gaze; my mother had tears in her eyes but was restraining her emotion, and her quivering lips expressed a feeling beyond words. I don't know how far the two women were aware of what they were speechlessly saying to each other. It was a silent communication, a sort of brief ritual which they were spontaneously rediscovering and which must have been handed down to them through the centuries; it was a sort of handing over of powers. At that moment my mother gave up her place, and gave me up too, to my wife. This was what my mother's expression said: he is no longer mine, he is yours. What silent injunctions, what sadness and what happiness, what fear and hope, what renunciation there was in this expression! It was a dialogue without

words, in which I had no part, a dialogue between one
woman and another.

Fragments of a Journal

Piri Thomas

I turned and saw Nita. I dug the maid of honor and the escorts. I watched Nita all dressed in white and wondered on
how come I hadn't really noticed how tiny she was. She was
barely five feet.

"You have the ring?" James whispered.

And the rest was a beautiful jumble of my getting up
and being next to Nita and Reverend Hernandez's words of
"togetherness," and ring being given and best man and "I
do" and "I do" and "man and woman" and till death do us
in, or something like that, and a raising of a veil and a warm
gentle kiss and mucho congratulations and Sis and Don and
Tia and La Vieja and her revelations and all made a
warmness into a Puerto Rican symphony of getting married
sounds.

I made my way cool up the aisle that had all kinds of
mickey mouse flashbulbs going off and pictures being taken
by the dozens.

There was a studio for more picture taking—
There was a reception—
There was a wedding cake—
There was soda and ice cream—
There was *arroz con gandules* and *lechon asado*—
There was many well-wishers, poems and prayers—
There was many presents and promises of them—
There was my Sister Miriam and Don—

There was my brother James and his get-away car—

There was us getting away—and James driving us around—

And finally—there was just us, Nita and I, standing there with mucho presents scattered all over the red and blue linoleum carpet, looking at each other in the middle of a forest green living room on 117th Street between Second and Third avenues in El Barrio.

Savior, Savior, Hold My Hand

Malcolm Muggeridge

Marriage (whether registered or not) begins, not with setting up house, counting wedding presents, blowing kisses, looking at wedding groups, but with two bodies confronting one another like two wrestlers. To clinch and struggle and contend with one another. Rolling about, now one on top, now another; grunting, coaxing, sweating, murmuring, yelling. So the world began, with vast turbulence in the genitalia of space. Each bodily union is a microcosm of the same process; a continuation of creation, a reaching after creativity through the fusion of two beings—the flesh first; then the soul, the totality, to make a third. This achieved, peace follows; the work done, we may sleep, letting an arm grow numb rather than wake a sleeping head cushioned there. So serenely asleep after the battle, and maybe already ovum and sperm seizing the interlude to enact their own drama; the expense of passion quickening in its peaceful aftermath. We exist to continue existence; unite to be united; love in order to go on loving.

Kitty and I, after all, were children of our time. How

could we be otherwise? We looked to our bodies for gratification, which we felt they owed us, and that we now owed one another. "To our bodies turn we then, that so Weak men on love revealed may look." It was inevitable that this pursuit should become the prevailing preoccupation, the obsessive quest, of our restless and confused generation. Sex is the only mysticism offered by materialism, whose other toys—like motor-cars and airplanes and moving pictures and swimming-pools and flights to the moon—soon pall. Sex pure and undefiled; without the burden of procreation, or even, ultimately, of love or identity. Just sex; jointly attained, or solitary—derived from visions, drug-infused; from spectacles, on film or glossy paper. Up and down moving stairways, with, just out of reach, legs and busts and mouths and crotches; ascending to no heights, descending to no depths, only movement upward and downward, interminably, with the trivial images of desire forever in view, and forever inaccessible. As enlightened readers of D. H. Lawrence and Havelock Ellis, with even a peep at Kraft-Ebbing, we looked for rarer pleasures than these. Our moving stairway, as we hoped, climbed into a paradise where ecstasy was attainable through sensation pure and undefiled. The Blessed Orgasm itself leaned out from the gold bar of heaven; and, rubber-stopped against any adverse consequence like birth, sealed and sterilized and secured for *coitus non interruptus* that is guaranteed *non fecundus,* we pursued happiness in true twentieth-century style.

Chronicles of Wasted Time

Groucho Marx

Man will never learn. When first he meets the girl of his dreams, it may be on a Sunday morning in church, it may be at a tennis match, or it may be at the restaurant where he daily gulps the businessman's luncheon (with dessert, 25¢ extra). Girls, it has been said, are everywhere, so it could be almost anywhere that the male is stung by the love bug.

What attracted him to her? Her eyes? Her legs? Was it something mysteriously feminine about her that no other girl seemed to possess? She is young, cute, and romantic and her speech is fairly intelligent. As they get to know each other more intimately (I mean in a nice way, of course), they both discover that they are ecstatically happy when together and miserable when apart. And then, oh happy day, if she is smart enough not to spring her mother on him too unexpectedly, they will get married.

No matter how many married couples they know, some unhappy, some happy, it seems inconceivable that anything could ever mar the joy they presently find in each other. I am sure that if they ever had any doubts or misgivings about their future happiness, neither wild horses nor her father could drag them to the altar.

It is well known that young love is a temporary form of insanity and that the only cure for it is instant marriage. What these pathetic innocents don't know is that the stresses and strains of matrimony don't appear until they have gone through what, in the navy, is termed a "shakedown cruise."

When one considers the pitfalls and traps that await them it seems to me incredible that so many couples remain married. There are so many obstacles to overcome; the intrusion of the children at the wrong moment, the intrusion of the children at any moment, the breakdown of the garbage disposal, and money. Don't ever underestimate the importance of money. I know it's often been said that money won't make you happy and this is undeniably true, but everything else being equal, it's a lovely thing to have around the house.

As a marriage grows older, sex eventually recedes to its proper proportions. Oh, you think not? Well, let's say it's not as important as it was those first three wonderful days in Niagara Falls or that weekend in a San Antonio motel. But my guess is that, in the average home five years after the marriage takes place, there is more bickering and acrimonious debate over money than any other subject.

Memoirs of a Mangy Lover

Max Frisch

QUESTIONNAIRE

1. Do you still find marriage a problem?

2. When are you more in favor of marriage as an institution, when you consider your own marriage or when you consider other people's?

3. Have you more frequently advised others:
   a. to separate? or
   b. not to separate?

4. Do you know of reconciliations that have *not* left a scar on one or both of the partners?

5. What problems are solved by a happy marriage?

6. How long on average can you live with your partner without losing your self-integrity (meaning, that you no longer venture even in secret to hold views that could shock your partner)?

7. How do you explain to yourself the urge, when contemplating a separation, to look for blame—either in yourself or your partner?

8. Would you of your own accord ever have invented marriage?

9. Do you feel in harmony with the mutual habits of your present marriage? If not, do you believe your partner is happy with them, and on what do you base your assumptions?

10. When do you find marriage most of a strain:
    a. in everyday matters?
    b. on journeys?
    c. when you are alone?
    e. when just the two of you are together?
    d. in company with others?
    f. in the evenings?
    g. in the mornings?

11. Does marriage produce common tastes (as the furnishing of the marital home seems to suggest), or does the purchase of a lamp, a carpet, a vase, etc., always mean a silent capitulation on your part?

12. If you have any children, do you feel a sense of guilt toward them when a separation occurs? That is to say, do you believe that children have a right to unhappy parents? If so, up to what age?

13. What induced you to marry:
    a. a desire for security?
    b. a child?
    c. the social disadvantages of an irregular union, for example, difficulties in hotels, gossip, the tactlessness of others, complications with officials or neighbors?
    d. custom?
    e. simplification of household arrangements?
    f. consideration for your families?
    g. the experience that irregular unions can equally lead to habit, boredom, disenchantment, etc.?
    h. the prospect of an inheritance?
    i. a trust in miracles?
    j. the feeling that it is only a formality anyway?

14. Would you like to add anything to the marriage oath as used in church or registry office ceremonies:
    a. as a woman?
    b. as a man?
    (Please give precise wording)

15. If you have been married more than once, at what point did your marriages most closely resemble one another, at the beginning or at the end?

16. If you find after separation that your former partner does not cease blaming you, do you conclude from this that you were more loved than you had realized, or do you feel relieved?

17. What do you usually say when one of your friends gets a divorce, and why didn't you say it to the person concerned before?

18. Can you be equally frank with both partners in a marriage when they themselves are not frank with each other?

19. If your present marriage can be called happy, state briefly to what you attribute this.

20. If you had to choose between leading a happy marriage and following a call that might endanger your marital happiness, which would you consider more important:
    a. as a man?
    b. as a woman?

21. Why?

22. Do you think you know how your present partner would answer this questionnaire? If not:

23. Would you like to see your partner's answers?

24. Conversely, would you want your partner to know how you have answered this questionnaire?

25. Do you consider that having no secrets from each other is a necessary part of marriage, or do you feel that it is precisely the secret between two human beings that binds them?

Sketchbook 1966–1971

John Wain

I was married in July 1947, and divorced in the autumn of 1956. It is out of the question for me to try to tell the unhappy story in full, since it would involve an unwarranted intrusion on someone else's privacy; in any case, I do not think I could bring myself to dwell on the details. My duty as an autobiographer is simply to place the episode in some sort of relation with the rest of the story.

Oxford, as I have said, led me into a desert. Along with the lavish gifts I took away from my years there, I had one great disability: my settled, middle-aged pessimism, my conviction that the hordes of barbarians were already within the gates and that the only thing left was to guard the few fragments in one's possession and accept a backward-looking, stoical melancholy as one's portion in life. At twenty-one I had far less curiosity about the world, far less faith in the future, far less urge to travel and see the different lives of men and nations, than I have today. All I wanted to do was to dig in, cultivate my knowledge of the glorious past, and stand firm as the tidal wave of modernity swept over me.

Given this attitude, it was no doubt an excellent plan to get married. And if anyone had pointed out to me the folly of marrying in the greenness of my youth, with every important discovery about my own character still to be made and every serious problem still to be faced, I expect I should have brushed the advice aside. I did not believe there was anything to come. As I was now, so I would always be; entrenched, unheeding, sternly absorbed in the pursuit of sacred knowledge. I did not see, because I would not let myself see, that my present set of attitudes was simply a temporary disguise, assumed to help me give some unity to the disparate elements in my character and my upbringing.

In a word, I lacked the maturity even to recognize myself as immature. Circumstances conspired against me: the normal obstacles which usually prevent very young men from precipitating themselves into marriage melted away. One year after taking Schools, I traveled down from Oxford to Reading for the day, was interviewed for a post at the University, and was successful. The regulations governing my research fellowship at St. John's allowed the holder to be a pluralist; no objection was made to my receiving the money for another two years in addition to my salary from Reading. The two together amounted to £700 a year, which I considered wealth; at any rate, it was enough to support two young people.

The economic barrier was removed, and there was no other that I recognized. I knew, of course, that getting married would put me out of the immediate running for a teaching job at Oxford; since every college must have a statutory number of bachelor dons living within its walls, it is usually accepted that a man who hopes for a college fellowship must keep clear of marriage until he has served a term of residence; but I was too high-minded to let this kind of thing weigh with me, just as I was too pessimistic and distrustful of life to feel the young man's normal urge to wander about the world and pile up experiences, emotional and otherwise. All that, I told myself, was an illusion. Emptiness was everywhere, except in the past; a man of twenty-two had no business frittering years away in idle travel and desultory work. It was time to be about the task of one's lifetime.

That was myself in 1947, moving my few possessions down the line from Oxford to Reading and settling down, as I thought, to the outwardly uneventful life of a scholar and teacher. I don't say that my mood was buoyant; I seem to have done everything in a spirit closer to resignation than happiness. I had taken one look at the wider world, found it wanting, and had done with it. Henceforth I would live a quiet, intensely dedicated life within the small enclosure I was staking out.

This, as a stage in a man's development, is intelligible enough; but why the marriage? Why involve someone else in this fantastic act of renunciation at the beginning of one's twenties? I cannot explain the decision fully without more detail than I feel at liberty to give; but, if one element in the situation was the mood of Johnsonian pessimism I took away from Oxford, another was the revolt against my family. Simply, I was still young enough to feel a compulsion to demonstrate to my parents that I could live my own life. My fiancée's parents came down heavily against the marriage, on the perfectly reasonable grounds that I was young and untried; and they spent many hours in hammering at her to give me up. The more they hammered, the more loyal to me she became (when, *when* will parents understand their children?), and ultimately matters reached the point at which to cancel or even postpone the marriage would have seemed like submitting to an enemy. Something of the kind happened to my side; my parents tried to keep off the subject, but one day at lunch my father exploded and said that if I married at this stage of my life it would be the greatest misfortune that could befall me. He was right—but no twenty-one-year-old is going to take that kind of talk from his father, and when I reckon up the reasons for my having married so unsuitably young, I have to realize that one of the motives was the wish to show my father how wrong he was.

Not all marriages between very young partners come to grief, but ours did; slowly, messily, in a welter of tears and agony. Even if I could bring myself to write about it, there is nothing constructive to say. If only we could have hated each other it might have been easier. As it was, we slowly tore apart, wounding and wrenching where we longed to give love and comfort. It was, as far as I can see, completely useless; from nearly a decade of suffering neither of us learned any particular lesson. For my own part, it has left me only with the knowledge that parting from someone you care for is the worst kind of pain, the slowest to heal and the most deeply felt; that the moment when two people face each other and realize that they have reached the end of the journey is the nearest thing to hell that life can offer; and that the most terrible of all words is Goodbye.

Sprightly Running: Part of an Autobiography

William Carlos Williams

To Florence Herman Williams

On Board S.S. Pennland
Sept. 28, 1927, 7:45 A.M.
Wednesday

Dearest Flossie:
This is mid-ocean. The wind has shifted again to the north where there is a small freighter on the horizon streaming in the same direction as ourselves. It is a gray threatening sort of day but not too cold. The sea is fairly quiet. I have slept well, thank you, and my bath was splendid.

This simple life on the ocean, without close companions, without work to do and without temptation or irritation of any sort about me—unless there be a temptation to read too much—has put me in a thoughtful mood—full of love for you and of interest in that America ahead of me where the gay hell will be lit for me pretty soon.

I was really an unhappy, disappointed child—in general—during my early years. It was due to the mood of our home and to my eager desires, which no world, and certainly not the Rutherford of those days, could satisfy. I do not say it was not good for me but I never could do what I really and violently wanted to—either in athletics, studies, or amorous friendships—so I was gnawing my insides all day long.

And yet underneath it all there was an enormous faith and solidity. Inside me I was like iron and with a love for the world and a determination to do good in the world that was like the ocean itself. I had a mountainous self pride and a conviction that I could afford to adventure and decide for myself.

But if, one way and another, I was a disappointed and unhappy—lit by wild flashes—boy, though this is true I am a most happy man. And the greatest thing which has caused that has been yourself.

I don't need to discuss our history. For some uncanny reason you saw through me and you saw me good. I in my turn recognized in a flash of intuition that you were the queen of the world for me at that moment. I tell you now that that feeling went through my whole body like sweetest nectar and that I knew it would last forever. And I mean just exactly forever. There was the eternal in that and I knew it at once.

I was wild then, hurt and crazy, but that tremendous reserve of strength in me was touched and it responded. No one else had seen that as you had. For me that was a stroke of genius on your part.

What "love" is I don't know if it is not the response of our deepest natures to one another. I went direct to you through my own personal hell of doubt and hesitation and I have never changed the millionth part of one inch since that first decision.

You know and I do not deny my irrational—and I still believe necessary faults—but the result of whatever I have done to lessen myself in your eyes has merely brought me back to you the stronger. All my life I have grown from that moment when I asked you to marry me, always into a clearer and more satisfying realization of what really took place at that time. I love you and you love me and so only at the end will I know what love is—and that is my answer to the world and to you.

It is wise that we have adventured once again, this time on a separation. You are a corker in your power to think and decide over emotional and other situations and wring the good out of them. You are the one to have made this "necessary evil" of separation possible. I am sure it is good. I feel it all over me in many ways not yet fully come to light: in power to work, in clarity of conception of some of my emotional difficulties, in firmness within myself, and in decision and fuller realization concerning my love for you.

But you too are alone and you too are thinking. It is certain that I do not know everything in your mind. All I ask is, Isn't it good? Tell me.

I believe that with love—(how I hate the word, mistrust it I mean) with love we can dare to understand each other.

There, I'm written out on that topic. I wanted so much to say it, but it is so hard to say well. The damned words keep jumping and slipping, until before long we've said just the opposite of what was intended. But a strong emotional bias keeps the words straight—pretty well. And that's what they mean when they say that in spite of faults the truth shines through.

Money, my dear! You must write at once, for I rely on you absolutely in this, to tell me what of our funds you want me to send you. Figure out about what you'll need and figure it *large* and thus I'll be able to keep my plans clear. Of course sometimes you'll get five cents extra for candy, but do figure it so that you will be *easy*. I shall be disappointed and angry at you if you try to skimp. Now do what I tell you. If we are going broke I'll tell you in plenty of time, so while you are abroad do what you please to do and do not consider twice an expenditure of two or three or even more hundreds here and there extra if you want to. Mind me now, I am your husband.

If the boys need small extra things buy them if necessary or tell Mr. Schwarts to buy them—but in either case let *me* have the bill. It is not to come out of your money.

The Legion is still going strong. It seems some woman called them "cattle." Well, I am still fearful that something may happen.

One man was criticizing them to another fellow whom he did not know was the leader of the Legionnaires on this ship. The man spoken to said to the other: "What port did *you* sail from ten years ago?" The other fellow said, "I worked in a shipyard."

Biff! he got it between the eyes.

On the way over to Europe on the *Celtic* one ex-gob, dead drunk, climbed to the very tip of the aftermast. They had a hell of a job to get him down.

Sweetheart, do have a fine time in Europe. Do, do, do it for me. We are not separate, we are one. I am the half that is home working (and having fun too, of course) but you must not be sulky. Go on out and *see*!

Breakfast.

Love,
Bill

The Selected Letters of William Carlos Williams

August Strindberg

To Harriet Bosse

About *29 August, 1901*

In this spook tale, which is called our marriage, I have some times suspected a crime. Will it surprise you that I momentarily have believed that you have been playing with me, and that you—like Emerentia Polhem—had sworn you would see me at your feet.

This suspicion I expressed later to Palme after the inexplicable scene at the dress rehearsal of *To Damascus.* I still believed, from your first visits in February, that you were toying with me, but that your feelings gradually would change and that you would become sincerely attached to me. I presume you know it to be true that there was wickedness in your eyes and that you never gave me a friendly glance. But I loved you and hoped unceasingly that I would finally meet with love in return.

When—following the wedding—I saw your spiritual decay; the forms your maliciousness took; how cynically you regarded what to me was holy; how you despised me; how melancholy and anguish took hold of you—then I thought you were tortured by a bad conscience, for it is in this manner it asserts itself.

That you had betrayed the secrets of the yellow room, that I could understand—and I forgave you, even though I was horrorstricken and wept inwardly.

When I saw your portrait hanging in the shop windows between two similar portraits of a certain actor, I trembled with dread. And when this actor was struck by a bullet in the chest, I felt as if a protecting Power stood watch over me and saved our holy union.

I once thought you loved me: when you returned from the visit to Inez in the skerries . . . then there was harmony—and it was then, I think, that our child was given its life.

In the evening you radiated a supernatural beauty at the dinner table and you gave vent to these words: "Oh, now I feel that I am a woman!" Our child has been conceived in love, after all, and not in hatred; in pain and not in pleasure! Therefore it is legitimate; and that is the difference between legitimate and illegitimate offspring! For where sensual pleasure is sought, there will be no children!

Your absolute distaste for seeing Richard Bergh again I have sought to explain, by guessing, in this manner: that the secrets of the yellow room had been confided to him last spring and that you now had a feeling of shame. It is possible that I have been mistaken. In which case he must have behaved indiscreetly toward you, and if so, you ought to have indicated this to me so that I could have broken off the friendship without explanation.

This—our marital relationship—is to me the most inexplicable thing I have ever experienced: the most beautiful and the ugliest. At times the beautiful stands forth by itself—and then I weep, weep myself to sleep that I may forget the ugly. And in such moments I take all the blame upon myself alone! When I then see you, melancholy, agonized—in May and June—in your green room, sorrowing over your lost youth, which *I* have "laid waste," then I accuse myself, then I cry out in pain because I have been wicked to you and wronged you. . . . I kiss the sleeve of the garment from which you stretched out your little hand, and I plead with you to forgive me all the misery I have inflicted upon you!

When I have shed all my tears and the Angel of the Lord has consoled me, I can think a little more calmly . . . this is the way all young girls have grieved over their youth and through these portals of grief have entered into the domain of motherhood, where woman comes into the greatest joy of life, the only true joy—and which she divines instinctively beforehand. . . . You have already sensed and experienced it!

But I—who was a partner in this grief—I am not permitted to share the happiness!

Is it my fate to give life to children, to be weighted down by worries and ingratitude, and then to have all the joy torn from me? Then do not say that it is I who flee from happiness!

When I once made a remark that our home was like a ghost home, you answered: "If you knew what took place in this house, you would die from horror."—What was it that happened here, of which you were aware but not I?

Suppose that our relationship is tainted by hate and suspicion—everything becomes soiled in the autumn—but the new Spring that the child is bringing us will destroy and place in the background our selfish love. Can we not put aside our personal illusions and be joined only in mutual interest as parents and friends, and meet in artistic endeavor, which is our common ground?

And have you given no thought to our child that cries out to be born in a home; that demands a father and a mother, tenderness, consideration, support, and later, an introduction to life?

A child, growing up without knowing its own father who is known to everyone else. . . . And should you die, do you think I would be prepared to receive a child brought up to hate me?

What does all this matter to you?

What is to happen now? I don't know, but I long for an end of this—even if it be the very worst!

Letters of Strindberg to Harriet Bosse

Bertrand Russell

In 1929, I published *Marriage and Morals,* which I dictated while recovering from whooping-cough. (Owing to my age, my trouble was not diagnosed until I had infected most of the children in the school.) It was this book chiefly which, in 1940, supplied material for the attack on me in New York. In it, I developed the view that complete fidelity was not to be expected in most marriages, but that a husband and wife ought to be able to remain good friends in spite of affairs. I did not maintain, however, that a marriage could with advantage be prolonged if the wife had a child or children of whom the husband was not the father; in that case, I thought, divorce was desirable. I do not know what I think now about the subject of marriage. There seem to be insuperable objections to every general theory about it. Perhaps easy divorce causes less unhappiness than any other system, but I am no longer capable of being dogmatic on the subject of marriage.

The Autobiography of Bertrand Russell: 1914–1924

Alan Watts

Now I have what might be called a temperamental incapacity to understand conventional sexual mores. I can see no association of sex, per se, with dirt—unless, perhaps, one takes the flea's-eye view of sex often found in our new full-color pornographic magazines. Perhaps that is most people's view. Perhaps the idea of its being dirty is just what arouses them. I can see no good reason for regarding anyone as my exclusive sexual property, or being so regarded myself, just as no one else is my exclusive property for dining, walking, talking, or working together. What two human beings do together in private, by mutual consent, is as little other people's business as anything can be, though if they have accidents—such as pregnancy or disease—as a consequence, they must together be as responsible as if they had had an accident while driving, and although it is hard to know which of the two adventures is the riskier, people seldom get killed by intercourse.

My own sexual mores are largely principles of style and taste concerning how and with whom I should participate in the most intimate pleasure that people can give to each other. By nature, I enjoy such pleasure only with the feminine sex, and only if it is equally pleasurable to my partner. Thus the Augustinian saying, *Omne animal post coitum triste est,* is true for me only if I fail to delight her. Otherwise, I could crow. For this reason I have never employed a prostitute, imagining most of them to be difficult to please. I do not believe that I should be passionately in love with my partner—though it is the best of pleasures under such circumstances—and still less, married. For there is a special and humanizing delight in erotic friendships with no strings attached. If marriages are holy and made in heaven, the proverb still applies that God gives us our relations, and let us thank him we can choose our friends. My life would be much, much poorer were it not for certain particular women with whom I have most happily and congenially committed adultery, and the value of such friendships is not to be measured by the calendar. There are women to whom I am permanently grateful for but one or two embraces, and I have every reason to believe that they feel the same way toward me, for our sexual communion was the natural culmination of our admiration for one another as people.

And what a person is includes the so-called physical body, which is not simply a given chunk of flesh and bones, statically considered, but the way it moves, its rhythms, its voice, and its perfume. For the body is as much a streaming pattern of energy as a flame. Indeed, I hesitate in speaking of the body as "it." Nobody likes to be treated as an it, to have shapely breasts, chest, shoulders, neck, hips, bottom, genitals, or legs considered as if they were external appendages that might go with just any body. For all that, they are nonetheless admirable, and one must not feel treated as an it if fondled in certain particular places. To a discerning and sensitive eye, a bottom shows character as clearly as a face, for the whole organism is manifested in every one of its features. Yet, as of today (1972), I am vaguely aware of a growing prissiness among intelligent women as a, nevertheless, understandable reaction against being treated as lust dolls. But if you disown your body, and think of yourself and want to be appreciated purely as your soul or character, your body does indeed become a doll, a mere vehicle in which the abstract "you" goes around.

Men's attitude to women invariably reflects their attitude to nature as a whole, and thus I have often said that if the tacit goals of technological progress were realized, if all events were predictable, and all natural phenomena perfectly controlled, life would be like having intercourse with a plastic doll. You cannot have an experience called "self" without an experience called "other." This is why the two are really one, which is both self and other and yet neither, as may be realized in the climax of sexual love.

As for marriage, there is nothing wrong with it except the legal institution. The natural event of a man and woman living in constant companionship, with or without children, is an admirable arrangement which works to the degree one does not insist that it *must* work, and does not treat one's partner as property. Another being regarded as property is automatically a doll. Whenever I perform a ceremony of marriage for personal friends, I give some such discourse as this:

"What I am about to say may at first sound depressing and even cynical, but I think you will not find it so in practice. There are three things I would have you bear in mind. The first is that as you now behold one another, you are probably seeing each other at your best. All things disintegrate in time, and as the years go by you will tend to get worse rather than better. Do not, therefore, go into marriage with projects for improving each other. Growth may happen, but it cannot be forced. The second has to do with emotional honesty. Never pretend to a love which you do not actually feel, for love is not ours to command. For the same reason, do not require love from your partner as a duty, for love given in this spirit doesn't ring true, and gives no pleasure to the other. The third is that you do not so cling to one another as to commit mutual strangulation. You are not each other's chattels, and you must so trust your partner as to allow full freedom to be the being that he and she is. If you observe these things your marriage will have surer ground than can be afforded by any formal contract or promise, however solemn and legally binding."

A couple that would object to this discourse should not marry.

My first marriage came to an end from neglect of the third of these precepts, and my second from mutual neglect of the first. In the summer of 1949 I was writing *The Supreme Identity* in an attempt to put Christian theology and Indian philosophy into a constructive relationship, and at the same time Canterbury House was a buzz of activity, with seminarists, professors, students, clergy, and wandering seekers from all over. I was also being invited, more and more, to give lectures and conduct retreats away from home. Inevitably, the problems of sex and marriage came into these discussions, and Eleanor was increasingly disturbed by my libertarian views. Under the circumstances she acted with great tact and consideration, for in the autumn she simply feigned sickness as a result of the pressure of work, and went to live with her mother in New York. A little later she went quietly to Nevada and, without fanfare, had our marriage annulled for the interesting reason that, if I believed in free love, I could only have contracted a monogamous marriage under false pretenses. I made no contest, and handed back the capital assests she had made over to me.

In My Own Way: An Autobiography

D. H. Lawrence

We lack peace because we are not whole. And we are not whole because we have known only a tithe of the vital relationships we might have had. We live in an age which believes in stripping away the relationships. Strip them away, like an onion, till you come to pure, or blank nothingness. Emptiness. That is where most men have come now: to a knowledge of their own complete emptiness. They wanted so badly to be "themselves" that they became nothing at all: or next to nothing.

It is not much fun, being next to nothing. And life ought to be fun, the greatest fun. Not merely "having a good time," in order to "get away from yourself." But real fun in being yourself. Now there are two great relationships possible to human beings: the relationship of man to woman, and the relationship of man to man. As regards both, we are in a hopeless mess.

But the relationship of man to woman is the central fact in actual human life. Next comes the relationship of man to man. And, a long way after, all the other relationships, fatherhood, motherhood, sister, brother, friend.

A young man said to me the other day, rather sneeringly, "I'm afraid I can't believe in the regeneration of England by sex." I said to him: "I'm sure you can't." He was trying to inform me that he was above such trash as sex, and such commonplace as women. He was the usual vitally below par, hollow, and egoistic young man, infinitely wrapped up in himself, like a sort of mummy that will crumble if unwrapped.

And what is sex, after all, but the symbol of the relation of man to woman, woman to man? And the relation of man to woman is wide as all life. It consists in infinite different flows between the two beings, different, even apparently contrary. Chastity is part of the flow between man and woman, as is physical passion. And beyond these, an infinite range of subtle communication which we know nothing about. I should say that the relation between any two decently married people changes profoundly every few years, often without their knowing anything about it; though every change causes pain, even if it brings a certain joy. The long course of marriage is a long event of perpetual change, in which a man and a woman mutually build up their souls and make themselves whole. It is like rivers flowing on, through new country, always unknown.

But we are so foolish, and fixed by our limited ideas. A man says: "I don't love my wife any more, I no longer want to sleep with her." But why should he always want to sleep with her? How does he know what other subtle and vital interchange is going on between him and her, making them both whole, in this period when he doesn't want to sleep with her? And she, instead of jibbing and saying that all is over and she must find another man and get a divorce—why doesn't she pause, and listen for a new rhythm in her soul, and look for the new movement in the man? With every change, a new being emerges, a new rhythm establishes itself; we renew our life as we grow older, and there is real peace. Why, oh, why do we want one another to be always the same, fixed, like a menu-card that is never changed?

If only we had more sense. But we are held by a few fixed ideas, like sex, money, what a person "ought" to be, and so forth, and we miss the whole of life. Sex is a changing thing, now alive, now quiescent, now fiery, now apparently quite gone, quite gone. But the ordinary man and woman haven't the gumption to take it in all its changes. They demand crass, crude sex-desire, they demand it always, and when it isn't forthcoming, then—smash-bash! smash up the whole show. Divorce! Divorce!

I am so tired of being told that I want mankind to go back to the condition of savages. As if modern city people weren't about the crudest, rawest, most crassly savage monkeys that ever existed, when it comes to the relation of man and woman. All I see in our vaunted civilization is men and

women smashing each other emotionally and psychically to bits, and all I ask is that they should pause and consider.

For sex, to me, means the whole of the relationship between man and woman. Now this relationship is far greater than we know. We only know a few crude forms—mistress, wife, mother, sweetheart. The woman is like an idol, or a marionette, always forced to play one role or another: sweetheart, mistress, wife, mother. If only we could break up this fixity, and realize the unseizable quality of real woman: that a woman is a flow, a river of life, quite different from a man's river of life: and that each river must flow in its own way, though without breaking its bounds: and that the relation of man to woman is the flowing of two rivers side by side, sometimes even mingling, then separating again, and traveling on. The relationship is a life-long change and a life-long travelling. And that is sex. At periods, sex-desire itself departs completely. Yet the great flow of the relationship goes on all the same, undying, and this is the flow of living sex, the relation between man and woman, that lasts a lifetime, and of which sex-desire is only one vivid, most vivid, manifestation.

We Need One Another

John Fowles

TRANSPOSITION: MARRIAGE AS MODEL

136 Transposition is the avoidance of wasted energy, of pointless battle, of unnecessary suffering.

137 Self-control, instead of self-slavery.

138 Tensions not only rack man; they support him.

139 It is necessary to drink water; but it should not be necessary to drink polluted water.

140 I live in New York, I need urgently to be in London. Do I set out in a dinghy, as if there were no airplanes?

141 The journey is vital, therefore the means of transport is vital.

142 Marriage, as a model.

143 Joining is a first principle; the proton joins the electron, the atoms by joining grow in complicacy, make molecules by joining, amoeba joins amoeba, man joins woman, mind mind, country country: existence is being joined. Being is joining, and the higher the being the more the joining.

144 Marriage is the best general analogy of existing. It is the most familiar polar situation, with the most familiar tension; and the very fact that reproduction requires a polar situation is an important biological explanation of why we think polarly.

145 As with all tensional states, marriage is harassed by a myth and a reality. The myth is that of the Perfect Marriage, a supposedly achievable state, akin to Parahades, of absolute harmony between the partners. The reality is whatever is the case, every actual marriage.

146 Almost all married couples normally try to give the public, their friends, and even their children, a Perfect Marriage version of their own marriage; if they do not, then

they still express and judge the extent of their failure by the standards of the Perfect Marriage.

147 The characteristic gauges of the supposedly Perfect Marriage are passion and harmony.

148 But passion and harmony are antipathetic. A marriage may begin in passion and end in harmony, but it cannot be passionate and harmonious at the same time.

149 Passion is a pole, an extreme joining; it can only be achieved as height is on a swing—by going from coital pole to sundered counterpole; from two to two ones.

150 *Amantium irae amoris integratio est.*

151 *Post coitum tristitia; sed post tristitiam coitus.*

152 All duration annuls. Duration is a counterpole of whatever is.

153 The price of passion is no passion.

154 During the White Terror, the police caught two suspects, a man and a woman, who were passionately in love. The chief of police invented a new torture. He simply had them bound as one, face to face. To begin with, the lovers consoled themselves that at least they were together, even though it was with the inseparability of Siamese twins. But slowly each became irksome to the other; they became filthy, they could not sleep; and then hateful; and finally so intolerably loathsome that when they were released they never spoke to each other again.

155 Marriages without mutual hatred or quarrels from their very beginning; I could also write music in which every interval was of a perfect fourth. But I would not call it perfect music.

156 Most marriages recognize this paradox: that passion destroys passion. That we want what puts an end to wanting what we want. This is the Midas Situation.

157 An intelligent married couple might therefore come to this conclusion: we wish to retain passion in our marriage, and so we should deliberately quarrel, and hate, in order to swing back together with more force.

158 Quarreling should be as frequent as coupling.

159 Perhaps women initiate marital quarrels more frequently than men; they know more about human nature, more about mystery, and more about keeping passion alive. There may be biological reasons for menstruation; but it is also the most effective recreator of passion. And the Adam-women who resist emancipation also know what they are about.

160 There comes a time when passion costs too much in quarrels. To survive familiarity, dailiness, it needs more and more violent separations.

161 Either the two poles quarrel more and more violently inside marriage, or they look for new passion, a new pole, outside it.

162 For every Don Juan, a hundred who would like to be

Don Juan; for every Clytemnestra, a hundred Clytemnestras in their dreams.

163 The marriage full of hate: the partners may come to enjoy it. It provides frequent opportunities for inverted pleasures. It is a mistake to think that overt hatred in a marriage is a sign that the partners would be happier apart.

164 In the early stages of marriage passion is good, a great human experience; and must be fed. But harmony is attained by controlling passion, or the nostalgia for it.

165 Passion can be controlled in only one way: by being sacrificed.

166 A misconception: that the transposition from passion to harmony is no more than the death of passion, a first sign of old age.

167 The situation is exacerbated by twentieth-century art, both serious and commercial, which propagates this misconception.

168 Another exacerbation: the sexual act remains the best ritualization of the War and of the polar nature of reality. It is not only sexual desire that drives a man and woman nakedly together.

169 But passionate marriage is animal; harmonious marriage is human.

170 In passion we feel near the heart of things; but we are near the heart of *things*—nearer them than the heart of man.

171 Plenty of books that instruct sexual technique; we need books that instruct transpositional technique.

172 The first step: sacrifice the passion to control the hate.

173 The second step: accept the oneness of the marriage.

174 In passion everything is between thee and me; in harmony it is between them and us. I-thou is passion, we-they is harmony.

175 Egocentric; noscentric.

176 To become noscentric, find a counterpole. A harmonious marriage cannot be all harmony. To have harmony the partners must have no harmony on occasion.

177 They can find this in two ways: by uniting against some discord outside their marriage, so that a public discord replaces their private one; a universal, their individual; or by substituting the true for the practical pole.

178 The practical pole of harmony is discord; the true pole of harmony is not-harmony, nothingness or notness.

179 Not uncontrolled and active hostility between partners, but controlled not-harmony. Periods of disconnection from the relationship.

180 Having conquered the passion tension, a couple can transpose to socially more useful, or socially less harmful, tensions outside their marriage.

181 Passion is necessary in its season. We do not really possess anything until we have possessed it with passion.

182 Growth = passion, transposition, harmony.

183 Evolution = feeling, thinking, science.

184 Being human = conditioned reflexes, awareness of them, freedom.

185 Self, abnegation of self, society.

186 All I say about marriage is stale: every middle-aged and still happily married couple knows it. . . .

The Aristos: A Self-Portrait in Ideas

Havelock Ellis

It may seem to some that the spirit in which we approached marriage was not that passionate and irresistible spirit of absolute acceptance which seems to them the ideal. Yet we both cherished ideals, and we seriously strove to mold our marriage as near to the ideal as our own natures and the circumstances permitted. It was certainly not a union of unrestrainable passion; I, though I failed yet clearly to realize why, was conscious of no inevitably passionate sexual attraction to her, and she, also without yet clearly realizing why, had never felt genuinely passionate sexual attraction for any man. Such preliminary conditions may seem unfavorable in a romantic aspect. Yet in the end they proved, as so many conventionally unpromising conditions in my life have proved, of inestimable value, and I can never be too thankful that I escaped a marriage of romantic illusions. Certainly, I was not a likely subject to fall victim to such a marriage.

The union was thus fundamentally at the outset, what later it became consciously, a union of affectionate comradeship, in which the specific emotions of sex had the smallest part, yet a union, as I was later to learn by experience, able to attain even on that basis a passionate intensity of love. It was scarcely so at the outset, although my letters to her in the early years are full of yearning love and tender solicitude. We were neither of us in our first youth. I was able to look on marriage as an experiment which might, or might not, turn out well. On her part it was, and remained to the end, a unique and profound experience which she never outgrew. Yet, had anything happened to prevent the marriage, it is not likely that either of us would then have suffered from a broken heart. The most passionate letters I wrote her were, as she realized, not written until some years after marriage. I can honestly say that, by a gradual process of increased knowledge and accumulated emotional experience, I am far more in love with her today than twenty-five years ago.

Yet to both of us our marriage seemed then a serious affair, and with the passing of the years it became even more tremendously serious. She, at heart distrustful of her own powers of attraction, would from time to time be assailed by doubts—though such doubts were in conflict with her more rooted convictions—that she was not my fit mate, that I realized this, and that it might be best if we separated in order to enable me to marry someone else. This was never at any moment my desire. Much as each of us suffered through marriage I have never been convinced that our marriage was a mistake. Even if in some respects it might seem a mistake, it has been my belief, deepened rather than diminished, that in the greatest matters of life we cannot safely withdraw from a mistake, but are, rather, called upon to conquer it, and to retrieve that mistake in a yet greater development of life. It would be a sort of blasphemy against life to speak of a relationship which like ours aided great ends as a mistake, even if, after all, it should in a sense prove true that we both died of it at last. Each of us exhibited a constant process of spiritual and intellectual development during the whole of that quarter of a century of close intimacy. My own work in life had been more or less definitely planned before I knew her, yet it was altogether carried out, and to a more triumphant conclusion than at the outset I had ever imagined, during my fellowship with her.

She on her part was developing during all that period, and she only attained the complete adult maturity of her spiritual and intellectual powers a year or two before the end. Though I failed at first to perceive that she was the most difficult woman in the world to marry, I always knew that she was unique, and though there were other qualities I craved from a woman which she could not give, yet those other qualities had their chief value, I always well knew, in supplementing hers and could never replace what she had to give. She was far more to me than a "liberal education" to enrich, she was also a constant discipline to fortify. The presence of her naked and vital spirit moved my more dreaming and aloof spirit to a realization of the fundamental facts of living which has been beyond all estimation. In some respects I am what she has made of me.

On her part, again, although she too, craved qualities which I could not give and which I never grudged her finding in others, she yet always affirmed, and never denied, that I was the one person in the world who understood her, and it was on me that in all moments of difficulty or terror she instinctively called. That she altogether realized how entirely in this matter my attitude was the counterpart of her own I do not positively affirm, nor even that I made great efforts to explain my attitude, for in such matters I have always held that protestations are suspect, and even worthless, and that what cannot be divined must be left. Moreover, in matters of love I have ever been shy of promises, always so facile, always so meaningless; I can honestly say that my performances excelled my promises. Certainly it was so in the deep sense with marriage. At the outset it seemed to me—though never, I think, to her—as possibly only an experiment. It was an experiment to such an extent that to many if not most people it might seem no marriage at all. Yet it was a relationship so deep and so binding, so gripping the heart by its tenderness, and so compelling the whole being by the intensity of its spiritual passion, that the thought of any second relationship of the same kind seemed a sort of sacrilege. It is probable, however, that this feeling largely rests on the ritual formality which surrounds marriage and sets it apart, making it appear a unique relationship. It is always possible for me to imagine a more or less sexual relationship with another woman which sprang from a scarcely less deep root, for the varieties of relationships are infinite. But to repeat in exact detail a relationship, the closest of all, which had seemed and remained unique, to repeat publicly to another person the old formula of binding words, to place on another hand the same kind of ring, to confer on another the same right to bear the precisely same name before the world—all that, however tenderly I might love the new person, seems to arouse within me a deep repulsion. It may be an artificial feeling, not lying in the essence of things, but only in conventions. Yet it remains.

My Life

Henry Miller

People always ask if there's a similarity in the women I marry, and I suppose there must be. Sometimes I am aware of it. *Sometimes.* And yet, if I place one beside the other, they're completely different individuals. One would have to say no, they had nothing in common. But they must have had something in common *for me.* I'll tell you what I think the attraction is. I like strong women. I'm a passive sort of man, weak in a way. You know, I'm not the "he-man" type and I'm always attracted to women of strength and character. I've noticed that. My battle with them is a battle of wits. Also, I find that I'm intrigued by women who are devious, who lie, who play games, who baffle me, who keep me on the fence all the time. I seem to enjoy that!

Actually, I have found very great differences, both mentally and physically, although I must say that virtually all the women I loved were beautiful. Most of my friends agreed with me on that. They were sexually attractive. There had to be a sexual attraction, but I was never preoccupied with that aspect. It's the character of the woman, the personality, the soul, you might say, which concerns me. Believe it or not, the soul of woman is what gets me most.

Men always say, "The women *I* select." I say they select *us.* I give myself no credit for selecting. Sure, I ran after them, I struggled, and all that, but I can't say, "Oh, that's gotta be mine. Now that's the type I want and I'm gonna get it." No, it doesn't work that way.

So many men look upon a relationship with a woman from the sexual angle. It's the *thought* of sex that's interesting to me. Everything about it, everything connected with the realm of sex intrigues me. Of course, I have a great imagination. I can wonder and be mystified about how it's done here and there, everywhere, by what variety of types, and so on. But sex isn't an imperative. I can go without too.

I do think women find it difficult to live with me. And yet, you know, I think I'm the easiest person in the world. But it turns out that there is something tyrannical in me. And maybe my critical side comes out very strongly when I live with a person, whether man or woman. I have a great sense of caricature. I discover quickly one's foibles, one's weaknesses, and I exploit them. I can't help it.

That's the kind of person I am. I start out by putting women on a pedestal, by idealizing them, and then I annihilate them. I don't know if what I say is exactly true—but it does seem to work that way. And yet I remain friends with them, all of them except one woman, warm friends. They write me and tell me they love me still, and so on. How do you explain it? They do love me for myself, but they can't live with me.

My Life And Times

Dalton Trumbo

To Cleo Trumbo

Federal Correctional Institute
Ashland, Kentucky
March 11, 1951

My darling—

Two days hence will be our thirteenth wedding anniversary. I have been lying her on my bunk thinking about it. The thirteen years seem so short a time because it has been so happy a time for me. All that is any good in my life has grown out of it. I think back on each year of it with pride. I think our children take pride in it, too, and will take more pride as they grow older. Being married to you has made these months in prison tolerable, and when I have thought of you, which is very often, happy. We shall have many more years together, under cloudier skies or sunnier, but our love for each other will make its own climate—the climate of springtime which surrounds me tonight as I think of you. Many happy returns!

Dalton Trumbo—#7551

Additional Dialogue

John B. Koffend

I have thought about returning to you, assuming that I could, but I don't think it would work out on either side. You're not the forgiving kind, and I'm not penitent anyway. I'm reasonably confident that you don't want me back, just as I'm reasonably confident now that you didn't want me in the first place. Seldom has anyone put up more resistance to marriage than you, right up to the altar and beyond. I can guess how you interpret that resistance now—as rational. Somehow you knew or sensed the marriage wouldn't be compatible. My sharpest memory of our wedding day is not a sweet one. That may have been the beginning of the end, though it was some time coming. At the intellectual level I blame you for nothing. After all, I did marry you. I got into something I obviously wanted to get into. I qualified then, and perhaps still do qualify, as one of those guys who will

suffer a string tied around his big toe, who really believes it
when a girl says that a bed invitation, like the one extended
to me one Christmas before we were married, is just that
and no more. At the heart, or feeling, level, I don't deny
some resentment; I'm sure you nurse a good deal of it for
me. With just such a little effort, on both sides, it would
have worked. It kind of worked anyway. Maybe it's just because the memory retains pleasure and rejects pain, but I
look back with considerable fondness over all those years we
had together, and, in many ways, feel married to you still.
Even though I am the shithead of record, I can't make the
first move toward a reconciliation; it has to come from you,
and I know it never will. I'm not looking for a successor, because I have other things in mind, and hesitate to do so since
I'm not in a position to guarantee consortium to any woman,
but I keep thinking I should at least get back into circula-
tion. Early last spring Wendy Fernbach called me at the office, said the right things about the divorce, and then in effect indicated that I was an eligible unattached man whom
she would like to invite to her do's. At the time, I had the
roommate I told you about earlier. When I said as much to
Wendy, her interest declined at once and she suggested I get
back in touch when that temporary arrangement was over.
Which, of course, I could scarcely do. That roomie, by the
way, is back where she came from, pursuing the scholastic
life. She's a lovely girl but a thorough emotional jumble—
like me in some ways: common, garden-variety sex problems. Of course, I'm a fine one to talk. I was still writing
Time book reviews under Bobby Baker the last time I balled
with a woman (a way of putting it that you will doubtless
find offensive). Maybe we can get together some time to discuss our separate excursions into infidelity. I cheated on you,
as the custodians of conventional morality so disapprovingly
put it, more than you realized, but I never considered it

cheating really. The equipment doesn't deteriorate with use, affairs have nothing at all to do with marriage, and what you don't know can't hurt you. In any event, those days are over for me, at least until and unless some wise counselor picks the lock. Solitary experiment—no need for detail—indicates either that my resistance is terrific or else that I am old before my time. As I've said, this doesn't in the least deter me from getting into bed situations. But it sure as hell deters the woman. I understand some of the psychodynamics of it. Holding out is hostility, isn't it? I'm depriving the woman at the same time that I'm depriving myself. I'm sure I unconsciously deliberately held out on you—just as you unconsciously deliberately held out on me. But you're simply incapable of accepting the latter half of that equation. You still feel that a wife is well within her rights, during the early stages of marriage, to cry and accuse and carry on like a banshee whenever, in intercourse, the man reaches a climax first. The rationale being that he's doing it to her deliberately, frustrating her sexually out of pure malice. Just as you used to say that I wielded my insomnia like a weapon to interrupt your sleep. These positions, needless to say, were the ones I resented, with some justice I think. It's true that we stack the deck in our favor but I feel, nonetheless, that the marriage and I never really had a fair chance. You had a point to demonstrate, and you demonstrated it. Toward the end, I doubt that you would have noticed the total and absolute absence of Grosser. His dereliction, in fact, helped confirm your point.

A Letter to My Wife

Lenny Bruce

The bad break-up is like a long-time break-up. If you're married seven years, you gotta kick for two. Oh yeah. I think if you're married fifteen, eighteen years, then you get divorced, then you must lose your mind. Yeah. They get senile, then, the people. They get whacked out.

There's a certain critical area there, you been married about seven, eight years, where you really throw up for a coupla years. Really, just go throw up.

And if you broke up and you go anywhere alone, there's always *momzas* that ask about your wife. Which is really a hang-up. Especially if you've been married about, well, ten years, say. And you're very tight with your old lady—you'd go everywhere together. And now, you start to go places solo—whether it's a supermarket, laundromat, or a Chinese restaurant:

"Where's the missus?"

"Oh, I got divorced—"

There's an embarrassed silence, while the guy'll identify you—

"Oh, you're a lovely couple. You should get together. She'll come back to ya."

"Can I have my stamps? Yeah, I just wanna get the hell outta here."

Chinese restaurant. Same waiter, week after week, for ten years. First time you go in alone, the waiter goes:

CHINESE VOICE: Where's maw-maw? How come you don't bring maw-maw in? Ma-maw sicka? Ah so, maw-maw velly sick. You better bring maw-maw some cookies. Tell maw-maw say hello. Tell her say hello to her.

HUSBAND: I'm divorced.

CHINESE VOICE: *Ohhhh. You bettuh awf.*
You bettuh awf. Christ, that's really going with the winner. What's he tell *her*?

And what kind of chicks you going to hang out with, if you're over thirty-five? You just can't—I can't—go out

with any chick under twenty-five. I really do feel funny. Cause you just, you just know if you met her father, you know, he'd say, "*You're* not going to *marry* her."

So you hang out with chicks that are divorced. But you *never* can go over to their pad. Every chick that I know who's divorced has got a seven-year-old kid. It's really a prop from central casting.

"Listen, I'd like to have you over the house, but I have a kid—"

"I know."

I know I'm going to get *schlepped* into the bedroom, right, to look at the kid.

(whisper) "*Shhhhhhh*, don't wake him up."

"No, I don't *wanna* wake him up."

He's sweating in his pajamas. Boy, that really kills the image, man. Or if they don't have a kid they'll have a French poodle that wants to stay in the bedroom all the time:

"Hey, why don't you let the dog go out?"

"He's a *little* dog. He's not gonna bother anybody."

"I know. I just feel uncomfortable with the dog here. Has no function. What's he doing here?"

"Looking at us."

"*Pervert! Get outta here!* . . . Look, I'm not an exhibitionist. I can't, the dog is making me uncomfortable."

Sick red eyes, tap dancing on the linoleum. Dumb French poodles.

The Essential Lenny Bruce

Paul Goodman

Under present urban conditions, it is hard to define Marriage of our American-European kind without finding neurotic components in the essence: ties of infantile dependency, fear of abandonment, jealousy, conceit, super-ego, Oedipus complex. It is hard to conceive of an aware and independent person as being "married," even though one might start by rationally choosing monogamous marriage as an economy of energies, the most efficient way of managing one's time and feelings. The chances of life soon confuse and dissolve such a merely prudent choice. There is always looming a more attractive and somewhat practical opportunity. It seems to be the play of non-rational clinging, resentment, guilt, dependency, need to imitate one's own parents, that preserves the marriage. The prudential advantages look like a "secondary gain of illness." But in a society where everybody is pretty impractical, a healthy man might paradoxically find himself frustrated and left out just on statistical grounds, because he does not get the secondary advantages of remaining married!

Marriages get a more rational meaning by being obliged to real necessities, primarily the children, that must be coped with unquestionably. These limit the working of the underlying fantasies that wreak havoc with the happiness of the partners. Objective necessity provides a workable and sharable tie. And in the course of time too, those shared necessities become a fund of shared memories and experience, unsoured by hurt feelings and with demonstrable achievements. This is a rational bond of union, a friendship.

Let us distinguish two levels of irrationality in marriage. (1) More superficially, the way in which the partners are suckers for each other's manipulations. This is likely what gets them to marry in the first place, for it is only with this one partner that either can become involved and feel anything at all. When the going gets rough at this level, the irrationality can often be worked through and the persons be made aware of what they habitually do to each other. (2) This means working down toward the underlying non-rational level, of jealousy, fear of abandonment, the Oedipus complex. The person says, "I see that we are bad for each other, but I cannot leave him (her) anyway." At this level there are several cheerful possibilities: there may be a diminution of the energy of the neurosis by working out unfinished needs when the superficial barriers to contact have been eliminated; there may be a compromise in which the marriage survives as a home base for outside exploration—"I am reconciled to my parents since they let me have fun and friends"; there may be growth through simple aging and increasing *self*-justification—"I can do what I want since I have spent so many years doing what I must."

Confronted with persons who cannot abide their marriage, try to find out if there is ever *any* real satisfaction that they get from each other, occasionally a pleasant shared meal, agreement on the children, a moment of teasing, a moment of feeling protected, a good fuck once a month. If there is this much, say three good hours a week, it is probably best to try to keep the couple together. It means that there is no inexorable positive principle of separation—e.g. somebody else whom one of them might marry; and to have something, in a lonely and difficult world, is better than nothing at all. There is no doubt—it leaps to the eye as we look about—that in most cases married couples would for a time be healthier and happier if they separated; but they would be less real; and when the feeling of emptiness begins to irk, they would marry again even more foolishly.

We must then speak of the "normal neurosis" of marriage (as we speak of "normal jealousy," etc.). The normal neurosis has important secondary gains, which are enhanced by the fact that it is epidemic and that everybody concurs in its rationalizations: "A husband has no right to—you cannot blame her if—"

*

Perhaps the concept of "Normal Neurosis" is the defining mark of an "Institution." It is the non-rational system that seems to be, and is taken as, a law of nature, and so it generates its own persistence. If the permanence of an Institution is threatened, there is at once anxiety and a fear of emptiness. It is believed that except in the Institution, a particular social function could not be carried on, though indeed it might be carried on better. As if bridges could not exist without tolls, or children be born and reared without marriage licenses, or education occur without schools. Wherever there is an Institution, like Marriage or the School System or the State, look for the repression and transference.

*

That I have been getting little sexual pleasure from most sexual acts these days has caused me qualms about my health. But I guess the case is simpler. Because of my frustrations, I have adopted a quite negative standard of choice. I do not ask that such and such a face or motion or trait of character be beautiful and rouse my desire, but simply that there are not, or not too many, desexualizing features or traits. I go ahead not because I want her kisses, but because her breath does not smell bad. Giving myself such very plain bread, I have no appetite. I eat in order not to starve. . . . But this raises a problem, for people do not starve to death so readily. Why don't I bide my time? . . . And indeed, if I may judge by the analogy of the food, it is more the time that is

unappetizing than the food. I rarely eat my family dinner
with pleasure; and this is not because it is my family dinner,
and usually the food is pretty good. Rather, just at that hour
I am not usually hungry. So my sexual life with my wife is
ruined because she does not make herself available at my
spontaneous moments.

*

After a long, slightly chilly walk, I have a bowl of hot
soup, and I find myself singing.

*

She uses him for her dildo and he her for his water-
melon. Her love she reserves for an unavailable young man
who rouses her jealousy, and he reserves his love for his
business and the affairs of the city. It is a pity that they cannot get a simpler happiness, but we do not live in paradise.
Rather than evaluating these things, let us merely try to
make sure that no important functions of life are entirely
unaccounted for.

Five Years: Thoughts During a Useless Time

Ernest Jones

I will not speak here of the happiness of that marriage nor
of its difficulties that had to be overcome. It is not to be
counted on that genius of such an order should go hand-in-
hand with a completely harmonious personality, nor does
this often happen. Singularly mature, and with unerring integrity of soul in all that concerned her art, Morfydd's men-

tal evolution had not proceeded evenly in all directions. Her attachment to her father was so great that she had misgivings at "deserting" him for anyone else. Her faith and devotion, so admirable when related to her country and her people, were also unfortunately attached to very simpleminded religious beliefs, and it was at first a great grief to her that I did not share them. This had also its practical inconveniences, since she wished to attend her church services, and even Sunday school, on the Sabbath, whereas I had long been in the habit of devoting that day to worship of the country. As time went on, however, love began to tell, and her ideas broadened. As may be imagined, my notion of adjustment in such matters consists in persuading the other person to approach my view of them, and that is what gradually and painlessly happened.

Our happiness grew more and more complete, but after eighteen months it came to an abrupt end. We were paying a summer visit to my father in Wales, and I was looking forward to taking her over my familiar Gowerland; though a native of the same county, she had never visited that beautiful peninsula. On the way down I wanted to buy her a box of chocolates, which for some reason she declined; it was poignant to reflect later that it would probably have saved her life. Life and great issues are always at the mercy of meaningless trivialities. Soon after arriving she fell obscurely ill, and it was a couple of days before it became plain that there was an appendicitis, which was going on to form an abscess. An operation was urgently indicated. I spent four or five hours at the telephone trying to reach Trotter; communications late in 1918 were poor, both by telephone and by rail. He advised me to secure a local surgeon and not risk the delay of waiting till he could come the next day; it was, of course, a simple operation. She did not do well, however, and after a few days became delirious with a high temperature. We thought there was blood poisoning till I got Trotter from London. He at once recognized delayed chloroform poisoning. It had recently been discovered, which neither the local doctor nor I had known, that this is a likelihood with a patient who is young, has suppuration in any part of the body, and has been deprived of sugar (as war conditions had then imposed); in such circumstances only ether is permissible as an anesthetic. This simple piece of ignorance cost a valuable and promising life. We fought hard, and there were moments when we seemed to have succeeded, but it was too late.

The grief I then had to endure was the most painful experience of my life, though it did not persist indefinitely as a later similar experience has. Life lost most of its value, or at least savor. The acuteness of the pain had the effect of bringing out all the gentleness and kindliness in my nature. I felt that with such possibilities of pain in the world it behoved everyone, or at all events those who knew of them, to be as kind as they could be to their fellows. If only mankind could learn that lesson! Nature sees to it that misfortune, sickness, and grief provide all the suffering in the world that the sternest moralist could demand for our improvement, so that the senseless additions we make to it by cruelty are truly superfluous. At least I was spared one agony. I did not have the insuperable task of having to reconcile this tragedy with a belief in a benevolent Deity. How I pitied Morfydd's father, a devout believer, in that struggle! Poor man, death took from him his wife and all his children, his darling daughter and two sons, within the space of a year. Even his religion broke under the strain. After all, the belief in God owes much of its value to the expectation that He will protect and comfort in critical situations, particularly those affecting our loved ones. If, on the contrary, He deals the chief of these a frightful blow, for which His omnipotence makes

Him by definition responsible, then one is faced with the predicament of accepting His conduct, which would involve a disloyalty to the loved one, or of repudiating Him. When the human love reaches a very high order no ordinary religious belief will vie with it.

Free Associations: Memoirs of a Psychoanalyst

Aldous Huxley

M.* was in hospital for two periods of about two weeks each, with an interval of a week between them. During these two periods she underwent a long series of tests and was given twelve X-ray treatments to relieve the pain in the lower spine and to guard against the spread, in that area, of what was suspected to be malignancy. These treatments were tolerated at first fairly well; but the last of them produced distressing symptoms of radiation sickness. These symptoms were aggravated, a few days later, by the appearance of jaundice, due, as it turned out, to cancer of the liver. During the last few days in hospital M. was unable to keep any food or liquid on the stomach and had to be fed intravenously.

She was brought home in an ambulance on Monday, February 7th, and installed in her own room. The nurse who had taken care of her after her operation, four years before, was waiting for her when she arrived. M. had a real affection for this good, deeply compassionate woman, and the affection was warmly reciprocated. Three days later a second nurse was called in for night duty.

On the Monday afternoon her old friend L., the psycho-

*Maria, Huxley's first wife, who died in 1955.

therapist, came in for half an hour, put her into hypnosis and gave her suggestions to the effect that the nausea, which had made her life miserable during the preceding days, would disappear, and that she would be able to keep down whatever food was given her. Later that evening I repeated these suggestions, and from that time forward there was no more nausea and it was possible for her to take liquid nourishment and a sufficiency of water for the body's needs. No further intravenous feeding was necessary.

The progress of the disease was extraordinarily rapid. She was still able to find a great and fully conscious happiness in seeing her son, who had flown in from New York on Tuesday morning. But by Wednesday, when her sister S[uzanne] arrived, her response was only just conscious. She recognized S. and said a few words to her; but after that there was very little communication. M. could hear still; but it was becoming harder and harder for her to speak, and the words, when they came, were wandering words, whose relevance was to the inner life of illness, not to the external world.

I spent a good many hours of each day sitting with her, sometimes saying nothing, sometimes speaking. When I spoke, it was always, first of all, to give suggestions about her physical well-being. I would go through the ordinary procedure of hypnotic induction, beginning by suggestions of muscular relaxation, then counting to five or ten, with the suggestion that each count would send her deeper into hypnosis. I would generally accompany the counting with passes of the hand, which I drew slowly down from the head toward the feet. After the induction period was over, I would suggest that she was feeling, and would continue to feel, comfortable, free from pain and nausea, desirous of taking water and liquid nourishment whenever they should be offered. These suggestions were, I think, effective; at any rate there was little pain and it was only during the last thirty-six hours that sedation (with Demarol) became necessary.

These suggestions for physical comfort were in every case followed by a much longer series of suggestions addressed to the deeper levels of the mind. Under hypnosis M. had had, in the past, many remarkable visionary experiences of a kind which theologians would call "pre-mystical." She had also had, especially while we were living in the Mojave Desert, during the war, a number of genuinely mystical experiences, had lived with an abiding sense of divine immanence, of Reality totally present, moment by moment in every object, person, and event. This was the reason for her passionate love of the desert. For her, it was not merely a geographical region; it was also a state of mind, a metaphysical reality, an unequivocal manifestation of God.

In the desert and, later, under hypnosis, all M.'s visionary and mystical experiences had been associated with light. (In this she was in no way exceptional. Almost all mystics and visionaries have experienced Reality in terms of light— either of light in its naked purity, or of light infusing and radiating out of things and persons seen with the inner eye or in the external world.) Light had been the element in which her spirit had lived, and it was therefore to light that all my words referred. I would begin by reminding her of the desert she had loved so much, of the vast crystalline silence, of the overarching sky, of the snow-covered mountains at whose feet we had lived. I would ask her to open the eyes of memory to the desert sky and to think of it as the blue light of Peace, soft and yet intense, gentle and yet irresistible in its tranquillizing power. And now, I would say, it was evening in the desert, and the sun was setting. Overhead the sky was more deeply blue than ever. But in the West there was a great golden illumination deepening to red; and this was the golden light of Joy, the rosy light of Love. And to the south

rose the mountains, covered with snow and glowing with the
white light of pure Being—the white light which is the
source of the colored lights, the absolute Being of which
love, joy and peace are manifestations and in which all the
dualisms of our experience, all the pairs of opposites—positive and negative, good and evil, pleasure and pain, health
and sickness, life and death—are reconciled and made one.
And I would ask her to look at these lights of her beloved
desert and to realize that they were not merely symbols, but
actual expressions of the divine nature—an expression of
pure Being; an expression of the peace that passeth all understanding; an expression of the divine joy; an expression
of the love which is at the heart of things, at the core, along
with peace and joy and being, of every human mind. And
having reminded her of these truths—truths which we all
know in the unconscious depths of our being, which some
know consciously but only theoretically and which a few
(M. was one of them) have known directly, albeit briefly
and by snatches—I would urge her to advance into those
lights, to open herself up to joy, peace, love, and being, to
permit herself to be irradiated by them and to become one
with them. I urged her to become what in fact she had always been, what all of us have always been, a part of the
divine substance, a manifestation of love, joy, and peace, a
being identical with the One Reality. And I kept on repeating this, urging her to go deeper and deeper into the
light, ever deeper and deeper.

So the days passed and, as her body weakened, her surface mind drifted further and further out of contact, so that
she no longer recognized us or paid attention. And yet she
must still have heard and understood what was said; for she
would respond by appropriate action, when the nurse asked
her to open her mouth or to swallow. Under anesthesia, the
sense of hearing remains awake long after the other senses

have been eliminated. And even in deep sleep suggestions will be accepted and complicated sentences can be memorized. Addressing the deep mind which never sleeps, I went on suggesting that there should be relaxation on the physical level, and an absence of pain and nausea; and I continued to remind her of who she really was—a manifestation in time of the eternal, a part forever unseparated from the whole, of the divine reality; I went on urging her to go forward into the light.

At a little before three on Saturday morning the night nurse came and told us that the pulse was failing. I went and sat by M.'s bed and, from time to time, leaned over and spoke into her ear. I told her that I was with her and would always be with her in that light which was the central reality of our beings. I told her that she was surrounded by human love and that this love was the manifestation of a greater love, by which she was enveloped and sustained. I told her to let go, to forget the body, to leave it lying here like a bundle of old clothes, and to allow herself to be carried, as a child is carried, into the heart of the rosy light of love. She knew what love was, had been capable of love as few human beings are capable. Now she must go forward into love, must permit herself to be carried into love, deeper and deeper into it, so that at last she would be capable of loving as God loves—of loving everything, infinitely, without judging, without condemning, without either craving or abhorring. And then there was peace. How passionately, from the depth of a fatigue which illness and a frail constitution had often intensified to the point of being hardly bearable, she had longed for peace! And now she would have peace. And where there was peace and love, there too there would be joy and the river of the colored lights was carrying her toward the white light of pure being, which is the source of all things and the reconciliation of all opposites in unity.

And she was to forget, not only her poor body, but the time in which that body had lived. Let her forget the past, leave her old memories behind. Regrets, nostalgias, remorses, apprehensions—all these were barriers between her and the light. Let her forget them, forget them completely, and stand here, transparent, in the presence of the light—absorbing it, allowing herself to be made one with it in the timeless now of the present instant. "Peace now," I kept repeating. "Peace, love, joy *now*. Being *now*."

For the last hour I sat or stood with my left hand on her head and the right on the solar plexus. Between two right-handed persons this contact seems to create a kind of vital circuit. For a restless child, for a sick or tired adult, there seems to be something soothing and refreshing about being in such a circuit. And so it proved even in this extremity. The breathing became quieter, and I had the impression that there was some kind of release. I went on with my suggestions and reminders, reducing them to their simplest form and repeating them close to her ear. "Let go, let go. Forget the body, leave it lying here; it is of no importance now. Go forward into the light. Let yourself be carried into the light. No memories, no regrets, no looking backward, no apprehensive thoughts about your own or anyone else's future. Only the light. Only this pure being, this love, this joy. Above all this peace. Peace in this timeless moment, peace now, peace now." When the breathing ceased, at about six, it was without any struggle.

Letters of Aldous Huxley

Raymond Chandler

Jan. 1955

TO LEONARD RUSSELL

... I have received much sympathy and many letters, but yours is somehow unique in that it speaks of the beauty that is lost rather than condoling with the comparatively useless life that continues on. She was everything you say, and more. She was the beat of my heart for thirty years. She was the music heard faintly at the edge of sound. It was my great and now useless regret that I never wrote anything really worth her attention, no book that I could dedicate to her. I planned it. I thought of it but I never wrote it. Perhaps I couldn't have written it. Perhaps by now she realizes that I tried, and that I regarded the sacrifice of several years of a rather insignificant literary career as a small price to pay, if I could make her smile a few times more.

Jan. 1955

TO HAMISH HAMILTON

... Please don't send me any more books, as they will only have to go into storage. I have sold the house and I will be out of here about March 15th or before. I'll let you know as soon as I know myself about when I shall be in London. I gather from your letter that you would like me to stay with you at your house for a little while. But if I may say so without sounding ungrateful, I should rather be on my own. I'd like to be at a hotel until you can help me find a service flat. I don't want to be a burden or a nuisance to anyone. I am pretty badly broken up, and for me it may last a long time, as my emotions are not superficial.

You probably realized when we were in London that Cissy was in rather frail health. When we got back she looked and felt better than she had in a couple of years, but it didn't last. She got weaker and weaker and more and more tired. She had an obscure and rather rare ailment, I am told, called fibrosis of the lungs. It's a slow hardening of the lung tissue, starting at the bottom of the lungs and progressing upward ... As far back as 1940 her X-rays showed the condition as existing, but it was quite a long time before I realized that it could have only one ending. I don't think that she herself ever quite gave up hope, or if so during the last weeks, she didn't let anyone else know that she had given up hope. . . .

She was in an oxygen tent all the time, but she kept pulling it away so that she could hold my hand. She was quite vague in her mind about some things, but almost too desperately clear about others. Then she would turn her head away and when I was no longer in her line of vision, she seemed to forget all about me.

A little after noon on December 12th, which was a Sunday, the nurse called up and said she was very low. When I got there they had taken the oxygen tent away and she was lying with her eyes half open. . . . The doctor had his stethoscope over her heart and was listening. After a while he stepped back and nodded. I closed her eyes and kissed her and went away.

Of course in a sense I had said goodbye to her long ago. In fact many times during the past two years in the middle of the night I had realized that it was only a question of time until I lost her. But that is not the same thing as having it happen. But I was glad that she had died. To think of this proud, fearless bird caged in a room in some rotten sanitarium for the rest of her days was such an unbearable thought that I could hardly face it at all.

I am sleeping in her room. I thought I couldn't face that, and then I thought that if the room were empty it would just be haunted, and every time I went past the door I would have the horrors, and that the only thing was for me to come in here and fill it up with my junk and make it look like the kind of mess I'm used to living in. It was the right decision.

For thirty years, ten months, and four days, she was the light of my life, my whole ambition. Anything else I did was just the fire for her to warm her hands at.

March 19, 1957

TO HELGA GREENE

... I wasn't faithful to my wife out of principle but because she was completely adorable, and the urge to stray which afflicts many men at a certain age, because they think they have been missing a lot of beautiful girls, never touched me. I already had perfection. When she was younger she used to have sudden and very short-lived tempers, in which she would throw pillows at me. I just laughed. I liked her spirit. She was a terrific fighter. If an awkward or unpleasant scene faced her she would march right in, and never hesitate a minute to think it over. And she always won, not because she deliberately put on the charm at the tactical moment, but because she was irresistible without even knowing or caring about it. So she had to die by half-inches. I suppose everything has to be paid for in some manner.

Feb. 7, 1955

TO ROGER MACHELL

... I sit up half the night playing records when I have the blues and can't get drunk enough to feel sleepy. My nights are pretty awful. And they don't get any better. I've been alone since Saturday morning except for Mabel the Marble, my Pennsylvania Dutch cook and housekeeper. She has a lot of fine qualities but she is not much company. Perhaps when I get away from this house and all its memories I can settle down to do some writing. And then again I may just be homesick, and to be homesick for a home you haven't got is rather poignant.

Tomorrow is or would have been our thirty-first wedding anniversary. I'm going to fill the house with red roses and have a friend in to drink champagne, which we always did. A useless and probably foolish gesture because my lost love is utterly lost and I have no belief in any afterlife. But just the same I shall do it. All us tough guys are hopeless sentimentalists at heart.

Raymond Chandler Speaking

Thomas Bell

A widow must live with her grief for a while; there is no escaping it. Edie told us it took her over a year to get back to what she called normal, which means it took her that long to develop a new habit, the habit of living without Ed. Marie might need less time; she is younger than Edie and presumably more resilient. But it might just as well take her longer, on the theory that a young body can endure more, exhaust less quickly, than an older one. I do think, however, that in a year or so she should be pretty well adjusted to her new way of life, a way that she may not like as well as her old one but which needn't be without its advantages. The chief of these, I think, is that for the first time in her life she will be her own boss, without either her mother or me to interfere. Not everyone wants or likes independence, and Marie's won't make up for what she has lost, but it *is* something, it *is* a gain. Its value will depend solely on herself. I think she'll use it wisely.

Women may make the best widows, . . . if only because they seem to be more self-sufficient than men, as cats seem more self-sufficient than dogs; but I don't really know. True or not, I find it small comfort. I wish, I keep forever wishing, that I could make what is coming easier on Marie. But how can I, except by not dying? And how can I do that?

Dear Marie, dear Mrs. B., dear Susie, dear wife. What can I say? One can do only so much with words; they are, after all, just the names of things, not the things themselves. And it is the thing itself that I am so conscious of now, the living richness of our years together. Something of the best of them is in the books I wrote, just as is much of the best of me. I was always my own hero; and after my first book I never had a heroine who didn't have more of you in her than of herself. But we did much more living during our years together than could be put into even a library of books, and it's that living I'm thinking about now.

We've made a good pair. We've been angry and impatient with each other, we've hurt and offended each other, we've been bad-mannered, stupid, mean, irritating, cruel and dull. But none of all that ever really mattered because there was always more than enough of the good things to make the bad unimportant. We have nothing to reproach ourselves with. I've been a damned good husband and you've been a damned good wife, and no man or woman could ask—or give—more. We've done a lot of fine living together, and I'd like nothing better than to start at the beginning and do it all over again.

Perhaps it would be easier on both of us now if we hadn't had it so good, but that's a small and miserly way of looking at it. I'm glad you came up to the apartment that April evening, and I'm glad we've had so many years together. That we can't have a dozen or so more is sheer bad luck, but the years we did have are still ours.

Your grief and loneliness won't last. (Look at all the widows around you.) As the days go by you'll discover that life is still worth living, that things are still worth doing. Time is the greatest of healers. Time and work. And in time you'll make another discovery: that your grief has been replaced by memories and that all the memories—this is the miracle—are pleasant ones. And from then on that's how it will mostly be: You'll have a headful of memories and all of them pleasant. And from then on, whenever you think or speak of me, you won't cry or feel sad. You'll smile. You'll remember me and smile.

What more could any husband want?

In The Midst of Life

Theodore Roethke

WISH FOR A YOUNG WIFE

My lizard, my lively writher,
May your limbs never wither,
May the eyes in your face
Survive the green ice
Of envy's mean gaze;
May you live out your life
Without hate, without grief,
And your hair ever blaze,
In the sun, in the sun,
When I am undone,
When I am no one.

4. Fathers

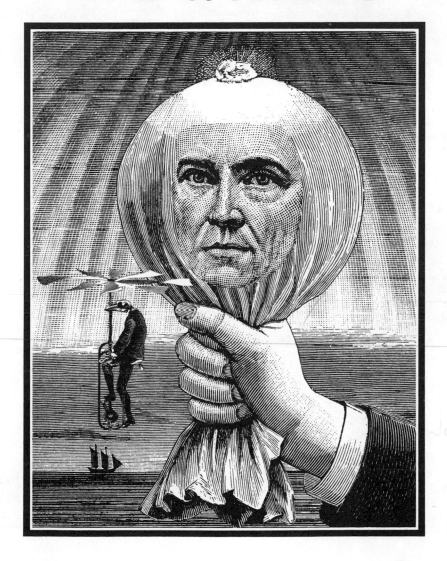

Eugène Ionesco

The libido, or love of life, is not a reassuring love, it is not a free love, it cannot be justified in spiritual terms; only creative love can be thus justified, fatherly love; the love that engenders, that seeks to create living beings. That, indeed, is divine love. Not to want to preserve one's own life but to make others live: to give life if we are not entitled to love ourselves; if it is not right to love ourselves, it is right to love others, not in order to meet one's own reflection in them but because they are truly other than oneself. In this way the world would not be lost.

Fragments of a Journal

Cesare Pavese

8th July 1938

"He has found a purpose in life in his children." So that they in turn may find the same in theirs? But what point is there in this endless procreation? We care so little about other people that even Christianity urges us to do good *for the love of God.* Man prefers to punch his fellow man in the mouth, and is such a fool that to give himself an object in life he has to produce a son.

The Burning Brand: Diaries 1935–1950

Malcolm Muggeridge

It was at this time that Kitty first became pregnant. I found the whole process utterly wonderful; her stomach gradually swelling up, and the thought that out of our fleshly gyrations, beautiful and hilarious and grotesque all in one, should come this ripening fruit, this new life partaking of us both, and breaking out of its cocoon—her womb—to exist separately in the world. I had seen death, now I was to see birth. A white stomach rounding out, and inside it something growing, moving, living. It gave a point to every touch and caress and heave and groan; like print in a foreign language, laboriously spelled over, until suddenly it says something, and one understands. How beautiful are the Magnificats, the songs of birth! How desolate and ultimately disastrous and destructive is the pursuit of Eros for its own sake! The sterile orgasm; the bow passed across the strings and no music coming, the paddle dipped in the water and no movement following.

Chronicles of Wasted Time

Jakov Lind

It wasn't only money, the Jews, the communists, the world, freedom, the Nazis, acting, writing, and traveling I had on my mind. I looked at Ida's big stomach and was frightened of the unborn. My problem was not who would look after the child—my father-in-law, Ida, or God Himself. My problem was inside my brain, where something didn't function as it should.

While Ida sat on the sun deck wrapped in blankets, staring into her own unknown future, and Fritz tried to seduce Nancy Sokoloff with his white teeth, I lay on my bunk, stared right above me, and imagined myself as the empty space in a long stippled line of warriors, horsemen, and nomads. Inside was neither Jew nor Gentile, neither male nor female, but all of them simultaneously, or the absence of all. Inside was something which could not speak for itself yet it was in a constant state of change, without either a body or a soul. Identification perhaps with an unborn son due in July? I wasn't him, but myself yet unborn, which confused me as I couldn't think where I could possibly be if not on a bunk on C deck. I am there, I presumed, but something in me isn't born yet—what, I absolutely could not figure out, and wanted to dismiss the whole thing as fantasy. It dawned on me gradually that I might still be in my own father's mind, just as my unborn son was in mine. In that case I am only an idea, nothing but an idea, but as an idea I definitely exist, though invisible to others and sometimes even to myself. How many circles will I have to go through to reach existence? I counted seven: doubt, fear, hesitation, consideration, projection, indecision, uncertainty. What chance did I have to be born into this world if the biologists are right and from the millions of small heads of sperm only one ever makes it? If a sevenfold shield protects one from becoming (which means birth for the unborn and death for the living), birth, I concluded, is neither necessary nor unavoidable, but happens all the same. Was the boat rocking me up and down? I felt distinctly that if it hadn't been for an incomprehensible force outside myself I would never have become. This self grows a body around itself. Does it first grow brain tissue or first the feet? I couldn't imagine myself to have been born without either, nor could I see all existence and nonexistence as a constant crossing from nothingness into something and back again and so on, which it is. I ate myself through ovum, placenta, womb, and my mother, and if there had been more inside, I might never have come out. To have eaten my mother hollow just as I was eating my life up now was not a cheerful conclusion to come to.

Numbers: A Further Autobiography

Edward Hoagland

We're to have a baby soon. I can feel him bang my wife's stomach, and already, even before he is born, we're losing sleep and discombobulated. During the night M. shifts in discomfort from the bed to the sofa and back, although her face is at a pitch of beauty much of the time, and occasionally we're seized with momentary panic that the event is now. Since we have not been married long, the pregnancy has brought us into an instant intimacy. We're hanging pictures and buying the furniture we hadn't bothered with earlier; a dozen times a day I nuzzle her—"Into the lion's mouth!" I say. Sometimes her belly seems very large, and that's a little alarming, but sometimes it seems to grow smaller and that's depressing. M. wears loose sweaters so that she can pull the neck open and look down the front, talking directly to him. I claim that he's a frog jumping under a towel, but she says his movements are like oatmeal slowly, irregularly bubbling—a cooking sensation—unless he stands painfully on her spleen. A girl in the prenatal class at the hospital startled the group by confessing she couldn't tell the difference between her baby's stirrings and gas. The instructor ignored this and returned to the subject of pushing: "Think vagina." Putting on diaperlike pads, the girls lay on their backs, opened their legs, and practiced the exercise: push, push and blow; push, push and blow. "Push, Mrs. Winograd. You're not pushing."

Alone we make babies of one another in preparation for the baby, or M. will poke her stomach sharply and look intently at it, as if she can see through inside. She pushes her stomach against me or lies on the couch wiggling her feet, but I tell her that she's too fat to kiss; I tell her the only reason she's still beautiful and hasn't turned from beauty into beast is that I've kissed her so much in the past.

This is my first baby but not my first marriage. Both marriages began in neurotic confusion and a sense of impasse, though they were honest in the fact that love quickly grew. Usually people love because they want to; we love when we're ready to love, which, as often as not, is when we think we have reached a dead end. There is also that agitating wait for the chance meeting—the meeting some people wait for their whole lives long—but unless we're ready to marry we're not likely to, no matter whom we manage to meet. As we climb in and out of bedrooms and run to parties, we're partly ransacking ourselves for the potential to tarry awhile and not lose hope or lose our temper or our trust.

Since, at first, love includes such a dose of the urgencies, in the weeks before the wedding ceremony one comes back and comes back to see that this really *is* the right person and that the marriage isn't simply being jumped into because each of you feels boxed in. M.'s mother, a widow for many years, married again shortly before we did, so she and her mother were mirroring one another's emotions. For my part, I'd thought ever since my divorce that I'd thrown my first marriage away carelessly, arrogantly, ignorantly, and so I'd been eagerly awaiting my chance to try again. That had been the blundering marriage of one's twenties; this was the marriage of which much is hoped.

On our wedding morning we spoke over the phone on tiptoe, not wanting to upset anything. Then the happiness, the confidence, the chatter afterwards—*at last*—and the exuberance of the word *wife*. I knew I was giving myself more wholeheartedly than before, with less wariness and self-distrust. I'd had four years of bachelorhood between marriages and was sick of it: I realized again how sick when I went on a business trip for several weeks, returning unexpectedly, and found the apartment a mess: earrings on the floor, dust in puffs, tumbled clothes. I'm a neatness bug, but this disorder just seemed like delicious complexity.

We had a short, auspicious honeymoon, with Edwardian meals, champagne, flowers, and strolls in the park, where I talked through the bars to the Bengal tigers in their own language by way of indicating my competence as a bridegroom. Now we own a wine-red Parego baby carriage and wait for the sea change which is under way. It's a peculiarly vulnerable juncture, like the month before one goes into the army, when every hearty soul who has preceded you is an authority on what you ought to expect. The natural-childbirth people speak of the penultimate pleasure which their program of yoga builds up to, while in the opposite camp are the jumpy ladies who confide to M. that labor is brutal beyond describing. Most people do neither; they simply say by the light in their faces that the childbearing years are about as gay as any they can remember. We're told, incidentally, that our Jeremy (as we think of him) is going to be a girl, because the heartbeat is strong and steady and the outline of M.'s stomach is generally round, not humpy, although as big as a pumpkin.

For the time being the preludes of sex bore me—the

whole repetitive preoccupation with the next pair of bob-bledeboobs. It's probably part of the conditioning for father-hood, but it should enable me to set down some erotica without wetting the page. Of course everything is fluids—kissing is fluids, babies are fluids, having a baby is fluids. Thank God a shapeless being is going to emerge instead of somebody already formed—a little loan shark or a beauty queen. In the pudginess is a new beginning.

The Lapping, Itchy Edge of Love

Charles Bukowski

BIRTH

I.
reading the Dialogues of Plato when the
doctor walks up and says

do you still read that high-brow
stuff? last time I read that I
was in
high school.

I read it, I tell
him.

well, it's a girl, 9 #, 3 oz. no trouble at
all.

shit. great. when can I see
them?

they'll let you know. good
night.

II.
I sit down to Plato again. there are 4 people playing
cards. one woman has beautiful legs that she doesn't hide
and I keep looking at her legs until she covers them with a
blue sweater.

III.
I am called upstairs. they show me the thing through glass.
it's red as a boiled crab and tough. it will make
it. it will see it through.

hey, look at this, Plato: *another broad!*
I can see her now on some Sunday afternoon
shaking it in a tight skirt
making Boulevards of young men warble in their
guts.

I wave the girl and the nurse
away.

IV.
the woman is still stunned with
drugs but I tell her

a great woman has arrived!
and make my fists into little balls and I
hold up my arms and
snarl-cry.

the nurse is fat and Mexican, has eaten too many
tortillas.

nice to have met you, sweetheart, I
tell her.

V.

then I am back at the shack. I sit down and listen to
the bathtub drip.
I go over and pull all the blinds down and fall on the
couch. all I can hear is tires on
steel streets.

VI.

there is a *meeow* from the screen and I let him
in: sober, indifferent,
hungry.

VII.

we walk into the kitchen
male, swaggering under the electric light;
4 balls, 2 heads
dominion over all the continent
over ships that sail in and out
over small female things and jewels.

I get down the can of
catfood and open
it. Plato is left in the
glove compartment.

Bertrand Russell

Ever since the day, in the summer of 1894, when I walked
with Alys on Richmond Green after hearing the medical

verdict, I had tried to suppress my desire for children. It had, however, grown continually stronger, until it had become almost insupportable. When my first child was born, in November 1921, I felt an immense release of pent-up emotion, and during the next ten years my main purposes were parental. Parental feeling, as I have experienced it, is very complex. There is, first and foremost, sheer animal affection, and delight in watching what is charming in the ways of the young. Next, there is the sense of inescapable responsibility, providing a purpose for daily activities which scepticism does not easily question. Then there is an egoistic element, which is very dangerous: the hope that one's children may succeed where one has failed, that they may carry on one's work when death or senility puts an end to one's own efforts, and, in any case, that they will supply a biological escape from death, making one's own life part of the whole stream, and not a mere stagnant puddle without any overflow into the future. All this I experienced, and for some years it filled my life with happiness and peace.

The Autobiography of Bertrand Russell: 1914–1924

William Gibson

It was a rainy dawn when I escorted my waddling wife into a hospital lobby, and three hours later I saw the tiny creature who had dwelt so long and anonymously in her womb: at the elevator a masked nurse bearing him from delivery to maternity waved me back, but lifted the cloth so I could spy the squeezed face and dark hair still matted with his mother's blood, and at last something in me found its pedalpoint. By what stumblings in the dark his mother and I had come to that beginning is another story, part and not part of this, but I had been a long way around and was home. Diminutive head, it pulled like magnetic bone at everything in my life, work, marriage, conscience, all was changed, and chiefly, whatever new griefs were in store, the oldest grief was gone under; a part of me dying as grown son was reborn, both as infant and as father resurrected, in a consciousness over three generations like the opening of a new eye. In so lengthened a perspective now the time between is shrivelled, and the two faces of death and birth swim up out of the darkroom fluids of the mind as contiguous as on a single snapshot.

And this very moment I spy him below me, homecoming from school between the pines along our mud road, his younger brother tagging behind; each in burly coat and long pants, bareheaded, dangling a briefcase bulky with learning, is almost no longer a boy. Tall as my thumbnail, they halt, talking and pointing at what I cannot see, but not seeing what I can, a decade gone in a snap of the fingers and my voice cannot reach them, but is in them, as they walk on among the puddles and into the disasters of young manhood. All I relive of mine in this workroom is only in words, happily, for in fact nothing then stood between me and insanity except my good sense, and so my bowels yearn upon and follow these two along their muddy road to the pillared corner of the dark green house, in which they are less safe than I; and here I write for their eyes, dear readers entering into the bloom of youth, do not despair, it is outlived. Another hour and I will go down to them and my duties in the house.

For if I dare to say salvation I mean a state which is neither simple nor enchanted, but conditional, and paid for by the day in the commonest coin of domesticity. Two years before we were parents we heard a mutter of these boys pester-

ing us to be born, and after half a lifetime of working only for myself I undertook to work for them. Seizing upon any offer that would make me a wage earner, a tardy ideal, I taught classes in music and literature, began a novel I saw would be publishable, sat with piano pupils, wrote to order an opera libretto and a pageant script, founded a theater group of psychiatric patients to direct, and on the run with my employments from breakfast to bedtime could not spare thirty minutes for lethargy; a feverish time, it was the most exhilarating of my life, and I lost the race to finish the novel only by a month; I scribbled its last pages in the hours after midnight in a rocker with my newborn son on my shoulder, a sleepless brat, and a writing board on my thigh. I had my witness, I wrote now in his service too, and I would never again fail to earn a living with a pencil, a revolution too timely to be luck. I took profound pleasure in becoming the provider to him, and later to his brother, that in another life my father had been. To be back in the human family was so long deferred a joy that for several years I was drunk on fatherhood; of every stranger I met I inquired into the number, sex, age, health, talents of his children, and could not but marvel at our skill.

Yet it was a dark mirror too, in which to this day I ponder reflections of me which are less than pleasant, the heart of the hope. I was a father not yet a month when at two in the morning our infant scrabbled on my shoulder in a refusal to sleep and, with my writing board blank, I shook all six pounds of him until he bawled in terror; my wife wept when I told her, and for days I was abased in that knowledge of myself. So it began, and though I recovered, confident that thereafter I would be the faultless father I had it in me to be, more than a decade later I am still making my own acquaintance with a painfulness no mortal other than these boys can evoke in me.

Now that they can breathe by themselves through the night their mother and I no longer hover so above a crib, nor do we sit a half-hour to jog it in rhythm to our lullabies; much of their innocence, and ours, is forgotten. Schoolboy faces, molded by purpose, they are not the babes we watched over when only the imagery of sentimentality, lambs, petals, angels, was apt. I understood heaven and hell at the cribside as I hung upon the face of our younger; it was his birth which restored my mother to me, who now lay dying, and I knew that never in this world would I find a word to tell him the love that rose like a grace or perfecting in me as he slept, for every morning we awoke to a language muddled by the parting of our wills, and I saw why heaven was populous with cherubs; heaven was my moment of grace made into an eternity, as hell is the burnings of will. "You're a good boy," my father teased in my childhood, "when you're asleep," but awake I am flesh like him, alive and imperfect, and our cherubs are themselves not without faults, some being mine. Once when this three-year-old in helping me dig a ditch was unshovelling my labors I spoke sharply, and still see on his happy face the panic come at work he had thought was good and I thought was bad; what melted in me was some ignorance that my word mattered as it never had in other ears. Of all they and my wife and I have forgotten, little is lost, and much of my voice in them is error I would undo.

I cannot, and can. I sat at the bedside as my wife suckled our firstborn, and the meeting of blind mouth and great mothering breast was the point it seemed not of my life but on which the world itself turned; it was a glimpse of verity not without a mystical blurring new to me, and passed, but I knew I would have a part in no event more important. To these boys whom I invited into the world I am answerable for every item in my life. It never occurs to me that I should not change for their sake; I can do better, to overcome my nature is a vow I will break and make while I have breath, and so help me what am I back to but my father circling a day on a calendar in the year of his vow to master his temper?

Lambs, who take away sins, I mean not too easily that in each child born is the future, so much of it reiterates the past, but that I had no parents until I had children, and in the mirror of them I see my falls from grace, as son, as father, which must be redeemed. It is as undeniable a claim as a diaper to be changed; and in such small labors of love is our judgment on the past, to reiterate this, to outgrow that, a work that expiates some sins and lays some ghosts. It is how the future comes, is woven out of and seamless with the past, even in the enmity between the generations, for the child escapes, but the voice of his begetter is in him, and in him the begetter lives on, but having changed for the child.

So the coming of children is a birth in us also, of will in the service of grace; only hell is barren of children, and with every birth the tale, not yet finished, begins anew, never done, is all beginnings, like man, and in each it seems the past need not be unredeemable.

A Mass For The Dead

Vladimir Nabokov

Throughout the years of our boy's infancy, in Hitler's Germany and Maginot's France, we were more or less constantly hard up, but wonderful friends saw to his having the best things available. Although powerless to do much about it, you and I jointly kept a jealous eye on any possible rift between his childhood and our own incunabula in the opulent past, and this is where those friendly fates came in, doctoring the rift every time it threatened to open. Then, too, the science of building up babies had made the same kind of phenomenal, streamlined progress that flying or tilling had—*I*, when nine months old, did not get a pound of strained spinach at one feeding or the juice of a dozen oranges per days; and the pediatric hygiene you adopted was incomparably more artistic and scrupulous than anything old nurses could have dreamed up when we were babes.

I think bourgeois fathers—wing-collar workers in pencil-striped pants, dignified, office-tied fathers, so different from young American veterans of today or from a happy, jobless Russian-born expatriate of fifteen years ago—will not understand my attitude toward our child. Whenever you held him up, replete with his warm formula and grave as an idol, and waited for the postlactic all-clear signal before making a horizontal baby of the vertical one, I used to take part both in your wait and in the tightness of his surfeit, which I exaggerated, therefore rather resenting your cheerful faith in the speedy dissipation of what I felt to be a painful oppression; and when, at last, the blunt little bubble did rise and burst in his solemn mouth, I used to experience a lovely relief while you, with a congratulatory murmur, bent low to deposit him in the white-rimmed twilight of his crib.

You know, I still feel in my wrists certain echoes of the pram-pusher's knack, such as, for example, the glib downward pressure one applied to the handle in order to have the carriage tip up and climb the curb. First came an elaborate mouse-gray vehicle of Belgian make, with fat autoid tires and luxurious springs, so large that it could not enter our puny elevator. It rolled on sidewalks in slow stately mystery, with the trapped baby inside lying supine, well covered with down, silk, and fur; only his eyes moved, warily, and sometimes they turned upward with one swift sweep of their showy lashes to follow the receding of branch-patterned blueness that flowed away from the edge of the half-cocked hood of the carriage, and presently he would dart a suspicious glance at my face to see if the teasing trees and sky did not belong, perhaps, to the same order of things as did rattles and parental humor. There followed a lighter carriage, and in this, as he spun along, he would tend to rise, straining at his straps; clutching at the edges; standing there less like the groggy passenger of a pleasure boat than like an entranced scientist in a spaceship; surveying the speckled skeins of a live, warm world; eyeing with philosophic interest the pillow he had managed to throw overboard; falling out himself when a strap burst one day. Still later he rode in one of those small contraptions called strollers; from initial springy and secure heights the child came lower and lower, until, when he was about one and a half, he touched ground in front of the moving stroller by slipping forward out of his seat and beating the sidewalk with his heels in anticipation of being set loose in some public garden. A new wave of evolution started to swell, gradually lifting him again from the ground, when, for his second birthday, he received a four-foot-long, silver-painted Mercedes racing car operated by inside pedals, like an organ, and in this he used to drive with a pumping, clanking noise up and down the sidewalk of the Kurfürstendamm while from open windows came the multiplied roar of a dictator still pounding his chest in the Neander valley we had left far behind.

Speak, Memory: An Autobiography Revisited

Henry Miller

My two children were a blessing. They weren't born at home—we had no conveniences. There was no doctor in Big Sur, not even a telephone nearby. From the time they were born, I was a very happy man.

When my children were very small I used to get up at night to feed them. And much more. I changed their diapers too. In those days, I didn't have a car; I would take the dirty diapers in a bag, a big laundry bag, and walk six miles to the hot springs (now taken over by Esalen) and wash them in that hot spring water, then carry them home! Six miles! That's *one* thing I remember about babies. For a time, after my wife left me, I was there with the children alone. That's the hardest thing to ask a man to do—take care of tots from three to five years of age, bouncing with energy, and shut up with them in one room, especially during the rains. In the winter when the rains came we were marooned. I fed them, changed their clothes, washed them, told them stories. I didn't do any writing. I couldn't. By noon every day I was exhausted! I'd say, "Let's take a nap." We'd get into bed, the three of us, and then they'd begin scrambling, screaming, fighting with each other. Finally I had to ask my wife to take them. As much as I loved them I couldn't handle the situation. It was something I'll never forget. That experience increased my respect for women, I guess. I realized what a tremendous job women have, married women, cooking meals, doing the laundry, cleaning house, taking care of children, and all that. This is something no man can understand or cope with no matter how hard his work may be.

The kids were fairly close together in age, two and a half years difference. They fought all the time, like sworn enemies. Today, of course they're good friends.

When Val was able to toddle beside me, when she was about three years old, I took her into the forest every day for a long walk beside a narrow stream. I pointed out birds, trees, leaves, rocks, and told her stories. Then I'd pick her up and carry her on my shoulders. I'll never forget the first song I taught her. It was "Yankee Doodle Dandy." What joy, walking and whistling with this kid on my back. Anyone who hasn't had children doesn't know what life is. Yes, they were a great blessing.

My Life And Times

William Saroyan

My kids came out to California from New York that summer, and mainly we had a lot of fun, but one thing happened that was no fun.

We drove up to San Francisco to spend a couple of weeks at my sister's home, and then we drove back to Malibu, by way of Fresno, and as we were driving around among the vineyards near Malaga my son asked me to stop, so we could pick some grapes. So we could *steal* some, if you like. I stopped, and ran out into the vineyard and began picking the grapes, only to notice that my son was just standing there looking at them. I told him to start picking, but he just went right on looking.

"I don't think they're ripe," he said.

"Even so," I said, "pick a couple of bunches."

I ran back to the car. He came back, taking his time, but he didn't have a single bunch of grapes with him.

This bothered me.

He had asked me to stop, and I had stopped, and then he hadn't done anything to make the stop worth anything.

I bawled him out about this, and about his boredom all during the drive, and then I bawled out my daughter, too. My sister said something, and I bawled her out too, and then for an hour or more nobody spoke.

By that time I felt foolish, but at the same time I couldn't understand my son, so I asked him if he had had a bowel movement in the morning.

He hadn't. And he'd had a headache all day.

I told him about myself when I had been his age. I had had nothing, but I had always been interested, fascinated even, by everything. On and on.

I knew it at the time, I know it now, and I suppose he knew it too: I was being angry at his mother.

It was stupid, but I couldn't help it, that's all.

I stopped somewhere for an aspirin for him, but he said he believed a Coke would do him more good, so he had a Coke, as everybody did, but whatever had been going on went right on going on.

My past was kicking me around, and with it I was kicking my son around, and every now and then my daughter, a little, too.

I tried to get out of it, to get myself out of being so mad at their mother, and at them, too, but it didn't work, and so I blamed my son.

Why wasn't he livelier, more comic, more alert, so that I would be driven out of the madness?

He didn't know. All he knew, but didn't say, was that he hated me, and I couldn't blame him, but I hated being hated.

I said that my trouble had been that I had loved them too much, had tried to do too much for them, had paid too much attention to every wish they had ever had, and of course they knew I meant their mother hadn't, which I believed to be true. From now on I would be different, I said. I would be like other fathers. I would give them orders. The other fathers were right, I was mistaken. I had looked upon them from the beginning as equals, or even superiors, and now I could see the folly of that.

I talked for hours and miles, and nobody replied, nobody dared, or cared, or needed to.

Now, I must point out that such talking is traditional in my family. It is invariably loud, intense, righteous, and critical of all others.

All families probably have their own procedure for the

achievement of psychiatric therapy or the restoration of balance, and the better part of this procedure is based upon talk, although it frequently moves along to shouting and fighting.

Six or seven times during the long recitation I tried to get out of the whole thing by laughing at myself, by making known that I knew I was being a fool, by saying things I believed were both true and amusing, but nobody laughed.

It was a very hot day in July, and from the beginning it had been a bad day.

In the back of the old Cadillac my daughter sat beside my sister, and beside me sat my son, drawn away on the car seat, the old Saroyan scowl all over his face.

At last the car began to climb the hills of Pacific Palisades, and soon we would be home.

I was still going strong when suddenly my son said in a tone of voice that still hurts me, and has twice come to me in my sleep: "Papa, Papa, will you stop the car, please?"

I stopped the car, he leaped out, and in the very leap began to buckle and vomit, trying to hide behind a tree whose trunk was too narrow for hiding. The sound of his sickness sickened me. Once, twice, three times, four times, five times. Silence. His face was drained of color and covered with sweat.

Immediately after he had jumped out of the car my daughter jumped out, saying, "Aram, what's the matter? What's the matter, Aram?"

My sister said in Armenian, "You've made the poor boy sick. He isn't like you. He's like himself."

We got home, and I got him into the shower, and then into a robe, and at the table for some hot chocolate and toast and boiled eggs, and then I had them both go to bed, even though it was only beginning to be dark, and their old friends in the neighborhood were coming to the door to ask them out for games.

That's the thing that bothered me in 1958, and will go right on bothering me the rest of my life.

I only hope it isn't the last thing I remember.

He told me the next day that it hadn't been my hollering at him that had made him sick, it had been other things.

I thanked him, but I didn't believe him, because I couldn't.

And my sister had been right in saying that he wasn't like me, only she'll never know how like him I was, but never vomited, because if I had, I might not be able to stop.

And I was sorry he wasn't like me, in that, because it is better not to get sick, it is better to find out how not to, it is better to insist on it, even, until it's almost impossible to get that sick, because getting sick doesn't get it, doesn't do it, at all.

But he hurt me, he hurt me deeper even than the failure and death of friends, and I loved him more than ever, and despised myself for never having been able to get sick that way, and for having made him sick that way, making him vomit for me forty years ago.

I went home one night from the winter streets of Fresno, possessed. Something had taken possession of me, hushed me, estranged me, put me aside from myself, and I wanted to get rid of it. The house was dark and empty when I got there, and cold, and I didn't know what to do. In the dining room was a bench my mother had made by placing planks over two apple-boxes and putting a coarse woven covering over the planks: red and black checks made out of some kind of sacking, made in Bitlis by somebody in the family. I couldn't sit and I couldn't lie down, so I kneeled on this bench and then put my head down, as Moslems do in praying, and I began to rock back and forth slowly because by doing that the thing that had taken possession of me, the sickness, the uselessness, whatever it was, seemed to go away. I half-slept, I half-prayed, and I thought, What *is* this, for God's sake? What's the matter? Why is my head like a damned rock?

At last I heard somebody at the door and quickly sat in the corner of the room, on the bench. My mother turned on a light, came in, and looked at me. I got up and fetched sawdust from the barn, so she could get the fire going, and in that way she wasn't able to notice that I was possessed, I was sick, I was useless, my head was a rock. Nobody would know.

The big event of 1958 was my son's sickness, known.

Here Comes/There Goes You Know Who:
An Autobiography

August Strindberg

"Better to be alone," I said to myself, and that was the last time I went out in the afternoon that summer. Keeping oneself company is best; still, one has to be on guard against the bad.

Consequently I stayed in the house, enjoyed my peace; imagined that I was beyond the storms of life; wished I were a little bit older so that I would not feel life's temptations; and believed that the worst was behind me.

And then one morning as I was having my coffee the maid came to me and said, "Your son was here, but I said you were still in bed."

"My son?"

"That's what he said."

"That's impossible! What did he look like?"

"He was tall, and ... well, he gave his name and said he would come again."

"How old was he?"

"Young—seventeen, eighteen."

I was struck dumb with apprehension, and the girl left. So it wasn't all over! The past was rising from its grave. Though it was piled with dirt and the grass on it was old, the past was not dead. My son who went off to America with respectable people when he was nine years old, and who I thought had made a career for himself. What had happened? Some accident, naturally—or several.

What would it be like to see him again? That terrifying moment of recognition, when you seek in vain for the familiar features of the child's face, those features that you helped shape from the cradle on, as you sought to make him as good as possible. In front of your child you always tried to show your best side, and for that reason you tried to catch the reflections of your better nature in that pliable and impressionable child's face, which you loved as a better version of yourself. Now I was to see it again, deformed and distorted. The growing adolescent is ugly, disproportioned, showing forth in terrible mixture both the angel in the child and the waking animal in the young man; filled with intimations of passion and conflict; fear of what is to come and remorse over what he had already experienced—and always that constant, restless sneering at everything; hatred of everything that is above him and represses him; which means hatred of the older generation and of those who are better off. And, above all, a distrust of life itself that had just transformed him from an innocuous child to a predatory man. I knew all this from my own experience and remembered how disgusting I was as an adolescent when all I thought of, however I tried not to, was food, liquor, and the coarsest pleasures. .... It wasn't necessary to remind me of this again; I already knew it, and I felt I could not be blamed for the way nature had arranged things. And, wiser than my own parents, I had never demanded anything from my son in return. I had brought him up to be a free and independent man and taught him from the first that he had certain rights as well as certain responsibilities to life, himself, and his fellow man. But I knew that he would come to me to make extravagant demands stretching back to infinity, although his claims on me ceased when he was fifteen. And he would grin and sneer when I spoke of his responsibilities, I knew that too—from my own experience.

If it was only a question of money, I wouldn't mind. But he would make demands on my person, even though he despised my company. He would lay claim on the apartment, which wasn't mine, my friends, whom I missed, my relatives, whom he thought I possessed, my name, with which to establish his credit.

I knew he would find me boring and that he would bring home ideas from a strange land with an entirely different outlook, with different manners, and attitudes; that he would treat me like an old fossil who didn't understand anything at all—since I was neither an engineer nor an electrician.

And what about his character and his propensities? How had they developed during these years? Experience has indeed taught me that one remains throughout life pretty much the same as one was born. No matter how he was rigged up, every human being that I had observed sailing through life from childhood on was as a rule still the same man at fifty, with a very few changes. It's true that many of them had suppressed some of their more glaring faults, unsuitable for social life; some had acquired a polish that

concealed their worst side; but at bottom they were the same
as they had been. In the case of the exceptions, certain traits
had grown and spread, sometimes moving from virtue into
vice. I remember one fellow whose firmness and tenacity
had turned into stubbornness, whose sense of order had
hardened into pedantry, whose thriftiness had taken root as
stinginess, whose love for civilized men had been converted
into hatred of the uncivilized. But I also remembered a man
whose bigotry had been slowly distilled into piety, whose
hate had turned to forbearance, and whose obstinacy had become firmness and strength. . . .

After brooding for a while, I went out for my morning
stroll, not in order to put aside painful thoughts but to face
them and to accommodate myself to the inevitable. I considered every possible course that the meeting with my son
might take. But when I came to the questions about what
had happened from the time of our separation until now, I
trembled and wanted to turn tail and run away. However,
experience had also taught me that one's back is the most
vulnerable side and that the chest is protected with a shield
of bones, evidently meant for defense. So I decided to stand
my ground and bear the blows.

Steeling my nerves and emotions, and adopting the dry
and matter-of-fact attitude of a man of the world, I drew up
my program. I would find a room for him in a boarding-
house, after having bought him some clothes. Find out what
he wanted to be. Get him a job immediately. Above all,
treat him as a respectable stranger who would be kept at a
distance by the absence of any confidences on my part. To
protect myself against any invasion of my privacy I would
pretend that the past didn't exist. I wouldn't give him any
advice, and I'd leave him completely free to do as he
pleased—he certainly wouldn't be likely to take my advice
anyway.

Done! And done with!

My mind made up, I headed back home. Yet I was fully aware that a change had taken place in my life, a change so radical that the streets, the country, and the town took on a different appearance for me. When I got halfway across the bridge and was looking up the avenue, the shape of a young man came within range of my vision. I shall never forget that moment. He was tall and gangling, walking hesitantly as if looking or waiting for something. I saw him stare at me. Just as he seemed to recognize me, a shiver coursed through his body, and then I saw how he pulled himself together, stood up straight, and crossed the avenue, headed straight for me. I grouped my forces for defense, heard myself clear my throat to summon up a light, pleasant tone of voice in which to say, "Hello, my boy!"

Now we were only a stone's throw from each other, I saw how *déclassé* he looked. Just what I was most afraid of: he had come down in the world. The hat on his head wasn't his: it didn't fit him. His trousers hung loosely: the baggy knees were too low. His whole appearance was shabby and out-at-elbow. Decay and corruption inside and out. Like a waiter out of a job. Now I could make out his face, thin and unpleasantly bony. And I could see his eyes, large blue eyes, in sunken blue-white sockets. It was he!

This down-and-out, up-and-growing boy had once been my little angel, whose very smile could make me throw out the ape theory and the origin of the species, who used to be dressed like a little prince and who once did in fact play with a real little princess down in Germany. . . .

Like a sharp blow I felt the whole rottenness of life. But without a vestige of self-reproach, for it was not I who had abandoned him.

We were only a few steps apart!—A doubt sprang up.

Was it he? And in the same second I decided to pass by leaving it up to him to give a sign of recognition.

One. Two! Three!!—

He went past!

Was it he, or wasn't it? I asked myself as I headed for home, certain that he would show up no matter what the circumstances.

Safe at home, I called in the maid to get more information from her and especially to find out if the man she had seen could have been the one I had passed. But it was impossible to settle the matter, and I was kept in suspense all morning. At one moment I would be hoping that he would come right away and put an end to the affair. The next moment I thought the situation had been so completely exhausted that nothing more could happen.

Lunch was over. The afternoon passed. And as it did, I got a new slant on the matter that made it even worse. He had assumed that I didn't want to say hello to him, that was it! I had frightened him and he had crawled away like a dog—was wandering dazedly in a bewildering town in a strange country—had taken up with bad company—perhaps fallen into despair. Where and how could I find him now? The police!

That's how my thoughts went round and round torturing me. I don't know why, since it was not I who had been in charge of his bringing-up. And I felt as if an evil power had forced me into this situation to put the blame on me.

Evening finally came. Then the maid entered with a calling card—on which was printed—the name of—my nephew!

When I was wrapped in my solitude again, I felt relieved that the anxious moments I had gone through had resolved themselves into projections of my imagination, which for me had had the same effect as the real thing. Still, these imaginings of mine had forced themselves upon me so importunately and so irresistibly that I felt there must have been some solid reason for their existence. Perhaps, I said to myself, perhaps my son in a faraway land was a prey to similar sensations. Perhaps he was in need, longed for me, "saw" me on some street just as I had "seen" him, and was torn by the same doubts. . . .

With that, I stopped worrying that particular bone and buried the incident away among other experiences I had had. But I didn't write it off as some kind of joke. Not at all. I kept it as a precious memory.

Alone

W. C. Fields

To Hattie Fields

Bushwick Theatre
Thursday May, 1915

Dear Hattie—
With reference to your letter of Monday, I do not feel offended with my son or his actions. He did not take his wheel and run away, it was you who grabbed his wheel and forced him to do what he did. You have him so scared that he is afraid to even think without consulting you first. This state of frightened obedience is only accomplished by unkind treatment.

You must consider me an awful dullard if you think I can't see what is going on. What is an enigma to me is, what you think you will gain by your strange behavior.

I was only fooling with son about carrying the wheel up-stairs, and had you stopped to think you would have known it. The other day you went to the dentist and left orders for son to remain indoors, strict orders were left that he must not go out with me; you should teach him to respect me as he does you, and he should be taught that my permission means the same thing to him as yours. But please understand this—I am not coming to you and ask your kind permission to take my son to a ball game, or a ride in a motor, and I'm not going to stand your abuse before a lot of stupid people with flapping ears. When son is older he will understand; but it is useless for me to talk seriously to him now, for he has been punished until you have his very heart and soul in your hands through fear. If I ask him a question he looks at you for his cue as to his answer. You have him frightened of me by your imaginary tales, which haven't the slightest foundation, of me stealing him. Son has no desire to please me, and he only thinks of me as he does of the bad man that steals little boys. You manufacture a lot of father and child stories which any fool can see through. I don't blame son, and please get this into your brain—I love him irrespective of what you have taught him to believe I am.

Please don't keep him in to wait for me or give him speeches or letters to write to me. When he is old enough to really know things as they are, then, I shall want to see him and talk. You are making him deceitful and dull by your primitive ignorant methods. And if I can get a line on your methods of punishment, let me inform you that you will not relish the stand I take in the matter. You are wholly to blame, my son has nothing to do in this matter. You are indeed a cowardly woman to try and shift the blame on his shoulders.

Most sincerely
W. C. Fields

To CLAUDE FIELDS

New York
Thursday June 1, 1915

Dear Son—
Unfortunately I did not receive your kind invitation to your teachers' Musicale until Monday or I should have attended same. However I did appreciate your thoughtfulness and I hope you will let me know when next you appear. Whenever you chance to get in N.Y. alone and have a wish to see me would be more than pleased to see you.

Father

W. C. Fields By Himself

Henry De Montherlant

Man strives, and makes it a point of honor, to go against nature and reason. The male human being is designed for short and numerous love-affairs: he is subject to marriage, which calls for fidelity to a single love. The child, if he follows his natural instincts, despises his parents and takes no interest in them, but he is required to respect, love, and support them, as well as to sacrifice himself for them, if need be, for half a century. From the age of twelve the adolescent feels the call of the flesh, but he is allowed no means of responding before, say, the age of eighteen. At a certain age every girl ought to become a woman. If she sees to it herself without benefit of marriage lines, the finger of scorn is pointed at her. Homosexuality is part and parcel of nature, but it is treated as a vice or an illness, and may lead to prison or the stake. These are only a few instances. We can add religions, which are all founded on unnatural or unreasonable premises. We can also add political and social idealogies, which are, in two cases out of three, crazy, and always pregnant with catastrophe, since common sense gets its own back, when it has been outraged for too long. It is hardly surprising that in these conditions humanity should always be involved in suffering. We are born under a layer of superstition and false ideas; we grow up under it, go on living under it, and say to ourselves that we shall die under it, without ever, *for one single day in our lives,* having lived otherwise than in subjection to the ideas of idiots and the customs of savages, which we cannot infringe or even denounce without danger to ourselves. Into this environment we throw our children, who are defenseless or have defenses as dangerous for them as the evils of the system. We say that life has always been like this and always will be, over the whole surface of the earth. We try to smile and bear things philosophically, but remain deeply impressed.

The Notebooks

Edward Weston

December 6, 1925

"While the cat's away the mice will play"—only I should not indicate Tina as a "cat"—not in the shrewish usage of the word. Nevertheless the "fiesta" of yesterday would not have been possible had she not been away posing for Diego.

Brett and X. and I sat down to the table for dinner together. There was a half keg of beer which we tapped—with unforseen consequences, for not always from a few glasses of beer does one attain such hilarity. But it was a day forecast for inebriety, Bacchus in the ascendancy, and we honored him well! First X.'s eyes began to roll heavenward, then Brett suddenly turned his beer upon the bread and with a gesture quite as bombastic as a matador tossing his velvet hat, let fly the empty glass over his shoulder.

There was no work that afternoon, but singing, dancing, grandiloquent words and nonsense. Brett was a burlesque worth a price of admission: we wept from laughter.

Yet how I would be criticized, berated for allowing my son to so shame himself—even taking part in his downfall!

But I know Brett! So full to overflowing with life! I did not scold him when an "obscene" drawing from his pen was turned over to me by his teacher; I put it in the waste-basket with a chuckle. He could be ruined by a tight rein or a long face. He needs to explode naturally. He is bound to adventure much, to experience much. He is open-faced, laughter-loving, amenable to suggestion. I hope to help him when he stumbles or give him a gentle kick in the right direction—if I am able to decide which is right, at the time!

I was forced to make a hasty decision when we first arrived. An obvious homosexual made pressing overtures to Brett. And what was I to do, with a personal distaste, but no moral objections? If a woman of the right kind had desired him, I would have aided the affair, but to have Brett at thirteen thrown into a perverse relation, unformed in tendencies as he is, perhaps to be physically drained by this very sophisticated older man, I could not give in to. So the person suddenly disappeared from his life. With my attitude toward so-called perversions, which is certainly understanding and tolerant, I retained some feeling of guilt over what I had done, for the man was infatuated, and wealthy, would have done for him in ways that I cannot. Well, in three years, I shall not stand in the way of any experience which opportunity may afford him.

The Daybooks

Georges Simenon

Sunday January 8, 1961

I have always had a horror of the father image and mother image as they have a tendency to be created in families. I do not want my children to have a monolithic memory of me, or to attribute to me qualities that I do not have. On the contrary, I would like them to know the vulnerable man that I am, as vulnerable as they and perhaps more so.

That's the point from which I took off last night in bed, and my thought followed parallel lines: one about faults and one about risks. I have not made a balance. I fell asleep before coming to a conclusion, but I was no less frightened by what I discovered.

Suddenly, I blamed myself for having been so apprehensive about Marc when he was fourteen or fifteen years old—and even now that he is married and an adult. I will be just as apprehensive about Johnny when he reaches the age of imprudence, more still, no doubt, about Marie-Jo. Then, if I live that long, it will be Pierre's turn.

However, am I not the one for whom someone should have been afraid? I've told in *Pedigree,* more or less romanticizing them, but remaining faithful basically, about certain of my experiences from before the age of sixteen.

Haven't I, later on, and even not so long ago, nearly foundered a hundred times? And by that word I mean every conceivable catastrophe imaginable.

Could I have become a criminal? I don't know. I have studied criminology a great deal, not only at the time when I was writing only Maigrets, but especially during these last years. One of the branches least known to the general public is victimology, that is to say the responsibility of the victim in almost seventy percent of crimes. Oh yes, I've deserved to be a victim a hundred times and I realize that I would have borne a large part of the responsibility.

But I have never been conscious of it. I am not particularly brave. I have a certain mistrust for physical bravery and, for example, I have a horror of getting involved in a scuffle, a scrap, even in a mob scene. I also have had a horror of brutality, of anything that injures the flesh, of what uselessly does harm.

How to explain my behavior, then? By a sort of innocence, of openness? I don't think so. More by a certain feeling that I am on an equal footing with men, whoever they are.

It is with the other column, of faults, that I want to start, since I began with my children.

Though, at the time of the *Gazette de Liège,* when I was sixteen and a half to nineteen years old, I had two women available to me each day, almost every day, at one moment or another, I would be like a dog in rut.

An example. A case that comes back to me. In Belgium at that time, as in Amsterdam to this day, there were strange houses: a dimly lit ground floor; half-open curtains behind which could be seen one or two women knitting or reading, raising their heads when they heard the step of a passerby.

These houses, the same as in Amsterdam, were not necessarily in deserted or disreputable streets. There was one on the Boulevard de la Constitution just opposite the largest secondary school, and I had to pass in front of it each time I came back from the center of town through the Passerelle.

I was passing this way one night at about ten o'clock. I did not see the familiar silhouette, but a splendid Negress, and suddenly I felt that it was absolutely necessary for me to enter and make love with her. I had never known a Negress.

I had only a small sum in my pocket. I hesitated. My father was already sick, dying. A little while before, he had given me his watch, a silver watch with the arms of Belgium on it, which he had won in a shooting match, for my father was an enthusiastic marksman (I still have three silver plates engraved with the same arms, won in the same way).

Shamefacedly, I paid with the watch, and it was one of the acts that I regret most, not for moral reasons, but because it would mean so much to me to have this souvenir of my father, who was to die a year later. At home, I was obliged to lie about it. Then to declare the loss of the watch to the police. And if it had been found it might have had far-reaching consequences.

It is only a small example. At the same time, I spent evening after evening all by myself in the most disreputable streets, where I risked being beaten up at every corner.

Later I did the same, almost all through my life, more out of curiosity than desire. When I was living on the Place des Vosges, as for instance around 1923-1924, the Rue de Lappe and other streets around the Bastille were not tourist attractions the way they are today.

In the dance halls they would pull a knife for a Yes or a No, and I have seen a woman's throat cut beside me in a bar.

At that time, my first wife was a painter and, to find models for her, I would go there to look for them, late at night. It was a curious world and one found girls there who had arrived in Paris from Brittany or Normandy only two months ago and were already on the streets.

I took them home. Men would follow me from a distance. Some of them threatened me.

During the same period I spent nights wandering, unarmed, on the old defense works which still existed, near La Villette, on the Rue de Flandre, and the neighborhood of the Canal Saint-Martin held no secrets for me.

I did the same thing in Montmartre and in the twentieth arrondissement and I admit that to my human curiosity was almost always added a certain sexual excitement. I have made love in the streets and the passageways where the un-expected arrival of a policeman could have changed my future.

Much later, in Cairo, I was wandering alone at night (with a revolver in my pocket) in the red-light district, which was as big as a Paris arrondissement, and I used to follow women through the alleys to houses that I could never have found by myself.

The same at Aswan, even in Panama, in Guayaquil, and almost all over the world.

I never had the sense of running risks. It is only now, retrospectively, that I feel fear.

As I feel it in the parallel area of which I have spoken. In Liège, at the *Gazette,* I already had the habit of borrowing two or three months' salary from the cashier and I wonder still how, finally, I managed to repay it.

In Paris I did the same thing, except that I had no salary. Having earned by a miracle, the day before the rent was due, the sum required to pay it, I would spend it in a night club. I earned money fast enough, with stories and popular novels, but even when the Maigrets brought me much more, when I had several houses at once, a car, a chauffeur, etc., I was only working to pay off debts.

"It's the only way to make myself work," I used to say.

Which was false, since I still have a middle-class soul and when I go several days without working I feel full of guilt, like a man who does not deserve the bread he eats.

I've owed money all over town. And I've seen too many cases where that has led to serious compromises.

Why did I have the luck to get out of it?

If I saw one of my children acting that way, I would shudder.

Sometimes when it seemed to be provoking fate, it appeared to me a natural act. I've mentioned my affair with a married woman. It has happened that I took her in her own house when her husband, busy in a neighboring room, was talking to us through the half-open door.

Isn't that a case where if there had been a tragedy I would really have been the one responsible?

The severity of American laws in sexual matters is well known. Well aware of it, one evening when I was feeling good I crossed the center of the city from east to west through the most brightly lit, the busiest streets and avenues, in a taxi with a woman, the two of us in a position ... which, aside from any scandal, would have got us at least five years in prison and expulsion from the country afterward.

Again, I did not mean it as a challenge. I am, by nature, a man who respects rules. If I do not believe in them, I pretend that they must be followed out of respect for others. And in forty years' driving I have never had a single ticket, not even for parking my car illegally.

I believe that I am a decent man, anyway in the sense that I give to that word. I have become more and more scrupulous in my own affairs and I am rarely satisfied with myself.

That is the reason why there are few years in my life which I can imagine reliving in a carefree way. I always feel uneasy in remembering myself as I was thirty, twenty years ago. Will I someday be ashamed of myself today?

When I sent out my first press copies (*Le Pendu de Saint-Pholien* and *M. Gallet, décédé*) I was foolishly proud enough to sign those for the greatest writers and critics with only a ridiculous and cocky "Cordially," as if from one day to the next I had become their equal.

I've spoken of my suits cut in London, of the pearl in my necktie, of the apartment done by a "decorator de luxe" on the Boulevard Richard-Wallace.

How, in spite of all that, did I manage to find my way? And how many times, with the slightest slip, could it have been a catastrophe?

All the same I have achieved a certain balance, at least I don't feel too ashamed of myself, I'm able, most often, to look myself in the face.

Then I think of others, some of them for a time my friends, my colleagues, or my relatives, who ended badly.

The responsibility of parents we talk so much about to-day! Would my parents have been responsible if something bad had happened to me? God knows they took their roles seriously, following to the letter the precepts of morality and religion.

Me, I don't presume any right to interfere, except to speak gently to them, and, as I do to Johnny, to tell them things of the sort I tell here.

I hope there won't be other details coming back to me, as with the preceding entry. There are hundreds, buried in my memory; I don't want to tell them, or to remember them. Not out of shame or embarrassment, but because they are without interest and this would take on the tenor of a pose.

Isn't it simpler to say, without searching further:

"I'm only a man."

Either my children will understand or they will not. I hope they understand, although that assumes certain risks. I mean that they must run some risks.

Amen!

When I Was Old

F. Scott Fitzgerald

To Frances Scott Fitzgerald

Metro-Goldwyn-Mayer Corporation
Culver City, California
July 7, 1938

Dearest Scottie:

I don't think I will be writing letters many more years and I wish you would read this letter twice—bitter as it may seem. You will reject it now, but at a later period some of it may come back to you as truth. When I'm talking to you, you think of me as an older person, an "authority," and when I speak of my own youth what I say becomes unreal to you— for the young can't believe in the youth of their fathers. But perhaps this little bit will be understandable if I put it in writing.

When I was your age I lived with a great dream. The dream grew and I learned how to speak of it and make people listen. Then the dream divided one day when I decided to marry your mother after all, even though I knew she was spoiled and meant no good to me. I was sorry immediately I had married her but, being patient in those days, made the best of it and got to love her in another way. You came along and for a long time we made quite a lot of happiness out of our lives. But I was a man divided—she wanted me to work too much for *her* and not enough for my dream. She realized too late that work was dignity, and the only dignity, and tried to atone for it by working herself, but it was too late and she broke and is broken forever.

It was too late also for me to recoup the damage—I had spent most of my resources, spiritual and material, on her, but I struggled on for five years till my health collapsed, and all I cared about was drink and forgetting.

The mistake I made was in marrying her. We belonged to different worlds—she might have been happy with a kind simple man in a southern garden. She didn't have the strength for the big stage—sometimes she pretended, and pretended beautifully, but she didn't have it. She was soft when she should have been hard, and hard when she should have been yielding. She never knew how to use her energy—she's passed that failing on to you.

For a long time I hated *her* mother for giving her nothing in the line of good habit—nothing but "getting by" and conceit. I never wanted to see again in this world women who were brought up as idlers. And one of my chief desires in life was to keep you from being that kind of person, one who brings ruin to themselves and others. When you began to show disturbing signs at about fourteen, I comforted myself with the idea that you were too precocious socially and a strict school would fix things. But sometimes I think that idlers seem to be a special class for whom nothing can be planned, plead as one will with them—their only contribution to the human family is to warm a seat at the common table.

My reforming days are over, and if you are that way I don't want to change you. But I don't want to be upset by idlers inside my family or out. I want my energies and my earnings for people who talk my language.

I have begun to fear that you don't. You don't realize that what I am doing here is the last tired effort of a man who once did something finer and better. There is not enough energy, or call it money, to carry anyone who is dead weight and I am angry and resentful in my soul when I feel that I am doing this. People like————and your mother must be carried because their illness makes them useless. But it is a different story that *you* have spent two years doing no useful work at all, improving neither your body nor your mind, but only writing reams and reams of dreary letters to dreary people, with no possible object except obtaining invitations which you could not accept. Those letters go on, even in your sleep, so that I know your whole trip now is one long waiting for the post. It is like an old gossip who cannot still her tongue.

You have reached the age when one is of interest to an adult only insofar as one seems to have a future. The mind of a little child is fascinating, for it looks on old things with new eyes—but at about twelve this changes. The adolescent offers nothing, can do nothing, say nothing that the adult cannot do better. Living with you in Baltimore (and you have told Harold that I alternated between strictness and neglect, by which I suppose you mean the times I was so inconsiderate as to have T.B., or to retire into myself to write, for I had little social life apart from you) represented a rather too domestic duty forced on me by your mother's illness. But I endured your Top Hats and Telephones until the day you snubbed me at dancing school, less willingly after that. . . .

To sum up: What you have done to please me or make me proud is practically negligible since the time you made yourself a good diver at camp (and now you are softer than you have ever been). In your career as a "wild society girl," vintage of 1925, I'm not interested. I don't want any of it— it would bore me, like dining with the Ritz Brothers. When I do not feel you are "going somewhere," your company tends to depress me for the silly waste and triviality involved. On the other hand, when occasionally I see signs of life and intention in you, there is no company in the world I prefer. For there is no doubt that you have something in your belly, some real gusto for life—a real dream of your own—and my idea was to wed it to something solid before it was too late—as it was too late for your mother to learn anything when she got around to it. Once when you spoke French as a child it was enchanting with your odd bits of knowledge—now your conversation is as commonplace as if you'd spent the last two years in the Corn Hollow High School—what you saw in *Life* and read in *Sexy Romances*.

I shall come East in September to meet your boat—but this letter is a declaration that I am no longer interested in your promissory notes but only in what I see. I love you always but I am only interested by people who think and work as I do and it isn't likely that *I* shall change at my age. Whether you will—or want to—remains to be seen.

Daddy

P.S. If you keep the diary, please don't let it be the dry stuff I could buy in a ten-franc guide book. I'm not interested in dates and places, even the Battle of New Orleans, unless you have some unusual reaction to them. Don't try to be witty in the writing, unless it's natural—just true and real.
P.P.S. Will you please read this letter a second time? I wrote it over twice.

The Letters of F. Scott Fitzgerald

William Carlos Williams

To William Eric Williams

Sept. 25, 1942

Dear Bill:
Your letters recently have shown me the changes that are taking place in you, a maturity which I want to salute and acknowledge. Generally speaking, your present experience has been of decided benefit, something you could not achieve, at least not so quickly, in any other way. Part of it has been the enforced separation from any protecting influence I may still have had on you, a very good thing. What you're facing is your world, a world in which I haven't the slightest part. We are now two individuals, two men, closely bound by mutual beliefs and interests but completely independent as to the future. Strangely enough, this separation has brought me much closer to you. I'm glad that early phase is at an end.

That relationship between father and son is one of the toughest things in the world to break down. It seems so natural and it is natural—in fact it's inevitable—but it separates as much as it joins. A man wants to protect his son, wants to teach him the things he, the father, has learned or thinks he has learned. But it's exactly that which a child resents. He wants to know but he wants to know on his own—and the longer the paternal influence lasts the harder it is to break down and the more two individuals who should have much in common are pushed apart. Only a sudden enforced break can get through that one.

But I've sweated over wanting to do and say the right thing concerning you boys. Certain things stick in my mind—I just didn't do the right thing and I suffered for it. Once when you were a little kid some question of veracity came up between you and Elsie, that goofy girl we had here. I should have known that you were just a baby but I lost my temper, insisting one of you was lying when I should have known, if I had thought for a moment, that it wasn't you.

Or if it was, then what the hell anyway? It might have been from fear—no doubt of me. Then one day at the close of Watty's camp in Maine you were in some sort of a canoe race and were about to win when someone quite unfairly cut you out and you cried. I like a God-damned fool laughed at you. Why? Just to hide my own embarrassment. You looked at me and said, "It was my only chance to win anything!" I tell you that hurt. I've never forgotten it. Such are a father's inner regrets. Stupid enough. And what in the hell is a parent to do when an older child is tormented by a younger child, finally smears his younger tormentor and then comes up for punishment? I've never solved that one. I've done many more seriously stupid things than those mentioned— but I wanted so hard to give you the best.

On the other hand, when you say you've got so much more in the bank than some of the men you have to deal with, I feel that what we did for you wasn't too bad. The same for what you say about the kitten and the spiders. That you can get the good out of such trivia is a tribute to your mind which I have always respected and which I'm glad to see maintaining itself with distinction in the situation in which you are placed. I don't know what kind of a father I was but in things like that at least something "took" of what I intended and that it wasn't all beside the point.

You say you'd like to see my book of poems. What the hell? Let 'em go. They are things I wrote because to maintain myself in a world much of which I didn't love I had to fight to keep myself as I wanted to be. The poems are me, in much of the faulty perspective in which I have existed in my own sight—and nothing to copy, not for anyone even so much as to admire. I have wanted to link myself up with a traditional art, to feel that I was developing individually it might be, but along with that, developing still in the true evolving tradition of the art. I wonder how much I have succeeded there. I haven't been recognized and I doubt that my technical influence is good or even adequate.

However, this is just one more instance of the benefits to be gained by breaking entirely with the father-son hook-up. It was logical for you not to have looked at my poems—or only casually to look at them. You had me in my own person too strongly before you to need that added emphasis. You did the right thing and I never cared a damn. Now, separated from me by distance and circumstance, it may after all be permissible for you to look at the poems. Not to do anything more than to enjoy them, man to man, if you can get any enjoyment out of them, I'll send them. I have a gold-edged copy reserved for you, one of the de luxe copies, but I'll not send that. Look, if you care to, at whatever I have done as if you had never known me. That's the only way for a father and son to behave toward each other after the son's majority has been reached. Then, if you still find something to cherish, it will be something worthwhile.

You in your recent letters have shown that you have a style of your own—another testimonial to your own character and a tribute to your parents for not trying, really, to press themselves upon you. You have an interesting prose style that everyone who reads your letters admires. It's really comical. Some say, "A chip off the old block;" others say, "He writes better than you do," and so it goes. You are entirely different from me in your approach, and yet we are alike in our interests. . . .

They finished insulating the attic today and are putting storm windows all along the front of the house. Better to be prepared for what may happen the coming winter.

Love,
DAD

The Selected Letters of William Carlos Williams

Dalton Trumbo

To CHRISTOPHER TRUMBO

Los Angeles, California
November 8, 1958

My dear son:
I have at hand your most recent letter addressed, I believe, both to your mother and to me. That portion which I assume was designed to capture my attention has. I refer to your addled account of an exchange between you and Mike [Butler] relative to mensal checks from home. You may be sure I shall give it much thought.

You also inform us you haven't made holiday travel reservations because you haven't the money to pay for them. Artful fellow! Do you truly think me so stupid as to send the fare directly to you, who'd only squander it in high living and end up stranded on Christmas Eve begging poor-man's pudding in some snow-swept Bowery breadline?

The procedure is this: go at once to an airline office and make round-trip reservations (not de luxe, not a milk-run either). Do it immediately, for the seasonal rush is already at hand. Notify me of the airline, flight number, date and hour of arrival, and within twenty-four hours a check made over to the airline will be delivered into your greedy fist. Take it to the seller and the deal is consummated without laying you open to temptation.

I am sending you two books I think appropriate for a young man spending five-sevenths of his time in the monkish precincts of John Jay Hall. The first is *Education of a Poker Player,* by Henry O. Yardley. Read it in secret, hide it whenever you leave quarters, and you'll be rewarded with many unfair but legal advantages over friend and enemy alike, not to mention that occasional acquaintance who has everything including money.

The second book I think you should share with your young companions. It is *Sex Without Guilt,* by a man who will take his place in history as the greatest humanitarian since Mahatma Gandhi—Albert Ellis, Ph.D. This good man has written what might be called a manual for masturbators. That is to say, in one slim volume he has clarified the basic theory of the thing, and then, in simple layman's language, got right down to rules and techniques. This in itself is a grand accomplishment; but what most compels my admiration is the zest, the sheer enthusiasm which Dr. Ellis has brought to his subject. The result (mailed in plain wrapper under separate cover) is one of those fortuitous events in which the right man collides with the right idea at precisely the right time. It makes a very big bang indeed.

It is Dr. Ellis's idea to spring masturbation from the bedroom's crepusculine gloom, where for endless generations it has lain a saprogenic curse on millions of little lechers, and turn it loose in the parlor where it rightfully belongs. This chap doesn't find anything wrong with it at all: indoors or out, he ranks it right up there with ping-pong, gin rummy, and "Maverick" as a time-honored, health-giving, red-blooded patriotic pastime.

What Ellis wants to do—and by gad he does it too!—is remove that gnawing sense of guilt so characteristic of the act, the awful tension of it, the leering, searing, sneering fear of it. (Oh Phalloform, dread Phallio— / Let never me deride / My onanistic, irresistic, post-pubescent bride!) Once all that unhealthy brooding is dissolved, nothing remains of a former vice but unadulterated fun. And that's what Ellis is after. He doesn't want American youth to go about guilt-twitching like a pack of inbred Chihuahuas for nothing more serious than a raging appetite for fescenninity. He doesn't want those golden hours of childhood festered over with concern about the imminent putrefaction of genitalia. He wants young people not to give a damn! He wants them to relax. He wants, in short, a world of *happy* masturbators.

This whole new approach—this fresh wind blowing under the sheets, so to speak—this large-hearted appeal for cheerful self-pollution, invokes perhaps a deeper response in my heart than in most. For I (sneaky, timorous, incontinent little beast with my Paphian obsessions) was never wholesomely at home with my penile problem, nor ever found real happiness in working it out—all because of that maggoty, mountainous pustule of needless guilt that throbbed like an abscess in my young boy's heart.

On warm summer nights while exuberant girl-hunting contemporaries scampered in and out of the brush beneath high western stars, I, dedicated fool, lay swooning in my bed with no companion save the lewd and smirking demons of my bottomless guilt. Cowering there in seminal darkness, liquescent with self-loathing, attentive only to the stealthy rise and Krafty-Ebbing of my dark scrotumnal blood, fearful as a lechwe yet firmer of purpose than any rutting buffalo, I celebrated the rites of Shuah's son with sullen resignation. Poor little chap on a summer's night, morosely masturbating. . . !

There *were* lads in Grand Junction, Colorado (most of whom became civil servants or evangelistic clergymen) who strode the sunlit streets of that never-to-be-forgotten town like fierce young gods, lean and supple, tall and strong, pace brisk, shoulders well thrust back, frank of face, forthright of smile, clear of eye, innocent of heart, clean of mind. But I was not one of them.

Oh no, not I. Not your poor father.

When I appeared in public, toad-blinking against the unwonted and revelatory blaze of day, I conveyed the immediate impression of ambulant filth—of obscenity, so to speak, in transit. I lurched through those years like some demented crab, shoulders at a goatish hunch, eyes a-scum with fantasies of defloration, my acneous skin (hot with crimson shames) exuding from every greasy pore that sour effluvia which marks imagined love. My sweaty nippers—ah, cursed, cursed paws!—I carried thrust to the very bottom of my trouser pockets, in which humid and forbidden depths they secretly envaginated that marvelous little pendant I knew must drop from its frazzled moorings the instant I withdrew my helping hands.

I turned thin and pale; my odor changed from sour to stercoraceous; reflexes vanished altogether; palpitations of the heart set in, accompanied by giddy spells and sudden faints. My left eye developed so fearsome a tic that its aftermath may be seen to this day in the crapulous squint with which you are perhaps far too familiar. My blood ceased to coagulate: for eleven months I went about completely swathed in bandages. Satyriasis, ever latent in my yielding genes, turned chronic and then acute: treatment consisted in the rapid alteration of ice packs with cauldrons of scalding water. I was placed on a diet of loblolly laced with seaweed extract.

It was this revolting dish even more than my rampageous libido that brought my nervous system to a state of utter dissolution. I would start up briskly at the slightest sound and begin to canter counterclockwise, and in ever widening circles, crepitating all the while like a Percheron at close trot (*you* know that horrid sound—thup-thup-thup-*thurp*-thup), and nickering suspiciously. I became so unhinged that the mere sight of a girl reduced me to mucilaginous pulp, identifiable as human only by a pair of inflamed eyes and a faint squinking sound that seemed to proceed from the hepatized heart of the mess. Ah, sweet suppurating soul of Satan, I thought I never *would* get adjusted!

Even now, more than three decades later (and I, as you know, a tower of moral strength, a civic leader, a respected—nay, beloved—community figure), even now when I forget a friend's name, or mislay my spectacles, or pause in mid-sentence idiocy (my thought having died twixt concept and delivery)—even now such lapses set a clammy chill upon my heart, while purulent memories of my secret shame incarnadine the sallow of these aging cheeks.

It's then, while panic tightens my sagging throat, that I whisper to myself: "It's true after all. It *does* make you crazy. It *does* cause the brain to soften. Why, oh why did I like it so much? Why didn't I stop while I was still ahead of the game? Was it only one time too many that caused this rush of premature senility? Or a dozen times? Or a thousand? Ah well—little good to know it now: the harm's done, the jig's up, you're thoroughly raddled, better you'd been born with handless stumps."

An instant later I blessedly recall the name, I find the spectacles, I complete the sentence—and the salacious ghoul of my sickened fantasies retreats once more into the shadows, not banished to be sure, but held off at least for a few more days or hours. I ask you, dear boy—if the mere memory of past guilt has such power to swoon my adult mind, can you imagine the effect upon a naturally depraved constitution of what then was *present* guilt?

I recall a certain chill winter night on which my father took me to one of those Calvinist fertility rites disguised as a father-and-son banquet. I was in no real shape to mingle with respectable society, being then at the dismal nadir of my lechery and much given to involuntary belching, squirching, belly-rumbling, wind-breaking, nasal pearl-diving and the like. The banquet consisted of dead fish, stale bread, soft-boiled potatoes and leather-bottomed pie.

Master of the revels was an acrid old goat named Horace T. McGuinness who kept a doxy, engaged in brutish orgies, and reserved his public hours for denunciation of everything dear to a little boy's heart. This excrementitious old fornicator was greatly venerated in our town, and much in demand for such festivities as that which I describe.

He buttoned his protruberant vest on discs of decayed egg yolk and brayed like Balaam's ass voiding hot barbed-wire. His nostrils extruded threads of ductile mucus which streamed downward in gay opalescent loops to a scraggle of brush which conccaled practically all of that moist, pink, vulviform cave of the winds that served him as a mouth. When speaking—and he always spoke—he displayed the carious ruin of what in his youth had been a gaggle of strong yellow teeth. With every phrase he emitted dense clouds of sewer gas, while his harsher consonants shot forth such poisonous showers of spittle that full-grown bull blow-flies fell stunned to the tablecloth the instant they flew in range.

The old debauchee opened his discourse with a series of blasphemous demands that the Almighty agree with his ghastly notions and make our young minds (his whole talk was addressed to us youthlets, never to pa) receptive to the bilge he proposed to pump into them. Then he got down to the meat of the program which, to no one's surprise, was girls. When you go out with a young lady, he slavered, you go out with your own sister. As you treat her, so will your sister be treated. It followed that you must not think of it in relation to her, you must not suggest it to her, and certainly you must not do it to her. If you did, you were a black-guard, a degenerate, a runnion, a cullion, and a diddle-cove.

To this day I don't know why that crazed old rake's clap-per-claw affected me as it did. I was a menace only to my-self. For all the harm I was able to do girls, or they me, their whole concupiscible tribe had just as well been my sisters. On the other hand, it seemed plain to me that if one day I did burst upon the world as the hymeneal Genghis Khan of my dreams, I'd be in for an extremely incestuous time of it.

Several winters later, when my headmaster at Mc-Teague's Chicago Academy for Distraught Boys, enraged by the nocturnal racket of my solitary revels, clapped hands on me and dragged my quaking hulk to a lupanar much favored by the faculty, I stood spellbound and terrified as the grisettes paraded for my selection. The vile, incestuous objurgations of old Reek-mouth still fevered my brain. These girls were my sisters—the tall one over there, and the tiny one with the dazzling blue curls, and that charming creature with the wise clitorial wink (the first I'd seen to that time)—all of them sisters! How could I even *think* of—

Piteously I tried to explain the taboo that held me apart from this naked herd of mooing female relatives. Headmaster (he was a good-hearted man but quick with his right) cuffed me about for something under an hour. Toward the end of the beating I was enabled to see the thing from head-master's point of view rather than that of old Stench-tooth. I began to regard the lovely denizens of that establishment with rising interest. My heart grew light. My temples ceased to throb. My eyes began to glitter brilliantly. I found myself laughing, as Columbus must have laughed when first he spied the shimmered green of Hispaniola.

Ah-ha, my darlings—no sisters ye nor brother I, blessed be the sapient gods! (Descend, Murgatoyd!) Flee for your lives, thou still unravished brides of quietness—thou foster children of slow time! (Down, slavering monster!) Weep, ye Sabine maidens—cringe, ye moaning seraphim! (*Abajo,*

little Sir M.!) That which ye greatly feared has come upon
you! The stuprator is at hand! *Estoy aqui! Me voici! Ad-
sum!*

I learned, so to speak, the hard way. (Ah, Chicago, Chicago—stud-barn of the western world!) Not once in those
three wild aphrodisiacal weeks did headmaster or I set foot
outside that house of ecstasy. We ordered the telephone dis-
connected, and had our meals sent in piping hot from the
Pump Room. I, who had barely matriculated, qualified for
graduate work in three fiery days. When finally we returned
to the vertical world (headmaster, being without tenure,
lost his appointment at the Academy, while I, poor lad, was
sent down for simple venery) I was a new boy: snake-lean,
rock-hard and ferociously determined that earth herself
should reel beneath the measured thunder of my copu-
lations. That, however, is a different story to be reserved for
later times and nicer problems. Returning now to that atro-
cious hugger-mugger which set me thus to dreaming:—

Having deranged our building psyches with this sister
business, old Pus-head passed on to the subject of procreation—or, more precisely, non-procreation. In unbelievable detail he shambled through the story of Judah, son of
Jacob, son of Abraham (nee Abram), son of Terah, son of
Nahor, son of Serug, son of Reu, son of Peleg, son of Eber,
son of Salah, son of Axpharaxed, son of Enoch, son of Jared,
son of Mahalalcel, son of Cainan, son of Enos, son of Seth,
who was born to Adam and Eve in their autumnal years.

Now to the story. Judah had three sons improbably
named Er, Onan, and Chezib. Er caroused so heroically that
"the Lord slew him," making his wife Tamar a widow.
Judah thereupon commanded his second son, this Onan
chap, to marry his brother's relict and have children by her.
Onan yielded to the first command and moved in with the
girl (note how that sister theme creeps in again?), but he

flatly refused stud service, devising instead an escape route that ensured his memory and made his name practically a household word to this day. He spilled his seed out onto the ground. (Hence onanism, onanistic, and the like, for you know what).

By closing my mind and abandoning all sanity I can still hear that demented old reprobate howling his bill of particulars against poor Onan, shaking his fist at us all the while and sweating like a diseased stoat. "He wasted his seed! Oh monstrous, shameful, nameless act—he spilled it right out into the ground! *All* of it! Yes sir, every last drabble of it! And this *displeased* the Lord and the Lord *slew* him!" This ringing period he concluded with a gust of spittle so noxious that a waitress, caught in its mere fallout, sank fainting to the floor beneath a tray of priceless cut-glass fingerbowls.

Without even a sideglance at his gasping victim, old Spruetongue rushed on to a warning against the most dangerous period of a boy's day, which he leeringly defined as those last ten minutes before the coming of blessed sleep. This period, he rasped, was Onan's hour, that dread time of temptation which separated the men from boys. He commanded us, on pain of Onan's fate, as we loved God, loathed sin, and cherished our immortal souls, thenceforth to sleep with our hands outside the covers "until, in the unpolluted glory of young manhood, that chaste girl of your dreams appears on the transept of God's heaven to give you, through holy matrimony, that love which no man deserves and all desire." Whereupon we were ordered to rise en masse, lift high our swearing arms ("All the perfumes of Arabia will not sweeten *this* little hand!") and take the pledge.

Well. You can imagine how I felt, poor shuddering pertinacious masturbating little dolt! My young companions, their faces shining with devotion, rose like eager chipmunks to recite that preposterous oath as solemnly as if it were a Te Deum. I felt compelled to join them, my skin flushing beet-red beneath a field of yellow pimples then riotously in bloom from the base of my throat to the farthest border of my scaly scalp. Seated once more, I vomited softly into a cannister of caramels my father took with him wherever he went. As for father—from that time forward a murk, a dark estrangement rose between us. How could I, degraded sperm-wasting voluptuary that I was, ever again look squarely into the calm serenity of his grave sperm-thrifty eyes? I couldn't and never did. For us, that moment was the end.

When I went to bed that night the thermometer shivered at twenty-three degrees below zero. I slept alone in public, so to speak, on an open porch with only a dismal flap of canvas to separate my quarters from those glacial winter winds that howled for three straight months each year on the other side of it. Shuddering like a greyhound bitch in heat, I burrowed beneath mounded covers. My congealing breath formed a beard of frost on the quilt beneath my chin. My pale hands, like twin sacrificial lambs, lay freezing outside the covers. It made no sense at all to me, yet I'd been gulled into taking their peccant oath, and now in my own dim-witted fashion I proposed to keep it. It was the witching hour.

While I lay there pondering Onan's fate, nerves twitching, gonaducts aflame, ten chilly digits convulsively plucking at my counterpane, I tried to divert my tumescent thoughts from their obsession. I thought on heroes and their heroism: on Perseus, Jason, Odysseus, Achilles—and it was on Achilles that I paused, evaluating again that dip in the Styx with only his left heel exposed. It occurred to me that the tragedy of his death stemmed directly from the triviality of the wound that brought him low.

At this point my incomparable flair for nastiness took charge. What would have happened, I asked myself, if Thetis had held the little tyke by his tippet instead of his heel? Since everyone understands there's utterly no point in living once your tassel's been shot off, all tears and sympathy would have been focused on that gory dopple, reducing his subsequent death to mere blessed anti-climax. The whole point of the yarn, it seemed to me, would have been changed, and for the better. Thus musing, I fell asleep. The next morning I was rushed off whooping to the hospital, brought low with quick pneumonia and seven frostbit claws. So much then, for keeping pledges.

There are still other stories I could tell you—tales of those corybantic pears that would inflame your bowels and thin your heart's young blood. They would, however, be merely cumulative: if my point isn't made by now it never will be. Yet the more I think on it the more positive I become that you will never truly be able to comprehend in all its horror that interminably sustained convulsion which was your father's youth. It's only reasonable that this should be so, since you've had so many advantages that were denied to me. To name but three of them—a private room, a mastur-bating father, and Albert Ellis, Ph.D.

Neither, I think, will you ever be able to understand that flood of savage joy which filled my heart on first read-ing *Sex Without Guilt*. I felt, with Keats, like "some watcher of the night skies. When a new planet swims into his ken." Having passed through such flaming pubic hells as would altogether carbonize a weaker lad, can anyone hope to imagine the wild surmise that stunned my soul on discov-ering that I'd been right all along? That all my Brob-dingnagian juvenile debaucheries had been as innocent as so many taffy-pulls? That I was, in truth, an example and a martyr for all who'd gone before me and for endless millions still to come?

For that's what it amounts to, son. I carried the ball for all of us, and carried it farther than anyone had a right to expect. I was the Prometheus of my secret tribe—a penile virtuoso, a gonadic prodigy, a spermatiferous thunderbolt; in fine, a masturbator's masturbator. In that sad hour when you lay me away, remember with awe what I did, and carve those words in ageless granite above my resting place, that your sons and your sons' sons may not forget the blood of champions coursing through their veins.

I am still, as you may suspect, somewhat distraught from reliving for your instruction the calamitous tale of my youth. That it's been painful I can't deny, but what is pain compared to the immeasurable satisfaction of being a proper dad to you? I am also, perhaps, still too deeply under the literary and erotic spell of *Lolita,* which I've read four straight times in four straight days. If you don't know the book, you must get it at once. This chap Nabokov, like Dr. Ellis, is a way-shower, one of those spirits who understands that everything under the sun has its time and place and joy in an ordered world.

His description of a two-year Saturnalia between an aging pervert and a twelve-year-old female (a "nymphet," as Nabokov so charmingly describes young girls in the immediate stages of pre- and post-pubescence) is something to make your mouth water. Now that *Lolita* has brought nymphetophilia into the world of fashion and made it, thank God, as respectable as ornithology, I'm willing to place it on record that my own sexual taste in young girls runs strongly to larvines, beside whom your average nymphet seems gross and dissolute. A larvine begins to glow at five-and-a-half and generally is quite hagged out before her eighth birthday. Perhaps it's the very brevity of her flower that so attracts me. The man fortunate enough to catch one of these delightful creatures at the very peak of larvineal bloom—provided, of course, no one catches *him*—will be rewarded indescribably.

A pair of them approach even as I pen these words. They live two houses down. I spy on them night and day with a 40-power Stankmeyer-Zeitz. They're on the point of passing my study door en route to Sunday school. One of them's already in the third grade. Soon she'll be too old. Closer and closer they come. My excitement mounts like the fires of Krakatoa.

Now (squish-squish-squish) they draw even with the door. Glowing grandeur of tiny milk-fleshed thigh. Liquescent breath of gay vulvaginous pearl. (Psst! Speak to the nice old man. Come into my parlor. Ice cream? Candy? Morphine? Exciting photographs?) They continue down the drive. Patter of footsteps fainting with my heart. Nubescent rumplets winkling wild their nappled wonder. Scent of loin-wine sighing, crying, dying on soft amber-tawny singing little legs. Oh my God—

Goodbye, boy!

DAD

Additional Dialogue

Robert Graves

Parent To Children

When you grow up, are no more children,
Nor am I then your parent:
The day of settlement falls.

"Parent," mortality's reminder,
In each son's mouth or daughter's
A word of shame and rage!

I, who begot you, ask no pardon of you;
Nor may the soldier ask
Pardon of the strewn dead.

The procreative act was blind:
It was not you I sired then—
For who sires friends, as you are mine now?

In fear begotten, I begot in fear.
Would you have had me cast fear out
So that you should not be?

ACKNOWLEDGMENTS

Selections by J. R. Ackerley reprinted from MY FATHER AND MYSELF. Copyright © 1968 by the Executors of the late J. R. Ackerley. Reprinted by permission of Coward, McCann & Geoghegan, Inc. and Harold Ober Associates Inc. Selection by James Agee reprinted from LETTERS OF JAMES AGEE TO FATHER FLYE, Second Edition. Copyright © 1971 by James Harold Flye. Reprinted by permission of Houghton Mifflin Company, Boston, and Peter Owen, London. Selections by Sherwood Anderson reprinted from SHERWOOD ANDERSON'S MEMOIRS: A CRITICAL EDITION, edited by Ray Lewis White. Copyright © 1942, 1969 by Eleanor Anderson. Reprinted by permission of University of North Carolina Press and Harold Ober Associates Inc. Selection by Michael J. Arlen from EXILES. Copyright © 1970 by Michael J. Arlen. Reprinted by permission of Farrar, Straus & Giroux, Inc. Selection by James Baldwin reprinted from NO NAME IN THE STREET by James Baldwin. Copyright © 1972 by James Baldwin. Reprinted by permission of The Dial Press. Selection by Orson Bean reprinted from ME AND THE ORGONE. Copyright © 1971 by Orson Bean. Reprinted by permission of St. Martin's Press, Inc. Selection by Thomas Bell reprinted from IN THE MIDST OF LIFE. Copyright © 1961 by Marie Bell. Reprinted by permission of Atheneum Publishers, New York. Selection by Andrew Bihaly reprinted from THE JOURNAL OF ANDREW BIHALY. Edited by Anthony Tuttle. Copyright © 1973 by Josephine Bihaly. Reprinted by permission of Thomas Y. Crowell Company, Inc. Selection by James Blake reprinted from THE JOINT. Copyright © 1970, 1971 by James Blake. Reprinted by permission of Doubleday and Company, Inc. Selection by Lenny Bruce reprinted from THE ESSENTIAL LENNY BRUCE. Copyright © 1970 by Douglas Int. Reprinted by permission of Douglas Books. Selection by Charles Bukowski, "Birth," reprinted from THE DAYS RUN AWAY LIKE WILD HORSES OVER THE HILLS. Copyright © 1969 by Charles Bukowski. Reprinted by permission of Black Sparrow Press. Selection by Neal Cassady reprinted from THE FIRST THIRD. Copyright © 1971 by City Lights Books. Reprinted by permission of City Lights Books. Selection by Raymond Chandler reprinted from RAYMOND CHANDLER SPEAKING, edited by Dorothy Gardiner and Katherine Sorley Walker. Copyright © 1962 by Helga Greene Literary Agency, Hamish Hamilton, London. Reprinted by permission of Houghton Mifflin Company, Boston. Selection by Cyril Connolly reprinted from THE UNQUIET GRAVE. Copyright 1945 by Cyril Connolly. Reprinted by permission of Harper and Row, Publishers, Inc. Selection by Frank Conroy reprinted from STOP-TIME. Copyright © 1965, 1966, 1967 by Frank Conroy. Reprinted by permission of The Viking Press, Inc. Selection by Edward Dahlberg reprinted from BECAUSE I WAS FLESH. Copyright © 1963 by Edward Dahlberg. Reprinted by permission of New Directions Publishing Corporation. Selection by Salvador Dali reprinted from THE SECRET LIEF OF SALVADOR DALI. Copyright 1942, © 1961 by Salvador Dali. Reprinted by permission of The Dial Press. Selection by Floyd Dell reprinted from HOMECOMING. Copyright 1933, © 1961 by Floyd Dell. Reprinted by permission of Holt, Rinehart and Winston, Publishers. Selection by Henry de Montherlant reprinted from SELECTED ESSAYS. © George Weidenfeld & Nicolson Ltd. 1960. Reprinted by permission of Macmillan Publishing Co., Inc. Selection by James Dickey reprinted from SORTIES: JOURNALS AND NEW ESSAYS. Copyright © 1971 by James Dickey. Reprinted by permission of Doubleday and Company, Inc. Selection by Nelson Algren reprinted from CONVERSATIONS WITH NELSON ALGREN by H. E. F. Donohue. Copyright © 1963, 1964 by H. E. F. Donohue and Nelson Algren. Reprinted by permission of Farrar, Straus and Giroux, Inc. Selection by John Dos Passos reprinted from THE FOURTEENTH CHRONICLE: LETTERS AND DIARIES OF JOHN DOS PASSOS. Copyright Elizabeth H. Dos Passos. Reprinted by permission of the publishers, Gambit. Selection by Theodore Dreiser reprinted from DAWN: A HISTORY OF MYSELF. Copyright 1931 by Theodore Dreiser. Reprinted by permission of The Dreiser Trust. Selection by Havelock Ellis reprinted from MY LIFE by Havelock Ellis. Copyright, 1939, by Houghton Mifflin Company. Published by Houghton Mifflin Company, Boston. Selection by Richard Elman reprinted from FREDI, SHIRL AND THE KIDS. Copyright © 1972 by Richard Elman. Reprinted by permission of International Creative Management. Selection by W. C. Fields reprinted from W. C. FIELDS BY HIMSELF by Ronald J. Fields, Editor. Copyright © 1973 by W. C. Fields Productions, Inc. Reprinted by permission of Prentice-Hall, Inc., Englewood Cliffs, New Jersey. Selection by F. Scott Fitzgerald reprinted from THE LETTERS OF F. SCOTT FITZGERALD, edited by Andrew Turnbull. Copyright © 1963 Frances Scott Fitzgerald Lanahan. Reprinted by permission of Charles Scribner's Sons. Selection by John Fowles reprinted from THE ARISTOS: A SELF-PORTRAIT IN IDEAS. Copyright © 1964 by John Fowles. Reprinted by permission of Little, Brown & Company, Boston, and Anthony Sheil Associates Limited. Selection by Waldo Frank reprinted from MEMOIRS OF WALDO FRANK. Copyright © 1973 by the University of Massachusetts Press. Reprinted by permission of University of Massachusetts Press. Selection by Max Frisch reprinted from SKETCHBOOK: 1966-1971. © 1974 by Max Frisch and Geoffrey Skelton. Reprinted by permission of Harcourt Brace Jovanovich, Inc. and Methuen and Co. Ltd., London. Selection by William Gibson reprinted from A MASS FOR